GOD'S
Sovereignty, Grace, and Redemption
REVEALED IN
10 Women
of Christmas

GOD'S
Sovereignty, Grace, and Redemption
REVEALED IN

10 Women of Christmas
a Bible Study

by
SUSAN SLADE
and
SUSIE HALE

WYATT & SONS
PUBLISHERS, LLC

Mobile, Alabama

Copyright © 2024- Susan R. Slade - Precious Jewels Ministries, Inc.

P.O. Box 1343, Hurst, TX 76053

www.preciousjewelsministries.com

All rights reserved. Permission is granted to copy or reprint portions for any noncommercial use, except they may not be posted online without permission.

Wyatt & Sons books may be ordered through booksellers or by contacting:

WYATT & SONS PUBLISHERS, LLC
399 Lakeview Dr. W.
Mobile, Alabama 36695
www.wyattpublishing.com

Because of the dynamic nature of the Internet, any web address or links contained in this book may have changed since publication and may no longer be valid.

Cover design by: Mark Wyatt
Interior design by: Mark Wyatt
ISBN 13:978-1-954798-28-1

This book is also available at amazon.com, barnesandnoble.com, and other online retailers.

Printed in the United States of America

Unless otherwise noted, Scripture quoted from Berean Study Bible. The Berean Bible (www.Berean.Bible) Berean Study Bible (BSB) © 2016, 2020 by Bible Hub and Berean.Bible. Used by Permission. All rights Reserved. Free downloads and licensing available. www.biblehub.com

Scripture quotations marked (AMP) taken from the Amplified® Bible (AMP), Copyright © 2015 by The Lockman Foundation. Used by permission. www.Lockman.org

Scripture quotations taken from the Amplified® Bible (AMPC), Copyright © 1954, 1958, 1962, 1964, 1965, 1987 by The Lockman Foundation Used by permission. www.Lockman.org

Scripture quotations taken from the Complete Jewish Bible (CJB), Copyright © 1998 and 2016 by David H. Stern. Used by permission. All rights reserved worldwide.

Scripture quotations marked KJV taken from the King James Version, public domain.

Scripture quotations marked (MSG) taken from *The Message,* by Eugene H. Peterson, Copyright © 1993, 2002, 2018.

Scripture quotations marked (NASB) taken from the NEW AMERICAN STANDARD BIBLE®, Copyright © 1960, 1962,1963,1968,1971,1972,1973,1975,1977,1995 by The Lockman Foundation. Used by permission."

Scripture quotations marked (NIV) taken from THE HOLY BIBLE, NEW INTERNATIONAL VERSION®, NIV® Copyright © 1973, 1978, 1984, 2011 by Biblica, Inc.® Used by permission. All rights reserved worldwide.

Scripture quotations marked (NLT) taken from *Holy Bible*, New Living Translation, copyright © 1996, 2004, 2015 by Tyndale House Foundation. Used by permission of Tyndale House Publishers, Inc., Carol Stream, Illinois 60188. All rights reserved.

Scripture quotations marked (TLB) taken from The Living Bible copyright © 1971 by Tyndale House Foundation. Used by permission of Tyndale House Publishers Inc., Carol Stream, Illinois 60188. All rights reserved.

Scripture quotations marked (VOICE) taken from The Voice™. Copyright © 2008 by Ecclesia Bible Society. Used by permission. All rights reserved.

DEDICATIONS

First and foremost, we both dedicate this book to our Lord Jesus Christ who created and elevated women.

Susan: This book is dedicated to all the women who have shown Jesus' love to me, mentored me, and encouraged me in my walk with the Lord. Throughout my life, the Lord has sent godly women to guide me toward my calling.

Susie: This book is dedicated to my sisters, Jeanne Cloward and Jan Betz, who taught me to read and write before I entered school and continue to encourage me.

ACKNOWLEDGEMENTS

Don Tipps for the original painting from which the cover art was developed.

Steve and Chelsea Landsee who helped us proofread and edit the final draft of the book.

Jeanne Cloward and her great grandson, Isaiah, for doing the original proofreading for grammar, punctuation, and content.

Richard Albin, official PJM photographer, for help with the picture on the cover and our photos on the back cover.

Dr. Chyanna Mull-Anthony for not only writing the beautiful foreword but for all of her encouragement along the way. She was Susan's pastor from 1995-2008 and is still a prayer warrior and confidant.

Our precious friend Missy Blanchard who prays for us and allows us to "decompress" as needed.

Susan's long-time friend, Chrissy Thorpe, who prays for us and lets us bounce ideas off her.

Our Pastor, Ben Polson, and our church family for being there for us even when we are not able to make it to church on a regular basis.

Our PJM Board members, Dane and Dana Carr, Crystal Foster, Eric Little, and Nick Miller, and our Treasurer, Rick Ivey.

Soli Deo Gloria!

If the Lord leads you to contribute to our ministry monetarily, you may do so via our website found at:
https://www.preciousjewelsministries.com by PayPal, credit card, or debit card. Or you can send funds via Venmo @Susan-PJM. You may also mail a check made out to Precious Jewels Ministries to P.O. Box 1343, Hurst, TX 76053.

FOREWORD

Recently I attended a large gathering of Pastors and Church leaders representing several Christian groups and denominations. One dear sister was shocked to discover that I was the senior Pastor of a church! She politely asked me why I thought that I could serve in such a capacity. In the few minutes that followed, I did my best to help her see that the Bible is full of women serving is all areas of godly influence. My goal was not to "persuade" her to my theological viewpoint, but rather to suggest that she re-examine her Bible and glean encouragement from the stories and portrayals of women that it includes.

This is exactly what is proffered in *God's Sovereignty, Grace, and Redemption Revealed in Ten Women of Christmas*. Susan and Susie have produced a tool that can be placed in the hands of any sincere Bible student, church, community or home study group. Studies have proven that a childhood, or lifetime, of watching women pushed further to the periphery edges of leadership and visibility has had an immense impact on many women's self-worth. But those negative influences are not from our Lord, or His Word. The Bible always produces hope, life and positive expectancy.

As you go through this book, and the subsequent discussion questions, you will enjoy the unique way that the authors exchange ideas and discuss each woman, and you will be challenged to interact more with women's redemptive role in Bible history. These are the accounts of pivotal women and their involvement with the plan of God during some of the most momentous events in the Scriptures. These sisters stood on the frontlines of spiritual, political and historical events. And their presence and actions pay tribute to the God of all flesh - who honors the faith of His daughters.

Now, turn the page. Get comfortable. Be prayerful. And give these women the chance to influence you and your walk with the Lord.

Rev. Dr. Chyanna Mull-Anthony
Pastor, International Gospel Center, Tulsa
Vice-President, Osborn Ministries, Int'l
Women's International Network

ABOUT THIS BOOK

This Bible study is formatted differently than most. We invite you into our "boffice" to discuss the Scripture with us. What is a "boffice?" Glad you asked. It is our word for our workspace—bedroom/office. Our desk with our laptop is at the foot of Susie's bed. The big screen TV at the foot of Susan's bed serves as her computer monitor. The way we study God's word is to read a passage and discuss it. As we discuss a verse, cross references may come to mind, and we look them up to see if they should be included in our notes. If we are unsure the exact meaning of a word, we look it up in an English dictionary and/or a Hebrew or Greek dictionary. You will find some our favorite resources for word studies in the bibliography. If we disagree or are unsure of the meaning and/or application of a verse or passage, we will look at commentaries or study Bibles. We invite you to pretend you are in the "boffice" with us discussing God's word. Write in your own observations and or questions as you go or use a spiral journal if you make copious notes like we do. Or you may make notes in a computer document. If you are doing this study as a group, share your insights with the others. If you are leading a group study, ask the participants to come prepared to share and assure them the only "dumb question" is the one that remains unasked. We are here to learn together!

ABOUT THE AUTHORS

SUSAN SLADE is an ordained minister (Fellowship of Churches and Christian Ministries) with a bachelor's degree in English Bible with minors in Pastoral Counseling and Modern Hebrew and a master's degree in biblical literature from Oral Roberts University in Tulsa, Oklahoma. She is the founder and president of Precious Jewels Ministries, Inc. and has co-authored five devotional books with her ministry partner, Susie. She has been a guest on "Life Today" with James Robison. She has performed weddings, baby dedications, and served as a research assistant to her pastor from November 2010 to August 2015, helping him prepare for sermons. Susan began by writing scriptural blessing poems for "champions," children with special challenges, to encourage parents not to define the child by their limitations but by what the Lord says about them; but now she writes these for all children as all of them face challenges. Susan has expanded the scriptural blessings to Covenant Blessings for couples and Exhortation Celebrations for individuals. She is a powerful prayer warrior. And by the way, she has a combination of spastic and athetoid cerebral palsy affecting all four limbs.

KAREN SUE HALE (SUSIE) has a Bachelor of Arts degree in music education and a Master of Education with a focus on language arts and serves as vice president and secretary of Precious Jewels Ministries, Inc. She taught eleven years at Glenview Christian School in Ft. Worth, Texas serving as curriculum coordinator as well. She enjoyed teaching a senior adult ladies' class at North Pointe Baptist Church in Hurst, Texas from June 2014 to August 2016. Susie is Susan's "facilitator" as she types what Susan dictates and handles all the computer aspects of their work in addition to helping Susan with personal needs. In addition to books she has co-authored with Susan, Susie had two articles published in "Purposeful Singleness Monthly" and one published on a webzine called "Christian Women Today."

TABLE OF CONTENTS

Copyright and Sources
Dedication
Acknowledgements
Foreword
About the Authors

INTRODUCTION TO TEN WOMEN OF CHRISTMAS

EVE
Gen. 1   Creation of Man and Woman
Gen. 2   Man from Dust and Woman from Rib
Gen. 3   Deception, Sin and Shame
Gen. 3   Blame Game, Curses, and Promise

Summary   Great^{nth} Grandmother of Jesus

SARAH
Gen. 11, 12, & 20   Introduction to Sarah
Gen. 17   Change of Names and ROFL
Gen. 18   Name the Baby "He Laughs"
Gen. 21   A Child is Born to One Old and Worn
Gen. 22   Boy to be Burnt Offering

Summary   Chosen to Be The Mother of The Promise

TAMAR
Gen. 38   Widowed Due to Husbands' Wicked Ways
Gen. 38   She who was Deceived becomes the Deceiver
Gen. 38   Judgment Pronounced Due to Unwed Pregnancy Until Paternity Proven

Summary   Woman Who Ensured Judah's Line Continued

RAHAB

Josh. 2   Harlot Hides and Helps Spies
Josh. 6   People Yelled, Walls Fell

Summary   Prostitute Who Protected Spies becomes great-great-grandmother of King David

RUTH

Ruth	Introduction
Ruth 1	Tragedy Strikes Naomi
Ruth 1	Devoted Daughter-in-love Determined to Dwell with Naomi
Ruth 2	Ruth Gleans and Meets a Man of Means
Ruth 2	Naomi's Faith Rekindled
Ruth 3	Intriguing Instructions
Ruth 3	Ruth Proposes to Boaz, But Runs into a Snag
Ruth 4	Let's Make a Deal
Ruth 4	It's a Done Deal
Ruth 4	Naomi's Arms Empty No More and Matt. 1
Summary	Moabitess Ruth Redeemed to be Great-Grandmother of King David

BATHSHEBA

2 Sam.11	Bathsheba's Bath Leads David Down Sin's Path
2 Sam.12	David, You Are the Man!
1 Kings 1	Bathsheba's Son to Be Number One
Summary	Mother of King Solomon

ESTHER

Esther 1	Vashti Banished
Esther 2	Esther Made Queen
Esther 3	Haman Hatches Extermination Plan
Esther 4	For Such a Time as This
Esther 5	Haman's Ego Stroked, But Then His Anger Provoked
Esther 6	Mordecai Honored, Haman Humiliated,
Esther 7	Esther Saves Her Nation from Annihilation
Est. 8–10	God Orchestrates the Preservation of His Nation
Summary	She Saved Her Nation from Annihilation

ELIZABETH

Luke 1	Amazing Grace Announcement

MARY

Luke 1   Behold the Handmaid of the Lord

MARY & ELIZABETH

Luke 1   Spirit-Filled Unborn Baby Jumps for Joy!

ELIZABETH

Luke 1	He Shall be Called John
Summary	Barren Woman Blessed with Bouncing Baby Boy

MARY

Matt. 1	Mary's Baby Born to be Savior
Luke 2	Shepherds Honor the Good Shepherd
Luke 2	Redeeming the Long-Awaited Redeemer

ANNA

Luke 2   Anna - Intercessor, Prophetess, and Evangelist

MARY

Matt. 2	Treasures for the Greatest Treasure (Really Cool Baby Shower!)
Matt. 2	"Out of Egypt I have Called My Son"
Summary	Humble but Courageous Servant of the Lord

SUMMARY OF TEN WOMEN OF CHRISTMAS
IN TEN WOMEN OF CHRISTMAS WE FIND...
NOTES
BIBLIOGRAPHY

INTRODUCTION TO
God's Sovereignty, Grace, and Redemption
REVEALED IN TEN WOMEN OF CHRISTMAS

EVE – Genesis 1–3
SARAH – Genesis 17–23
TAMAR – Genesis 38
RAHAB – Joshua 2 & 6
RUTH – Book of Ruth
BATHSHEBA – 2 Samuel 11 & 12, 1 Kings 1
ESTHER – Book of Esther
ELIZABETH – Luke 1
MARY – Luke 1 & 2, Matthew 2
ANNA – Luke 2

INTRODUCTION: Some of the names in our list of "Ten Women of Christmas" ring with familiarity because they are included in sermons on the birth of Jesus regularly—Mary (Mother of Baby Jesus), Elizabeth (Mary's relative who conceived late in life), and Anna (adored the Baby Jesus in the temple). Others are brought out by some preachers and teachers because they are in the lineage of Christ found in Matthew (Tamar, Rahab, Ruth, and Bathsheba). You may be surprised at our inclusion of Eve, Sarah, and Esther; but stick with us to find out why we found these three to be crucial to the Christmas story as well. In each of these women, we see both God's sovereignty and His grace at work and a picture of His redemptive purpose. Therefore, let us agree on a working definition of those terms:

> SOVEREIGNTY of God, his absolute right to do all things according to his own good pleasure (Dan. 4:25, 35; Rom. 9:15-23; 1 Tim. 6:15; Rev. 4:11). (1)

> GRACE: To show grace is to extend favor or kindness to someone who does not deserve it and can never earn it and will never be able to repay. (2)

> REDEEMER, REDEMPTION. The heart of the Biblical message of redemption is the deliverance of the people of God from the bondage of sin by the perfect substitutionary sacrifice of Jesus Christ and their consequent restoration to God and His heavenly kingdom. (3)

> Our friend, Steve Landsee, gave this understanding: Redemption means to buy back. Biblical redemption is the deliverance of God's people by Jesus' blood shed on the cross to pay our debt.

We will present these women chronologically as they fit into history (aka HIS story), but they will appear again as they overlap with the other women on the list. Since these women are a part of His Story, they are a part of our story as believers as well because we have been adopted into the family of God by His grace. Our sincere desire is that you will be blessed and challenged through the studying of the Bible together. We are not alone in seeing how the Lord values the women in history. In *Twelve Extraordinary Women,* John MacArthur writes in the introductory paragraph:

> One of the unique features of the Bible is the way it exalts women. Far from ever demeaning or belittling women, Scripture often seems to go out of the way to pay homage to them, to ennoble their roles in society and family, to acknowledge the importance of their influence, and to exalt the virtues of women who were particularly godly examples. (4)

Genesis 1 - CREATION OF MAN AND WOMAN

Susie: Why are we starting a Christmas study with creation? When our sovereign God created the world and placed people in it, He knew they would sin. The Father, Son, and Holy Spirit were all present when man was formed from dust and woman from man's rib. And before the creation of the world, the Godhead had the plan for mankind's redemption – the baby Boy who would be born to die as the Lamb slain from the foundation of the world (Revelation 13:8).

> *Revelation 13:8 (NIV) And all the people who belong to this world worshiped the beast. They are the ones whose names were not written in the Book of Life that belongs to* **the Lamb who was slaughtered before the world was made.**

Genesis 1:26–28 Then God said, "Let Us make man in Our image, after Our likeness, to rule over the fish of the sea and the birds of the air, over the livestock, and over all the earth itself and every creature that crawls upon it." So God created man in His own image; in the image of God He created him; male and female He created them. God blessed them and said to them, "Be fruitful and multiply, and fill the earth and subdue it; rule over the fish of the sea and the birds of the air and every creature that crawls upon the earth."

Susan: God said, "Let US...". Father, Son, and Holy Spirit were all present when man was created. It was a collaborative process.

Susie: The Godhead, the Trinity, fashioned man in their own image. What exactly does that mean?

Susan: People were given the ability to reason, to communicate through speech, to make choices, and to be creative. People are also relational beings. God is relational within Himself—the Father, Son, and Holy Spirit.

Susie: Humans need meaningful relationships among themselves and with God.

Susan: Before they sinned, the man and the woman were in perfect unity with each other and with God. They were what we, as Christians, shall be on the New Earth when Christ returns.

Susie: However, as we will see, our relationship with God and one another was tarnished by the sin of the very first man.

Susan: Animals are instinctual and often act on impulses related to their physical needs, their appetites.

Susie: People were given dominion or rule over all other earthly beings (animals, fish, birds, reptiles, bugs, etc.) because of our ability to reason, because we are created in the image of God. And because we *are* created in the image of God, humans have a relationship of equality and willing submission to one another.

Genesis 1:27 So God created man in His own image; in the image of God He created him; male and female He created them.

Susie: God did not just create a brotherhood to satisfy the need for relationships. Nor did He create only a sisterhood. He created both male and female or they would not have been able to obey the command in the next verse!

Genesis 1:28 God blessed them and said to them, "Be fruitful and multiply, and fill the earth and subdue it; rule over the fish of the sea and the birds of the air and every creature that crawls upon the earth."

Susan: Once God had created both the man and the woman, then He *blessed* them and told them to have a family. He encouraged them to enjoy their marriage relationship and all that implies. Humans were supposed to protect and direct the earth in an orderly manner *to bring glory to the Creator.*

Susie: The animals were created for the benefit of mankind, and people were to rule over them. In the Garden of Eden, God gave man and woman equal authority over all of creation. God did not intend them to exercise this authority over one another. We are to rule over the animals, but we are to submit to one another as unto Christ.

REVIEW QUESTIONS

1. Who created man—the Father, the Son, or the Holy Spirit?

   _____
   _____
   _____
   _____

2. What meaningful work did God give to Adam?

   _____
   _____
   _____

3. What was the relationship between people and animals supposed to be?

_____

_____

_____

Ponder This...

People were created in the image of God. We have attributes and qualities the animals do not possess. We were intended to be a reflection of our Maker, but sin has tarnished our ability to reflect. The only cleaning agent that can wash away the grime of sin is the blood of Jesus Christ shed on the cross to pay the debt of our sin—the soap of His redeeming love. We cannot be "good enough" to purchase the cleanser. The only way to appropriate that which will make us clean and restore our ability to reflect our Creator is by trusting Jesus, believing He was God incarnate (Son of God), died to pay our sin debt, and was raised to life and now sits at the right hand of God the Father. As Jesus said, "I am the way and the truth and the life. No one comes to the Father except through Me." (John 14:6) Perhaps journal about the day you surrendered your life to the Lord, trusting Jesus alone for salvation.

Genesis 2 - MAN FROM DUST AND WOMAN FROM RIB

Genesis 2:7 Then the LORD God formed man from the dust of the ground and breathed the breath of life into his nostrils, and the man became a living being.

Susie: God spoke the animals into being, but He carefully molded Adam out of clay and breathed His very life into him. I wonder if the person who developed mouth-to-mouth resuscitation got the idea from this verse?

Susan: God created the animals at arm's length but chose to get up close and personal in order to breathe life into the man. He put vitality into the man with His own breath. This was an extremely intimate encounter.

Susie: The relationship between God and humans was to be uniquely different than God's relationship as Creator of the animals. He personally breathed life into the people. This reminds me of the giving of the Holy Spirit recorded in Acts chapter 2 when the Spirit came upon them like a rushing wind.

> *Acts 2:2 Suddenly a sound like a mighty rushing wind came from heaven and filled the whole house where they were sitting.*

Susie: In Acts, God breathed spiritual life into the disciples. This breath—the indwelling of the Holy Spirit—is what empowers our ability to communicate with God and receive communication from Him.

Genesis 2:15 Then the LORD God took the man and placed him in the Garden of Eden to cultivate and keep it.

Susie: God gave Adam meaningful work—to cultivate and keep the Garden of Eden.

Susan: Adam was not supposed to just sit back fat and sassy enjoying the fruit of the various trees and shrubs. He was supposed to take care of them and the animals. Adam was a caretaker of the Garden.

Susie: Adam was the first park ranger. However, he was not to eat from every tree.

Genesis 2:16-17 And the LORD God commanded him, "You may eat freely from every tree of the garden, but you must not eat from the tree of the knowledge of good and evil; for in the day that you eat of it, you will surely die."

Susan: God gave Adam this ONE rule, just one! Don't eat from the tree of the knowledge of good and evil.

Susie: And the consequences of disobeying the one rule were dire: "in the day that you eat of it, you will surely die." We know the rest of the story that they didn't keel over dead that moment, but before we go there, we need to point out another feature that is unique to humans out of all of God's creation:

> "Only man, of all creation, was given this instruction; human beings alone were given moral choice." (5)

Susan: Only human beings were created in God's own image—Imago Dei in Latin:

> *Genesis 1:26-27 Then God said, "Let Us make man in Our image^{H6754}, after Our likeness^{H1823}, to rule over the fish of the sea and the birds of the air, over the livestock, and over all the earth itself and every creature that crawls upon it." So God created man in His own image^{H6754}; in the image^{H6754} of God He created him; male and female He created them....*

> H6754 ṣelem: A masculine noun meaning an image, a likeness, a statue, a model, a drawing, a shadow. The word means image or likeness; its most celebrated theological and anthropological use was to depict human beings as made in God's own image (Gen. 1:26, 27; 5:3). People continue to be in His image even after the fall, although the image is marred (Gen. 9:6), and still serves as the basis of the prohibition not to kill human beings. (6)

> H1823 dem-ooth . . . of son in likeness of father Genesis 5:3 (P); so also of man in likeness of God Genesis 1:26. (7)

> When God said, "Let us make human beings in our image," He was saying, in effect, "Humanity will be unlike anything I have created. No other being has a heart to love Me. No other created being has a mind to know Me or a will to obey Me. Nothing else in all of My creation has a destiny of eternity like these creatures will have. I will make humans distinct. They will have imago Dei, 'the image of God,' stamped on them. Only they will have a capacity within them to love and know and obey Me. (8)

Susan: Are the words "image" and "likeness" different or are they two sides of the same coin?

Susie: The definitions are slightly different. However, "image" and "likeness" could be considered synonyms. This may be an example of parallelism—a technique often used by Hebrew authors to emphasize a point by stating the same idea in two different ways. This is often employed in the Psalms. For example:

> *Psalm 19:1 (NLT) For the choir director: A psalm of David. The heavens proclaim the glory of God. The skies display his craftsmanship.*

Susan: Humanity is the only part of creation to which God extended His divine nature.

Susie: Humans alone are given the ability to have intimate fellowship with their Creator and Sustainer, God.

Genesis 2:18-20 The LORD God also said, "It is not good for the man to be alone. I will make for him a suitable helper." And out of the ground the LORD God formed every beast of the field and every bird of the air, and He brought them to the man to see what he would name each one. And whatever the man called each living creature, that was its name. The man gave names to all the livestock, to the birds of the air, and to every beast of the field. But for Adam no suitable helper was found.

Susie: Up until this point, God has pronounced all of creation "good." But there was one thing God declared "not good." Adam being alone, the sole human, was "not good." Therefore, God paraded all the animals and birds before Adam and had him name them.

Susan: Man did not find his equal among the animals. Man needed a "helper." The Hebrew word is ☐ēzer-kenegdo which means a helper suitable and complementary to him in every way. The word ☐ēzer also referred to God as the Helper of Israel. The term implies a role of equality and not subordination.

> 5828. ☐ēzer: It indicates persons who give help: the woman created as Adam's complementary helper (Gen. 2:18, 20) (9)

> 5048. neged: A preposition indicating before, in front of, opposite; corresponding to. It has a special sense to indicate Eve's likeness to Adam (Gen. 2:18, 20), with the preposition ke prefixed. (10)

Susie: The man needed someone like himself, created in the image of God.

Susan: The fullness of the image of God is found in the man and woman together. In fact, El Shaddai literally means "many breasted" because God completely provides for His own, He is the fullness of all that we need, an endless supply.

Susie: He is like a mother nursing her infant.

Susan: As separate and unique expressions of the image of God, man and woman were products of the plurality of God and reflections of His unity and His nature.

Susie: Together, a man and a woman have the potential to be a picture of the relationship between Jesus and His bride, the church, the oneness of a believer and his/her Savior.

Susan: Women are not inferior to man in any way. We are equally created in God's image. A husband and wife do not complete each other. We are each complete in Christ.

> *Colossians 2:9-12 For in Christ all the fullness of the Deity dwells in bodily form. And you have been made complete in Christ, who is the head over every ruler and authority. In Him you were also circumcised, in the putting off of your sinful nature, with the circumcision performed by Christ and not by human hands. And having been buried with Him in baptism, you were raised with Him through your faith in the power of God, who raised Him from the dead.*

Susie: Some people think that since God said it was not good for man to be alone, our chief goal in life is to find a spouse. This is not so. We are complete in Christ! My prayer as a single was, "If there is a man out there with whom I could serve You more effectively, please lead me to him. If I am to dedicate my life in service to You as a single adult, help me to be content in my singleness." The following quote from "Table for One" ministries—https://tfoministries.org/—expresses this idea well:

> To be Complete in Christ means to have a deep and abiding relationship with Jesus Christ, and to find your identity and purpose in him. As a single adult you recognize that you are loved and accepted by God, not based on your own merits, but through the sacrifice of Jesus on the cross. Being complete in Christ also involves growing in spiritual maturity, becoming more like Christ in character and behavior, and using your gifts and talents to serve others and share the message of hope and salvation with the world! Our goal is to see single adults come to Christ, be complete in Him, and build communities that accept single adults. While marriage may be in the plan for some singles, the fact is that while you are single, your mission should not be marriage. You need to Be Complete in Christ!
> https://tfoministries.org/complete-in-christ#

Susan: A Christian is complete in Christ plus *nothing!* However, a Christian married couple can be complementary and meant to serve God as a united force together.

> The word Ezer Kenegdo might be old but the purpose of our existence as women is the same. You are an Ezer Kenegdo. A strong warrior, complementary to man. Entire article found at https://ezerkenegdo.org/ezer-kenegdo/

Susie: Whether single or married, male or female, for the Christ-follower, the main goal is, as Dawson Trotman, the founder of The Navigators Ministry, put it, is "To know Christ, make Him known, and help others do the same." Learn more about the Navigators here: https://www.navigators.org/about/history/

Genesis 2:21-22 So the LORD God caused the man to fall into a deep sleep, and while he slept, He took one of the man's ribs and closed up the area with flesh. And from the rib that the LORD God had taken from the man, He made a woman and brought her to him.

Susie: Woman was created from a piece of man, his rib, so it takes both men and women to fully express who God is. The way Eve was created shows that we need both aspects to fully express the Godhead, the relationship. Jesus was the fullness of God but completely human. He even expressed the mothering nature in this verse:

Matthew 23:37 O Jerusalem, Jerusalem, who kills the prophets and stones those sent to her, how often I have longed to gather your children together, as a hen gathers her chicks under her wings, but you were unwilling!

WOMAN, noun plural women. [a compound of womb and man.] The female of the human race, grown to adult years. (11)

802. ʾiššāh: A feminine noun meaning woman, wife, or female. The origin of this word has been recorded in Genesis 2:23, where Adam said, "She shall be called Woman (ʾiššāh [802]), because she was taken out of Man (ʾiyš [376]) (NASB)." While this word predominantly means woman or wife, it is further used in various ways: those able to bear children (Gen. 18:11); a widow (Ruth 4:5; 1 Sam. 27:3); an adulteress (Prov. 6:26; 7:5); female children (Num. 31:18); or female animals (Gen. 7:2). (12)

2332. ḥawwāh: A proper noun designating Eve. The name of the first woman created by the Lord God. Adam gave her the name Eve, meaning "living, making alive" (Gen. 3:20). She was the wife of Adam (Gen. 4:1). In Genesis 2:23, she was designated as a woman (ʾiššāh [802]), a female being apart from the male being, Adam, both sharing common humanity. As her name indicates, she then gave birth to the human race (Gen. 4:1–2). (13)

Susan: The man and the woman were to be sewn together in their hearts and minds.

Susie: They were to have that relationship of equality and unity as exhibited by the Father, Son, and Spirit.

Susan: The man and woman had no clothing and were not embarrassed at all. They had an intimacy with God and each other that knew no shame.

Susie: Their relationship with God and each other was such that they could be completely naked and feel no vulnerability. But then—enter the serpent.

REVIEW QUESTIONS:

1. What makes humans unique among all the created beings?
   _____
   _____
   _____
   _____
   _____

2. What value does God place on humanity?
   _____
   _____
   _____
   _____
   _____

3. What one thing out of all of His creation did God say was "not good?"
   _____
   _____
   _____
   _____
   _____

4. Why is the often-used statement, "My spouse completes me," not an accurate picture of a biblical marriage relationship?
   _____
   _____
   _____
   _____

Ponder This...

God breathed life into the first man. However, sin sucked the life right out of us. We are dead, incapable of relationship with God, until by His grace we believe and trust in what Jesus accomplished by being born as a man in order to become the perfect sacrifice for all individuals who believe. Once we place our trust in Jesus, God breathes spiritual life back into us by filling us with His Holy Spirit.

Colossians 2:13-15 When you were dead in your trespasses and in the uncircumcision of your sinful nature, God made you alive with Christ. He forgave us all our trespasses, having canceled the debt ascribed to us in the decrees that stood against us. He took it away, nailing it to the cross! And having disarmed the powers and authorities, He made a public spectacle of them, triumphing over them by the cross.

Colossians 2:13-15 (MSG) When you were stuck in your old sin-dead life, you were incapable of responding to God. God brought you alive—right along with Christ! Think of it! All sins forgiven, the slate wiped clean, that old arrest warrant canceled and nailed to Christ's cross. He stripped all the spiritual tyrants in the universe of their sham authority at the Cross and marched them naked through the streets.

WORSHIP OPPORTUNITY

The Gaither Vocal Band sings a great song that reminds us to be amazed as we ponder creation. Look up "You Amaze Me" on YouTube™ or follow this link: https://www.youtube.com/watch?v=CZ1AVjudjSE
Be sure to click on closed captioning and sing along!

GENESIS 3 - DECEPTION, SIN, AND SHAME

Genesis 3:1 Now the serpent was more crafty than any beast of the field that the LORD God had made. And he said to the woman, "Did God really say, 'You must not eat from any tree in the garden?'"

Susie: The first words out of the serpent's mouth (really the mouthpiece of Satan) were designed to make Eve question God. He implied that God was not letting them eat from *any* of the fruit trees.

Genesis 3:2-3 The woman answered the serpent, "We may eat the fruit of the trees of the garden, but about the fruit of the tree in the middle of the garden, God has said, 'You must not eat of it or touch it, or you will die.'"

Susie: Eve replied that there was only one tree whose fruit was forbidden. However, she got the command a little wrong. God warned them not to *eat* the fruit, but Eve added that they could not even *touch* it. Seems like a minor error, but perhaps when she saw that she did not keel over dead when she touched it, she was more willing to try eating it.

Susan: God had given the commandment not to eat of that one particular tree to Adam before Eve was even created. Perhaps Adam passed it on to her incorrectly, or maybe she just put the "or touch it" in there for emphasis. We don't know.

> *Genesis 2:15-17 Then the LORD God took the man and placed him in the Garden of Eden to cultivate and keep it. And the LORD God commanded him, "You may eat freely from every tree of the garden, but you must not eat from the tree of the knowledge of good and evil; for in the day that you eat of it, you will surely die."*

Susie: Cultivating the garden would imply touching the trees when Adam pruned them. We give Eve the benefit of the doubt for her adding to the command because the New Testament clearly names Adam as the one through whom sin came into the world.

> *Romans 5:12 (NLT) When Adam sinned, sin entered the world. Adam's sin brought death, so death spread to everyone, for everyone sinned.*

Genesis 3:4 "You will not surely die," the serpent told her. "For God knows that in the day you eat of it, your eyes will be opened and you will be like God, knowing good and evil."

Susan: Both Adam and Eve were participants in the distortion of God's plan. Because of their failure to exercise their dominion over all the creatures (specifically the serpent) and their adherence to other voices instead of complete obedience to God's sovereign voice only, the opportunity for the seed of doubt was planted by Satan.

Susie: Being the father of lies, Satan told half-truths to the woman. He said she would not die, but her eyes would be opened, and she would know good and evil. After all, that was the name of the tree—the tree of the knowledge of good and evil. We will see later that this was a twisted partial truth.

Susan: This is a prime example of how Satan works to tempt us. He plants a suggestion, not a blatant urge to sin, but a subtle suggestion. The suggestion that "No one will know" or "it's not that bad" or "what God told you isn't the entire picture or completely true" or "do you think God is being fair to you?" or as he did in the Garden of Eden, "Did God *really* say . . .?" Satan makes us question what we know of our Lord. We know that God is (as Chris Tomlin sings) "a good, good Father," but Satan works hard to make us doubt that truth.

> *James 1:17 Every good and perfect gift is from above, coming down from the Father of the heavenly lights, with whom there is no change or shifting shadow.*

Genesis 3:6–7 When the woman saw that the tree was good for food and pleasing to the eyes, and that it was desirable for obtaining wisdom, she took the fruit and ate it. She also gave some to her husband who was with her, and he ate it. And the eyes of both of them were opened, and they knew that they were naked; so they sewed together fig leaves and made coverings for themselves.

Susan: Note that Adam was standing right there with Eve when the serpent deceived her, and he said nothing and did nothing to prevent her from eating the forbidden fruit. Adam and Eve forfeited their trustworthy relationship with God, thinking that the attribute of pseudo-wisdom would be a greater source and provider than the Source for all wisdom and all good things, who is God. Instead of realizing that she could trust God and obeying His command not to eat of the tree, Eve was deceived by Satan into feeling that God was withholding something from them.

Susie: Eve did not make the decision to taste the fruit while by herself as much artwork depicts the event.

Susan: No, Adam was right there with Eve when she ate the forbidden fruit, offered it to him, and he, also, ate. Adam was the one to whom God directly gave the commandment not to eat of the tree. Therefore, Adam is held primarily responsible according to New Testament teaching.

> *Romans 5:12 Therefore, just as sin entered the world through one man, and death through sin, so also death was passed on to all men, because all sinned.*

1 Corinthians 15:22 For as in Adam all die, so in Christ all will be made alive.

Susie: That's correct, Susan. The New Testament does **not** say that sin entered the world through Eve or that we all die because of Eve's sin. Paul clearly attributes the fall of the human race to Adam as the head and protector of his household.

Genesis 3:7 And the eyes of both of them were opened, and they knew that they were naked; so they sewed together fig leaves and made coverings for themselves.

Susan: For one bite of beautiful fruit, Adam and Eve forfeited their innocence. The command God had given to not eat of this tree was truly to protect His children from the burden of becoming aware of evil.

Susie: They did become "wise," as Satan through the serpent had told them, wise to the fact that they were now naked. They became aware of guilt and shame. They had been "covered" by their relationship with God, but now that trust had been violated by both of them. Therefore, they made what sounds like loin cloths out of leaves. They did not immediately die physically, but from that moment their bodies began the process of dying, slowly decaying. Also, their union with the Lord died, man became dead in sin. Because of Adam's sin, we are all born with a sinful nature. We all need a Savior to redeem us from sin.

Ephesians 2:1a As for you, you were dead in your transgressions and sins . . .

Susan: . . . separated from the life and light of God. However, God's ultimate plan was to show us a way to return to life and His light. To walk in the light is to live in obedience to the knowledge and instruction of God's word—to live according to God's will and ways.

1 Peter 2:9 But you are a chosen people, a royal priesthood, a holy nation, a people for God's own possession, to proclaim the virtues of Him who called you out of darkness into His marvelous light.

1 John 1:5-7 And this is the message we have heard from Him and announce to you: God is light, and in Him there is no darkness at all. If we say we have fellowship with Him yet walk in the darkness, we lie and do not practice the truth. But if we walk in the light as He is in the light, we have fellowship with one another, and the blood of Jesus His Son cleanses us from all sin.

Susie: Because of sin, the need for atonement sacrifices arose. Jesus would ultimately be the final perfect sacrifice to reconcile believers to God, to restore that relationship that was torn by sin. As we will see in this study of the Women of Christmas, Jesus was truly born to die.

REVIEW QUESTIONS

1. Who was really behind the words of the serpent?
   _____
   _____

2. What did Eve add to the command God had given Adam about the tree of the knowledge of good and evil?
   _____
   _____
   _____

3. Who does the New Testament hold responsible for sin entering the world?
   _____
   _____
   _____

Ponder this...

Susan knows what decaying flesh looks and feels like. She suffered for seven years with necrotic ulcers on both legs from just below the knees to the soles of her feet. When I first started working with her, her feet appeared to be melting, literally rotting. She had been hospitalized and treated more than once for this condition to no avail. Finally, she was told her legs were literally "two ticking time bombs" that could become septic and kill her at any moment. So, she made the difficult but wise decision to have them amputated. All that to say, from the day we are born, we begin dying literally in the physical sense but are also dead spiritually, housing the rottenness of our sin nature. As soon as Adam and Eve disobeyed God, they became dead spiritually as well as in the process of dying physically. There is only one cure for our spiritual decay, we must allow God to cut it out—to circumcise our hearts—by trusting Jesus by faith and surrendering our lives to God's scalpel.

> *Romans 2:28-29 (NIV) "A man is not a Jew if he is only one outwardly, nor is circumcision merely outward and physical. No, a man is a Jew if he is one inwardly; and circumcision is circumcision of the heart, by the Spirit, not by the written code. Such a man's praise is not from men, but from God."*

GENESIS 3 - BLAME GAME, CURSES, AND PROMISE

Genesis 3:8-9 Then the man and his wife heard the voice of the LORD God walking in the garden in the breeze of the day, and they hid themselves from the presence of the LORD God among the trees of the garden. But the LORD God called[H7121] out to the man, "Where are you?"

Susan: The question in my mind that may be a "rabbit trail" is whether this was a theophany—an appearance of the pre-incarnate Jesus in the flesh—or did they merely hear a sound or see God as a cloud or what?

Susie: This would be a "rabbit trail" but an interesting one. I did a brief search and found a good article here: https://www.gotquestions.org/God-walk-garden.html . If this intrigues you, take time to read this article or even research the question elsewhere.

Susan: Enquiring minds want to know, and I'm an enquiring mind.

Susie: Perhaps we'll do some more research on it later. In whatever form, God showed up for their evening walk but found Adam and Eve hiding from Him.

Susan: When God "called out" to Adam, He was summoning him into His presence:

> H7121 qārā☐: A verb meaning to call, to declare, to summon, to invite, to read, to be called, to be invoked, to be named. The verb means to call or to summon, but its context and surrounding grammatical setting determine the various shades of meaning given to the word. (14)

Susie: Like a child who fears the consequences of disobedience as soon as Daddy gets home, Adam feared God for the first time and hid from Him.

Susan: What a terrible moment in the story of man's relationship to God!

Genesis 3:10 "I heard Your voice in the garden," he replied, "and I was afraid because I was naked; so I hid myself."

Susan: Adam and Eve lost their innocence when they ate from the tree and now feared the consequences of their disobedience. The voice of God was no longer friendly, comforting, and exciting. Instead, God was someone to be feared.

Genesis 3:11 "Who told you that you were naked?" asked the LORD God. "Have you eaten from the tree of which I commanded you not to eat?"

Susan: God knew for sure that Adam and Eve had eaten the forbidden fruit because He is omniscient (all-knowing) and omnipresent (everywhere at once). He sees everything and knows everything. We cannot hide anything from our Lord.

> *Hebrews 4:13 Nothing in all creation is hidden from God's sight; everything is uncovered and exposed before the eyes of Him to whom we must give account.*

Susie: And God was summoning Adam to give an account of his actions.

Susan: God, knowing what had happened, asked Adam three questions: How do you know you are naked? Who told you? And did you eat from the tree of the knowledge of good and evil?

Genesis 3:12 And the man answered, "The woman whom You gave me, she gave me fruit from the tree, and I ate it."

Susie: Thus, ensued the first "blame game." Adam blamed the woman and ultimately God by pointing out that God had given him this "helper." He did not take responsibility for the fact that he listened to Eve rather than standing firm in obedience to the command God had directly given to him.

Susan: Adam's problem was he placed his wife's advice above the command God had given him. We must always obey God rather than be swayed by other voices.

Genesis 3:13 Then the LORD God said to the woman, "What is this you have done?" "The serpent deceived me," she replied, "and I ate."

Susan: Then God turned to Eve and asked her what she did. She blamed the serpent who was really Satan, the enemy of God and all humankind, because he had deceived her. He had twisted God's words and planted the seed of doubt in her mind.

Genesis 3:14 So the LORD God said to the serpent: "Because you have done this, cursed are you above all livestock and every beast of the field! On your belly will you go, and dust you will eat, all the days of your life.

Susan: After hearing His family's case, God turned to the serpent and said, "For this you are cursed, crawl on the ground and eat dust all the days of your life." The serpent may not have been in the form of a snake before the curse. However, after its part in deceiving Eve, it was doomed to slither along the ground. A physical change took place as a result of God's curse.

Susie: God continued with the curse of the serpent; but in so doing, He was giving Eve the first prophecy concerning the Savior, the Messiah, to come. Therefore, Eve was the first to receive a hint about Jesus and hope for humankind.

Genesis 3:15 And I will put enmity between you and the woman, and between your seed and her seed. He will crush your head, and you will strike his heel.

Susie: We felt the Amplified made this verse a little clearer:

Genesis 3:15 (AMP) "And I will put enmity (open hostility) between you and the woman, And between your seed (offspring) and her Seed; He shall [fatally] bruise your head, And you shall [only] bruise His heel."

Susie: Yes, snakes (serpents) bite the heel and we stomp their heads; but there is more to this prophecy.

Susan: Satan would be jealous. Satan was thrown out of Heaven for desiring to "be like God". Adam and Eve were both made in the image of God, but even though Eve was deceived and Adam willfully disobeyed God, they were both given grace. Therefore, Satan is the enemy of man, constantly trying to prevent people from having a right relationship with their Creator.

Susie: Crucifixion is one of the few forms of execution that "bruises the heel" as the spike is driven through the feet and the heels pushed hard against the cross. But as Jesus' heels were bruised, He was delivering the deathblow to Satan's head. Satan is truly a "dead devil walking." Eve and Adam were the first humans to hear this promise that Satan would ultimately be destroyed by Eve's Seed (singular) which would be Jesus. Usually "seed" denotes sperm, but it was by the woman's seed that deliverance would come. Mary conceived Jesus by the Holy Spirit without the normally necessary benefit of a human man's sperm, so Jesus was Mary's Seed and ultimately that of Eve.

> *Romans 16:20 The God of peace will soon crush Satan under your feet. The grace of our Lord Jesus Christ be with you.*

> *1 Corinthians 15:22 For as in Adam all die, so in Christ all will be made alive.*

Genesis 3:16–19 To the woman He said: "I will sharply increase your pain in childbirth; in pain you will bring forth children. Your desire will be for your husband, and he will rule over you." And to Adam He said: "Because you have listened to the voice of your wife and have eaten from the tree of which I commanded you not to eat, cursed is the ground because of you; through toil you will eat of it all the days of your life. Both thorns and thistles it will yield for you, and you will eat the plants of the field. By the sweat of your brow you will eat your bread, until you return to the ground—because out of it were you taken. For dust you are, and to dust you shall return."

Susan: God then forecasted what would happen as a result of the fall. Note that He does not use the word "cursed" in relation to the man and the woman but details the consequences of their sin. The pain of the woman would be increased in childbirth, and Adam would have to work hard to bring food out of the ground. A physical change occurred in Eve making childbirth more painful than originally designed. These consequences passed on to all humankind.

Susie: Women would desire their husbands and for the sake of order, the husband would "rule over" the wife. However, the husband is the head of the wife in the sense that he is the provider and protector, and the one God holds responsible for the spiritual welfare of the household. This verse and the passage in Ephesians dealing with the marriage relationship have been misused to excuse domineering and sometimes abusive behavior. We must look at the rest of the picture Paul presents, the fact that both are to **submit to each other,** and that the husband's love should be **self-sacrificing**. The husband is to be a Christ-like servant-leader as in Luke 22.

> **3:16** God reinforced His word of hope to Eve by assuring her that she would bear children and therefore not immediately die. But the special privilege of woman as the childbearer (and ultimately the one who would bring the Redeemer into the world) would involve multiplied pain in pregnancy as well as submission to her husband. The New Testament makes it clear that husbands and wives who love each other and are filled with the Spirit will be mutually submissive (1 Cor. 7:1–6; Eph. 5:18ff.). (15)

> *Ephesians 5:21-25 (CJB) Submit to one another in fear of the Messiah. Wives should submit to their husbands as they do to the Lord; because the husband is head of the wife, just as the Messiah, as head of the Messianic Community, is himself the one who keeps the body safe. Just as the Messianic Community submits to the Messiah, so also wives should submit to their husbands in everything. As for husbands, love your wives, just as the Messiah loved the Messianic Community, indeed, gave himself up on its behalf . . .*

> *Luke 22:24-27 (NLT) Then they began to argue among themselves about who would be the greatest among them. Jesus told them, "In this world the kings and great men lord it over their people, yet they are called 'friends of the people.' But among you it will be different. Those who are the greatest among you should take the lowest rank, and the leader should be like a servant. Who is more important, the one who sits at the table or the one who serves? The one who sits at the table, of course. But not here! For I am among you as one who serves.*

Susie: The earth was cursed as well, as it would now yield thorns, thistles, and other unpleasant plants. It would be more difficult for Adam to work the land. It would be prone to drought, floods, earthquakes as well as many kinds of pestilence—locusts, mosquitoes, etc. Paul tells us that the earth longs for Christ's return as we do.

Romans 8:22-23 We know that the whole creation has been groaning together in the pains of childbirth until the present time. Not only that, but we ourselves, who have the firstfruits of the Spirit, groan inwardly as we wait eagerly for our adoption as sons, the redemption of our bodies.

Genesis 3:20 And Adam named his wife Eve, because she would be the mother of all the living.

Susie: We like the way the Amplified Version translates Genesis 3:20:

Genesis 3:20 (AMP) The man named his wife Eve (life spring, life giver), because she was the mother of all the living.

Susie: Since Eve, as the first woman, was the first mother, all other people are descended from her. This makes her crucial to the Christmas story in three ways:

1. Without Eve, there would be no other people because Adam could not procreate alone.
2. Without Eve's being deceived and Adam's following her advice in disobedience to God and in contradiction to what God had directly spoken to him, humans would not need a Savior-Redeemer; and there would have been no need for the incarnation of Jesus.
3. Eve was the first person to receive the promise of the Messiah even though the word was not used. Her "Seed" referred to Jesus who would destroy Satan.

Genesis 3:21 And the LORD God made garments of skin for Adam and his wife, and He clothed them.

Susie: God then made the first animal sacrifice in order to cover the nakedness of Adam and Eve. Ultimately, Jesus would become the final blood sacrifice, the Perfect Lamb of God, to cover us with His righteousness. One more way in which the account of Eve foreshadows the coming of the Son of God, God incarnate, the Baby Jesus of Christmas.

Susan: Of course, God knew beforehand that Adam and Eve would fall and would need redemption. Therefore, as far as God was concerned Jesus had already paid the price of sin:

Revelation 13:8b . . . the Book of Life that belongs to the Lamb who was slaughtered before the world was made.

Genesis 3:22-24 Then the LORD God said, "Behold, the man has become like one of Us, knowing good and evil. And now, lest he reach out his hand and take also from the tree of life, and eat, and live forever..." Therefore the LORD God banished him from the Garden of Eden to work the ground from which he had been taken. So He drove out the man and stationed cherubim on the east side of the Garden of Eden, along with a whirling sword of flame to guard the way to the tree of life.

Susan: Being kicked out of the Garden of Eden may seem harsh at first glance. However, God was being loving, gracious, and protective by barring humans from the location of the tree of life. Had they eaten of the tree of life in their unredeemed state, they would have been alienated from God's presence forever.

Susie: Throughout history, people have searched for a "fountain of youth" wishing to stay young in this world perpetually. They do not look at the possible consequences this would bring. Theoretically, they would be stuck here on earth with no hope of going to Heaven. Perhaps that would have been the result had Adam and Even eaten from the tree of life.

Susan: How does Eve fit into the lineage of Jesus?

Susie: One of Eve's first children, Cain, committed the first murder when he killed his brother Abel. However, we see that Eve did not cease to believe in God's goodness after being expelled from the Garden of Eden because when her third son was born, she credited God with replacing Abel.

Genesis 4:25 And Adam again had relations with his wife, and she gave birth to a son and named him Seth, saying, "God has granted me another seed in place of Abel, since Cain killed him."

Susie: Seth means "anointed; compensation". She believed God had compensated for her loss by allowing her to conceive another son.

Susan: God healed Eve's broken heart with the birth of Seth. She saw God as faithful to relieve her pain even though it was brought on by sin. We see God's mercy and grace even in the lives of Adam and Eve.

Susie: It was through this son, Seth, that Jesus, the Messiah came. You will find his name listed in the lineage of Jesus in Luke 3:38.

Luke 3:38 . . . the son of Enosh, the son of Seth, the son of Adam, the son of God.

REVIEW QUESTIONS

1. What consequences are given to Adam and Eve because they listened to the serpent and ate the forbidden fruit?

   _____
   _____
   _____
   _____
   _____

2. What consequences were given to the serpent?

    _____
    _____
    _____
    _____
    _____
    _____
    _____

3. God gave the first prophecy in Scripture Himself. What did He predict in Genesis 3:15?

    _____
    _____
    _____
    _____
    _____
    _____
    _____

4. From which of Adam and Eve's sons would Jesus descend? What is the meaning of his name?

    _____
    _____

Ponder This...

You are probably seeing clearly that Christmas is not just about a cute little baby, lying in a manger on a bed of hay, in a barn. It's not just about shepherds, wise men, and angelic messengers. It is about the all-powerful, all-knowing, everywhere-present God of the universe descending down to earth in the form of that helpless baby in order to grow into the God-Man who would become our perfect sacrifice and stomp Satan's head once and for all. Christmas leads to the death and resurrection of Jesus. If you have not already surrendered your life to Him, please do so today. If you are not sure how to surrender yourself to Jesus, read "Jewels of Salvation" in the back of this book, contact us on our website at www.preciousjewelsministries.com or talk with a Bible teaching pastor. Christmas is about each of us having the opportunity to be in right relationship with our Creator, to be brought from death to life, from the darkness of sin to His marvelous light.

> *1 Peter 2:9 But you are a chosen people, a royal priesthood, a holy nation, a people for God's own possession, to proclaim the virtues of Him who called you out of darkness into His marvelous light.*

Eve

Great[nth] Grandmother of Jesus

- Genesis 1:17 So God created man in His own image; in the image of God He created him; male and **_female_** He created them.

- Genesis 2:18 The LORD God also said, "It is not good for the man to be alone. I will make for him a **_suitable helper_**."

- Genesis 2:20 The man gave names to all the livestock, to the birds of the air, and to every beast of the field. But for Adam no **_suitable helper_** was found.

- Genesis 2:22-23 And from the rib that the LORD God had taken from the man, He made a **_woman_** and brought her to him. And the man said: "This is now bone of my bones and flesh of my flesh; she shall be called '**_woman_**,' for out of man she was taken."

- Genesis 2:25 And the man and his **_wife_** were both naked, and they were not ashamed.

- Genesis 3:15 (AMP) "And I will put enmity (open hostility) Between you and the **_woman_**, And between your seed (offspring) and **_her Seed_**; He shall [fatally] bruise your head, And you shall [only] bruise His heel."

- Genesis 3:20 And Adam named his wife **_Eve_**, because she would be the **_mother of all the living_**.

- Genesis 4:25 And Adam again had relations with his **_wife_**, and **_she_** gave birth to a son and named him Seth, saying, "God has granted me another seed in place of Abel, since Cain killed him."

- Luke 3:38 . . . the son of Enosh, the **_son of Seth,_** the son of Adam, the son of God.

Sarah
INTRODUCTION

Susie: If you grew up in church, you are probably familiar with the basics of the story of Abram/Abraham and Sarai/Sarah. Let us refresh your memory. Abram lived in Ur of the Chaldeans but believed in the one true God. The first mention of Sarai is found in Genesis chapter eleven.

Genesis 11:27-32 This is the account of Terah. Terah became the father of Abram, Nahor, and Haran. And Haran became the father of Lot. During his father Terah's lifetime, Haran died in his native land, in Ur of the Chaldeans. And Abram and Nahor took wives for themselves. Abram's wife was named Sarai, and Nahor's wife was named Milcah; she was the daughter of Haran, who was the father of both Milcah and Iscah. But Sarai was barren; she had no children. And Terah took his son Abram, his grandson Lot son of Haran, and his daughter-in-law Sarai the wife of Abram, and they set out from Ur of the Chaldeans for the land of Canaan. But when they arrived in Haran, they settled there. Terah lived 205 years, and he died in Haran.

Susie: Right off the bat, we are told that Sarai was barren which is a crucial factor in the story of her life.

Susan: In their culture, a barren woman was thought to be cursed by God; but God had made Sarai barren in order to show His power and glory later on in their story.

Susie: God told Abram to leave his country and travel to a place He would show him. Abram obeyed even though God gave him no map and no information other than the fact that He would make a great nation of him. Abram's wife, Sarai, was beautiful, and more than once he had her pretend to be his sister so people would not kill him to get her. (See Genesis 12 & Genesis 20).

Susan: Abraham wavered in his faith in God's ability to protect him and Sarai, but God was still faithful.

Susie: God always rescued Sarai from becoming a part of some harem! God had a purpose and a plan not only for Abram but specifically for Sarai as well.

Susie: God led them on a long journey to the land of Canaan, later known as the Promised Land, then Israel, the Holy Land. God had promised to make Abram the father of a great nation and changed his name from Abram (exalted father) to Abraham (father of a multitude). At first Abraham thought he might have to designate a servant as his heir because Sarah was barren. Then Sarah suggested that Abraham have a child with her handmaiden, Hagar, as was the custom in that day. As we study Sarah it will become quite clear that God called **Sarah specifically** to be the mother of the great nation promised to Abraham. According to J. Vernon McGee:

> The thing that Sarai suggested was the common practice of that day. When a wife could not bear a child, there was the concubine. Now don't say that God approved it. God did not approve of this at all. This was Sarai's idea, and Abram listened to her. It looks like he is surrendering his position as head of the home here, and he followed her suggestion. (16)

REVIEW QUESTIONS

1. Where was Abram from originally?

   _____
   _____
   _____

2. To what city did Terah and Abram move? Who died there?

   _____
   _____
   _____
   _____

3. What did Sarah propose as a way to fulfill God's promise that Abram would have a son? Would this be considered morally wrong in their culture?

   _____
   _____
   _____
   _____

Ponder This...

If God spoke to you, even in an audible voice, and told you to pack up your entire household and go on a road trip until He said to stop, would you obey Him, not knowing where you would land? If you were Sarai, and Abram sprung this idea on you, how might you respond to him? Remember: they were traveling on foot or by beast and using a tent for shelter: no cars, no RVs, no Holiday Inns.

GENESIS 17 - CHANGE OF NAMES AND ROFL

Genesis 17:15 Then God said to Abraham, "As for Sarai your wife, do not call her Sarai, for her name is to be Sarah. . .

Susan: Sarai's name meant argumentative or quarrelsome, not exactly what I would want to be called. God changed her name to Sarah which means princess. Sar means "chieftain,' so Sarah could be translated "chieftainess." When God gives a new name, it is meant to reflect a new identity in Him.

Genesis 17:16 ". . . And I will bless her and will surely give you a son by her. I will bless her, and she will be the mother of nations; kings of peoples will descend from her."

Susan: God renamed Sarah appropriately since she would be the mother of a son, and her lineage would be that of kings.

Susie: God promised to give Abraham a son specifically *through* Sarah. We plan to make a list of all the times God specified Sarah as the mother of the promised son.

Susan: Abraham was the father, the patriarch of God's chosen people, and Sarah was equally the mother, the matriarch, of the nation of Israel.

Genesis 17:17 Abraham fell facedown. Then he laughed and said to himself, "Can a child be born to a man who is a hundred years old? Can Sarah give birth at the age of ninety?"

Susan: Note that Abraham was the first to laugh at the Lord's proposal. Abraham was only thinking of the limitations of their human bodies. He was focusing exclusively on the natural: his mind could not fathom the supernatural entering into their union.

Susie: In fact, he "fell upon his face," ROFL (**R**olling **O**n the **F**loor **L**aughing). Not how we typically picture the patriarchs!

Susan: His true feelings were in his heart as he questioned how a hundred-year-old man and a ninety-year-old woman could possibly conceive a child.

Susie: However, God loves to use the people who seem unusable in order to bring glory to His name. What man says is all finished up, God can still use. Susan is waving her right arm as an "amen" to this statement.

Susan: Probably 90% of people would look at my cerebral palsied body and consider me unable to be used by God, that the limitations of my "earth-suit" would disqualify me from serving Him. However, God loves to display His splendor and power through weak vessels in order to draw people to Him.

> *1 Corinthians 1:27 But God chose the foolish things of the world to shame the wise; God chose the weak things of the world to shame the strong.*

Susan: That could almost be my life scripture! My strength is not in myself but in Jesus Christ.

> *Philippians 4:13(AMP) I can do all things [which He has called me to do] through Him who strengthens and empowers me [to fulfill His purpose—I am self-sufficient in Christ's sufficiency; I am ready for anything and equal to anything through Him who infuses me with inner strength and confident peace.]*

> *2 Corinthians 12:9 But He said to me, "My grace is sufficient for you, for My power is perfected in weakness." Therefore I will boast all the more gladly in my weaknesses, so that the power of Christ may rest on me.*

Susie: For sure. Society sees Susan's body— trapped by cerebral palsy, limited use of one arm, unable to do many daily living tasks by herself—and assumes she is weak. Yet, the Lord God in His wisdom and power has chosen her to be a megaphone for His message! She is also my strong, steady, faithful chosen sister.

Genesis 17:18 And Abraham said to God, "O that Ishmael might live under Your blessing!"

Susie: Abraham was missing the point...

Susan: ...so he tried to convince God that Ishmael could be his heir. Both Abraham and Sarah tried to help God out, as if He needed any assistance from humans.

Susie: Earlier Abraham had said his servant Eliezer of Damascus (Genesis 15:2) would be his heir since Sarah was barren. Then Sarah suggested that Abraham have a child with Hagar, and out of respect for his wife, he took her advice to have Ishmael. But God wanted *Sarah* to be the biological mother of His people. God had his own, perfect plan; and He, the Potter, did not need any help from the clay!

> *Isaiah 29:16 (NIV) You turn things upside down, as if the potter were thought to be like the clay! Shall what is formed say to the one who formed it, "You did not make me"? Can the pot say to the potter, "You know nothing"?*

Genesis 17:19 But God replied, "Your wife Sarah will indeed bear you a son, and you are to name him Isaac. I will establish My covenant with him as an everlasting covenant for his descendants after him."

Susan: God, in His gentle grace, did not get angry with Abraham for laughing (and by the way, Abraham laughed first, not Sarah). Instead, God instructed Abraham to name this future son Isaac which means "he laughs."

Susie: I believe this demonstrates that God has a sense of humor.

Susan: The barren woman, the childless couple, would certainly laugh with joy to have a son born to them in their old age. God chose Abraham to be the father of His chosen people, but God in His sovereignty selected Sarah to be the mother of the nation. Since Jesus was born as a Jew, Sarah was another great-great-etc. grandmother of Jesus.

Genesis 17:20 As for Ishmael, I have heard you, and I will surely bless him; I will make him fruitful and multiply him greatly. He will become the father of twelve rulers, and I will make him into a great nation . . ."

Susie: Ishmael did indeed father twelve sons, and some of the Arab nations (not all) are descended from him. But his is a story for another time.

Genesis 17:21 But I will establish My covenant with Isaac, whom Sarah will bear to you at this time next year."

Susie: God went on to tell Abraham that Sarah would have this baby in the next year. I find it amazing and miraculous not only that God opened Sarah's womb to conceive but that He strengthened her to carry a baby at 90+ years old and enabled her to live to raise him! Sarah's son would be the one to receive the promise, and later Mary's Son would be the complete fulfillment of God's promise.

REVIEW QUESTIONS

1. Where did Abram and Sarai live before they moved to Haran?

2. What covenant did God make with Abraham: what were the promises He made to him?

3. What two people did Abraham propose to be his heir before the Lord made it completely clear that Sarah was to bear him the son of promise? Who were these men to him?

4. How did Abraham respond when God made it perfectly clear that Sarah was to bear him a son?

Ponder This...

Barrenness was considered a curse at the time of Sarah, but God's sovereign plan was for Sarah to experience the miraculous—a baby conceived after menopause. The man born blind in John 9 was given the problem of blindness, so that God could show Himself mighty. After experiencing the miracle of receiving his sight, the man glorified God. What may seem like a problem today may be changed to a blessing tomorrow. Therefore, we can obey the command of 1 Thessalonians 5:18 and give thanks in EVERYTHING. Also, we can never say, "Oh, God could not use me! I'm too _____." God can and will use you by His grace and for His glory because He knows no limitations!

> *John 9:1-3 Now as Jesus was passing by, He saw a man blind from birth, and His disciples asked Him, "Rabbi, who sinned, this man or his parents, that he was born blind?" Jesus answered, "Neither this man nor his parents sinned, but this happened so that the works of God would be displayed in him.*

> *1 Thessalonians 5:18 Give thanks in every circumstance, for this is God's will for you in Christ Jesus.*

Sarah

GENESIS 18 - NAME THE BABY "HE LAUGHS"

Susie: Abraham was sitting at the entrance of his tent one day under some oak trees when three visitors appeared. He invited them to rest and share a meal. It is not stated that he immediately knew them to be the Angel of the Lord (a theophany of Jesus) and two angels, but his behavior and the prophecy given suggest this to be the case. He had Sarah prepare bread and a servant prepare a calf.

Genesis 18:9 "Where is your wife Sarah?" they asked. "There, in the tent," he replied.

Susan: Because of modesty and dignity, Sarah had remained inside the tent instead of coming out among the men.

Susie: Sarah's respect for her husband is demonstrated in her modesty and her submissiveness toward Abraham as the head of their household. But we cannot stop there. Peter also points out and praises Sarah's courage and lack of anxiety. Abraham was not the only one having to leave Ur for an unknown destination. Sarah, in obedience to her husband, and without fear, followed Abraham on that journey. Note how Peter explains that husbands are to be understanding of their wives and RESPECT and VALUE them as coheirs in Christ lest their own prayers be hindered.

> *1 Peter 3:5-7 (VOICE) This is how, long ago, holy women who put their hope in God made themselves beautiful: by respecting the authority of their husbands. Consider how Sarah, our mother, obeyed her husband, Abraham, and called him "lord," and you will be her daughters as long as you boldly do what is right without fear and without anxiety. In the same way, husbands, as you live with your wives, understand the situations women face as the weaker vessel. Each of you should respect your wife and value her as an equal heir in the gracious gift of life. Do this so that nothing will get in the way of your prayers.*

Susie: Note that Peter referred to Sarah as "our mother" recognizing her role as the matriarch of Israel. Isaiah recognized Sarah as the nation's matriarch as well because God selected Sarah specifically to be the mother of the promised son.

> *Isaiah 51:2 Look to Abraham your father, and to Sarah who gave you birth. When I called him, he was but one; then I blessed him and multiplied him.*

Susan: God hand-picked Sarah to be the mother of the nation of Israel rather than Hagar. Both

Isaac and Ishmael were Abraham's sons, but God insisted that *Sarah* was to be the biological mother of the son of promise.

Genesis 18:10 Then the LORD said, "I will surely return to you at this time next year, and your wife Sarah will have a son!" Now Sarah was behind him, listening at the entrance to the tent.

Susie: This heavenly visitor was reiterating what the Lord had already told Abraham. It is not clear whether or not Abraham had communicated to his wife God's earlier promise to him that Sarah would bear a son. This may have been the first she heard of it while listening from the entrance of the tent.

Susan: God gave Sarah a specific time that Isaac would be born. He is not only sovereign over her barren womb but over the timing of the birth.

Susie: Likewise, we are told that Esther became queen "for such a time as this," and we will explore God's sovereignty in that later in this study. Mary bore Jesus "in the fullness of time." We will get into the specifics of what that meant when we get to Mary in our study. Right now, the point is that timing is everything, and God is in control of the times.

> *Esther 4:14b ...And who knows if perhaps you have come to the kingdom for such a time as this?"*

> *Galatians 4:3–5 So also, when we were children, we were enslaved under the basic principles of the world. But when the time had fully come, God sent His Son, born of a woman, born under the law, to redeem those under the law, that we might receive our adoption as sons.*

Genesis 18:11–12 And Abraham and Sarah were already old and well along in years; Sarah had passed the age of childbearing. So she laughed to herself, saying, "After I am worn out and my master is old, will I now have this pleasure?"

Susan: As did Abraham before her, Sarah cracked up laughing at the prospect of two elderly people, way past the age of reproduction, having a baby together. Her reproductive equipment was dilapidated!

Susie: It seemed absurd to her. They knew how things worked even though they did not study it in science/health class as we did.

Genesis 18:13–14 And the LORD asked Abraham, "Why did Sarah laugh and say, 'Can I really bear a child when I am old?' Is anything too difficult for the LORD? At the appointed time I will return to you—in about a year—and Sarah will have a son."

Susie: The Lord asked Abraham why Sarah laughed but did not wait for an answer.

Susan: He asked, "Is anything too hard for the Lord?" Then He let them know He would be back, and they would see the power of the Lord manifest in their old bodies, seemingly past the age of reproduction.

Susie: By the time He came back, Isaac would have been born. Paul emphasized God's sovereignty in choosing Abraham's son *born to Sarah* as the son of promise by reminding his readers of this promise:

> *Romans 9:8-9 So it is not the children of the flesh who are God's children, but it is the children of the promise who are regarded as offspring. For this is what the promise stated: "At the appointed time I will return, and Sarah will have a son."*

Genesis 18:15 But Sarah was afraid, so she denied it and said, "I did not laugh."
"No," replied the LORD, "but you did laugh."

Susie: Sarah tried to deny the fact that she had laughed, but the Lord knows our hearts. He confirmed that she did laugh. We cannot hide our feelings from God.

Susan: God did not discount the covenant due to their laughter. He graciously fulfilled His promises to Abraham and Sarah.

1. Who laughed at the prospect of Sarah having a baby first? Sarah or Abraham?

   _____
   _____
   _____

2. Why did Sarah think that the idea of her having a child was absurd?

   _____
   _____
   _____
   _____

3. Can you think of other things God has done both in the past and in the present that were seemingly "impossible."

   _____
   _____
   _____
   _____
   _____

Ponder This...

Have you ever felt the Lord was asking you to do something absurd? Something like going to college for eight years in a power chair and training your own caregivers? (Susan) Or becoming a ministry partner and caregiver for someone you had known less than a year? (Susie) Sometimes it seems God is asking us to do the impossible or in the least, the improbable. But if you are certain the Lord is calling you to serve Him in a specific way, laugh if you want but go forward boldly. In His timing, you will see His glory when you rely on His grace and power.

> *Jeremiah 32:17 "Oh, Lord GOD! You have made the heavens and the earth by Your great power and outstretched arm. Nothing is too difficult for You!"*

Sarah

GENESIS 21 - A CHILD IS BORN TO ONE OLD AND WORN

Genesis 21:1–2 Now the LORD attended to Sarah as He had said, and the LORD did for Sarah what He had promised. So Sarah conceived and bore a son to Abraham in his old age, at the very time God had promised.

Susie: Flash forward to the time the Lord had predicted, and Sarah did deliver a baby as promised! God always makes good on His promises in His timing and in His way.

Susan: God reminds us that Abraham was over 100 years old but think about poor Sarah! She had the hard part of carrying and delivering a baby at 90+ years old! Who got the better and easier end of this deal?

Susie: However, Sarah must have been delighted to finally hold her own baby in her arms. Abraham was extremely pleased to finally have a son by the wife of his youth. He finally had an heir to receive all the Lord had given him in blessings as well as the promise of becoming a great nation.

Genesis 21:3–5 And Abraham gave the name Isaac to the son Sarah bore to him. When his son Isaac was eight days old, Abraham circumcised him, as God had commanded him. Abraham was a hundred years old when his son Isaac was born to him.

Susie: Abraham named his son Isaac as the Lord had instructed him, and it is certain that many people joined Abraham and Sarah in celebration and laughter at the birth of this miraculously conceived baby.

Susan: God had given Abraham the command to circumcise all the males of his household. You can read about when Abraham circumcised himself and every male belonging to him in Genesis chapter 17. Therefore, he circumcised Isaac when he was just eight days old in obedience to what the Lord had commanded as the sign of their covenant relationship.

> *Genesis 17:10-12 This is My covenant with you and your descendants after you, which you are to keep: Every male among you must be circumcised. You are to circumcise the flesh of your foreskin, and this will be a sign of the covenant between Me and you. Generation after generation, every male must be circumcised when he is eight days old, including those born in your household and those purchased from a foreigner—even those who are not your offspring.*

Susie: It is not coincidental that God the Great Physician prescribed that circumcision be done on the 8th day of a newborn's life:

> "Dr S.I. McMillen, M.D., in his book None of These Diseases (2000) confirms that pain caused by circumcising later in life can last for up to a week. Newborns, on the other hand, are extremely resilient. So the most humane time is to circumcise in the first month of life. He also confirms that prothrombin only jumps to 110% of the adult level on the eighth day. Thus the safest day for circumcision in a baby's life is day eight. The fact that the Bible records the exact and earliest "cut off" point for a newborn reveals a divine fingerprint. God knew exactly what he was doing." https://www.premierchristianradio.com/Topics/Church/Apologetics/How-circumcision-shows-God-exists
>
> An article shared by famous surgeon and New York Times bestseller, Dr Joseph Mercola also states: 'Day 8 is said to be the only time in a baby's life when his prothrombin level will naturally exceed 100 percent of normal.'
> https://hermeneutics.stackexchange.com/questions/31778/why-is-a-male-child-circumcised-on-the-8th-day
>
> Prothrombin is a protein produced by your liver. It is one of many factors in your blood that help it to clot appropriately.
> https://www.mayoclinic.org/tests-procedures/prothrombin-time/about/pac-20384661

Susie: The nation of Israel began with a miraculous birth of a baby given to a couple in their extreme old age. God told Abraham that all nations would be blessed through his seed.

> *Genesis 18:17–19 And the LORD said, "Shall I hide from Abraham what I am about to do? Abraham will surely become a great and powerful nation, and through him all the nations of the earth will be blessed. For I have chosen him, so that he will command his children and his household after him to keep the way of the LORD by doing what is right and just, in order that the LORD may bring upon Abraham what He has promised."*

Susan: All nations would be blessed through Abraham's seed because the Messiah, Yeshua, Jesus, would be a descendant of Abraham…

Susie: …specifically through the line of Isaac who was born of *Sarah*. Laughter, joy, would surely enter the world and spread to not only the Jews but the Gentiles as well through Abraham's descendant born in a stable and laid in a manger in Bethlehem.

Susan: The Baby born to die so that we may believe and trust in Him for redemption and live with Him forever!

Genesis 21:6–7 Then Sarah said, "God has made me laugh, and everyone who hears of this will laugh with me." She added, "Who would have told Abraham that Sarah would nurse children? Yet I have borne him a son in his old age."

Susan: "I did it! I did it!" Sarah marveled. At over 90 years old, Sarah experienced a childlike wonderment over her miraculous conception and delivery of Isaac.

Susie: And she realized that only the power of God had made it possible. God had chosen *Sarah* as much as He had chosen Abraham. There could be no doubt that this was true because of the miraculous nature of Isaac's conception and birth.

Genesis 21:8 So the child grew and was weaned, and Abraham held a great feast on the day Isaac was weaned.

Susie: Abraham and Sarah had the joy of watching their baby become a young child and celebrated the rite of passage from babyhood to boyhood with a great banquet.

REVIEW QUESTIONS

1. What did Abraham do to Isaac when he was only eight days old? Why?

2. How did Sarah react when she finally had a child of her own at 90+ years old?

3. Who was to be blessed through Abraham's Seed?

Ponder This...

Over and over, the Lord made it clear that *Sarah* was to be the mother of the promised son. Abraham even tried to settle for second best by asking the Lord to choose Ishmael. But what a blessing when Isaac was born! Do we try to settle for plan B instead of waiting on the Lord? Do we settle for good instead of best? Do we fail to remember Psalm 37:5a (ESV) "Be still before the Lord and wait patiently for him"? Think about something you are waiting for. It may seem you've been waiting on the Lord for a long time. How can you encourage yourself and/or others by remembering the story of Sarah?

Sarah

GENESIS 22 - BOY TO BE BURNT OFFERING

Susie: A bit of history before the next section of scripture. Sarah became upset that Ishmael, Abraham's son by her handmaiden Hagar, was present at the weaning celebration of her own son and was mocking Isaac. Therefore, she asked Abraham to send them away. God reassured Abraham that Ishmael, too, would become a great nation, and instructed him to do as Sarah asked. He sent Hagar and Ishmael away with some provisions, but the provisions wore out. God preserved them, showing Hagar a well of water. God kept his promise to make Ishmael the father of kings and nations as well. But His covenant relationship was with Isaac, the son of *Sarah*, the son of promise. Time passed, and Isaac grew into his teenage years. God tested Abraham by commanding him to journey to Mount Moriah and offer Isaac, the son of promise, as a burnt offering. An animal offered as a burnt offering was first slaughtered and then burned until consumed. It must have been a painful journey walking up that hill. Abraham confidently told his servants to wait while he and the boy went to worship and that THEY would return.

Genesis 22:5 "Stay here with the donkey," Abraham told his servants. "The boy and I will go over there to worship, and then we will return to you."

Susan: It was perplexing for the teenaged Isaac as he carried wood, and his dad carried a pot of hot coals to start the fire. He asked his father, "Where is the lamb for the offering?" Abraham's mind was already in the state of thankful worship; and by faith, he assured Isaac that God would provide the lamb.

Genesis 22:7-8 Then Isaac said to his father Abraham, "My father!" "Here I am, my son," he replied. "The fire and the wood are here," said Isaac, "but where is the lamb for the burnt offering?" Abraham answered, "God Himself will provide the lamb for the burnt offering, my son." And the two walked on together.

Susie: Isaac does not question Abraham's statement that God would provide the lamb. He has grown up observing his father's faith and trusts him and His God.

Genesis 22:9 When they arrived at the place God had designated, Abraham built the altar there and arranged the wood. He bound his son Isaac and placed him on the altar, atop the wood.

Susan: Abraham had to gather large stones and build the altar. All the while, he must have been praying, wondering how the Lord could command him to kill the son of promise, the child of the covenant. I am certain it made his brain go "tilt." Isaac could have overpowered his father, but he was willingly, submissively obedient to his earthly father and to God.

Susie: Isaac had observed his father's complete trust in God all his life and had been told the miraculous nature of his birth. Abraham may have had questions but was confident God was in control of the situation.

Genesis 22:10 Then Abraham reached out his hand and took the knife to slaughter his son.

Susie: Abraham was fully prepared by faith to obey his God and sacrifice the son of promise. Talk about a test of faith!

> *Hebrews 11:17–19 By faith Abraham, when he was tested, offered up Isaac on the altar. He who had received the promises was ready to offer his one and only son, even though God had said to him, "Through Isaac your offspring will be reckoned." Abraham reasoned that God could raise the dead, and in a sense, he did receive Isaac back from death.*

Susan: At this point in Scripture, there is no record of God raising anyone from the dead. However, Abraham, trying to figure out this seemingly contradictory command, reasoned that God must be able to raise the dead. Abraham was able to extrapolate this idea based on the miracle of Isaac's birth. God enabled a one-hundred-year-old man to have active sperm and a ninety-year-old woman to have a viable egg and the two to meet in the uterus. That could not have been coincidence!

Susie: Since God had been able to knit Isaac in Sarah's worn-out womb, He could surely raise him from the dead if Abraham obeyed the command to sacrifice him.

Susan: In the King James Version, Isaac is described as Abraham's "only begotten son." The only other time we see the phrase "only begotten son" is to describe Jesus as the Son of God.

Susie: The near sacrifice of Isaac is what is called a "type," a foreshadowing of another event. Abraham's willingness to offer his only official heir to the Lord foreshadows God's sending His Son Jesus as our perfect sacrificial Lamb.

Susan: Abraham had reasoned that even if he slayed his son, God could and would raise him from the dead.

Susie: As we already stated, we do not recall any account prior to the time of Abraham of God raising someone from the dead, so Abraham was believing God could do this completely by logic based in faith rather than by past experience.

Genesis 22:11 Just then the angel of the LORD called out to him from heaven, "Abraham, Abraham!" "Here I am," he replied.

Susie: Abraham stopped his hand in mid-air and breathlessly awaited the command given by the angel of the Lord.

Susan: Isaac may have been closing his eyes and holding his breath at this point, waiting for the pain of the knife before death. Then he, also, hears the angel of the Lord.

Susie: "Angel of the Lord" many times refers to the pre-incarnate Jesus. Therefore, Jesus, God Himself, stopped Abraham from actually sacrificing Isaac.

Genesis 22:12 "Do not lay a hand on the boy or do anything to him," said the angel, "for now I know that you fear God, since you have not withheld your only son from me."

Susie: You can breathe again, Isaac! The Angel of the Lord praised the faithfulness of Abraham in not withholding even the treasured, miraculous son of his old age from God. God called Isaac Abraham's ONLY son because he was the only legitimate heir of the promise as far as God was concerned. By faith Abraham knew that God would somehow fulfill His promise of making Isaac into a great nation and did not hesitate to obey the command to offer him as a burnt offering. God stayed his hand at just the right moment.

Susan: We must be sensitive to listen to the voice of God. Had Abraham not listened... Perhaps God would have raised Isaac from the dead. There is a constant tuning the heart to the Holy Spirit that takes place in those who trust and believe in the Father and are listening for direction, insight, and understanding.

Genesis 22:13–14 Then Abraham looked up and saw behind him a ram in a thicket, caught by its horns. So he went and took the ram and offered it as a burnt offering in place of his son. And Abraham called that place The LORD Will Provide. So to this day it is said, "On the mountain of the LORD it will be provided."

Susie: Another foreshadowing is seen in this account: God Himself provided the substitute to be sacrificed to Him instead of Isaac. He provided a ram rather than a lamb because His Lamb was yet to come in the fullness of time. We are under the death penalty for our sins, but God has provided the perfect, spotless, sinless Lamb of God, His only begotten son, Jesus, to die in our place as the final sacrifice to provide the only way to right relationship with God for those who believe.

Susan: In the Garden of Eden, we saw God sacrifice animals to cover the nakedness of Adam and Eve. Here God provided the ram to take the place of Isaac as an offering to Him. In the sacrificial system of the Mosaic Law, God provided an abundance of sheep, bulls, birds, etc. to be sacrificed rather than have the punishment of the people's sins fall on their own heads. Then, in the fullness of time, God, in the person of Jesus Christ, sacrificed Himself on the cross to pay the debt of sin once for all.

Then God tested Abraham, and when he kept the faith, God provided a substitutionary sacrifice, a ram. That ram is a beautiful picture of our Lord Jesus. You and I deserve to die, but Jesus provided Himself for the lamb. He rushed out to Calvary and took our place, bore our sin, died our death so we could live His life. He took our sin so we could take His righteousness. He is our substitutionary sacrifice and all-sufficient Savior! (17)

Genesis 22:15–18 And the angel of the LORD called to Abraham from heaven a second time, saying, "By Myself I have sworn, declares the LORD, that because you have done this and have not withheld your only son, I will surely bless you, and I will multiply your descendants like the stars in the sky and the sand on the seashore. Your descendants will possess the gates of their enemies. And through your offspring all nations of the earth will be blessed, because you have obeyed My voice."

Susan: The Lord swore an oath upon His own name. There is no greater power to swear by! God reiterated His promise that Isaac's descendants would be as innumerable as the stars and the endless grains of sand, they would be blessed, and they would overtake their enemies.

Susie: As stated before, all nations are blessed through the seed, the descendant of Abraham and *Sarah*, Jesus Christ. Salvation—freedom from sin and freedom to live in right relationship with a holy God—is available not only to the chosen people, Israel, but to any person in the world of any nationality who by faith trusts in Jesus as the only way to the Father.

> *John 14:6 Jesus answered, "I am the way and the truth and the life. No one comes to the Father except through Me."*

Susie: But back to our main reason for studying Abraham, Sarah, and Isaac. *Sarah's* faith and contribution to the birth of the nation of Israel is of equal importance with that of Abraham. She was the mother of Isaac through whom the Messiah would come. She was another one of the Women of Christmas.

Susan: Therefore, Sarah received a place of recognition in the Faith Hall of Fame found in Hebrews chapter 11.

> *Hebrews 11:11 By faith Sarah, even though she was barren and beyond the proper age, was enabled to conceive a child, because she considered Him faithful who had promised.*

11:11 Although Sarah laughed when first hearing that she was to have a child, her disbelief evidently turned to faith long before the birth of her son, Isaac (Ge 18:12). God gave the outstanding patriarch, Abraham, a woman of faith as his wife. She, too, had to believe that the God who made promises would honor his Word, despite how impossible it must have seemed to her as a woman long past childbearing years. Sarah was willing to have her attitude changed. Her faith grew as a result. (18)

REVIEW QUESTIONS

1. What did God tell Abraham to do with the son given to him as a part of the covenant God made with him?

2. What did Abraham reason that God was able to do even though it had never been done before?

3. Make a statement about Isaac's faith.

4. What animal did God provide to take Isaac's place on the altar?

5. Explain how this is a "type" or foreshadowing of future events.

Ponder This...

Christianity is often accused of treating women like second-class citizens. However, as we have seen with Sarah, the Lord went overboard to remind us of her important role in the birth of the nation of Israel. Women are of equal importance in the Lord's plans, co-heirs of the Kingdom with Jesus Christ. Have you ever had self-esteem issues? Search for verses about our value in Christ. Write about them.

> *Romans 8:16-17 The Spirit Himself testifies with our spirit that we are God's children. And if we are children, then we are heirs: heirs of God and co-heirs with Christ—if indeed we suffer with Him, so that we may also be glorified with Him.*

> *Galatians 3:28 There is neither Jew nor Greek, slave nor free, male nor female, for you are all one in Christ Jesus.*

Ponder This too...

One last thing to ponder as we wrap up the story of God's promise to Abraham and **Sarah.** Abraham's biological children down through the ages account for a great number of people. However, we who trust in Jesus by FAITH just as Abraham and Sarah trusted by FAITH, are also CHILDREN OF ABRAHAM!

> *Galatians 3:29 (NLT) And now that you belong to Christ, you are the true children of Abraham. You are his heirs, and God's promise to Abraham belongs to you.*

WORSHIP OPPORTUNITY

Please take the time to go to YouTube and listen to "We are the Sands, We are the Stars" written by Gloria Gaither with Reba Rambo-McGuire and Dony McGuire, and then worship along with the Gaither Vocal Band: https://www.youtube.com/watch?v=G8Bs20-3D-M

CHOSEN TO BE THE MOTHER OF THE PROMISE

- Genesis 17:15-16 Then God said to Abraham, "As for Sarai your wife, do not call her Sarai, for her name is to be **Sarah**. And I will bless her and will surely give you a son **by her.** I will bless her, and she will be the **mother of nations**; kings of peoples will descend from her."

- Genesis 17:17-19 Abraham fell facedown. Then he laughed and said to himself, "Can a child be born to a man who is a hundred years old? Can Sarah give birth at the age of ninety?" And Abraham said to God, "O that Ishmael might live under Your blessing!" But God replied, "Your wife ***Sarah will indeed bear you a son***, and you are to name him Isaac. I will establish My covenant with him as an everlasting covenant for his descendants after him.

- Genesis 17:21 But I will establish My covenant with Isaac, whom **Sarah** will bear to you at this time next year."

- Genesis 18:10a Then the LORD said, "I will surely return to you at this time next year, and your wife **Sarah** will have a son!"

- Genesis 18:14 Is anything too difficult for the LORD? At the appointed time I will return to you—in about a year—and **Sarah** will have a son.

- Genesis 21:1-3 Now the LORD attended to **Sarah** as He had said, and the LORD did for **Sarah** what He had promised. So **Sarah** conceived and bore a son to Abraham in his old age, at the very time God had promised. Abraham named his son who was born to him, the son whom **Sarah** bore to him, Isaac.

- Isaiah 51:2 Look to Abraham your father, and to **Sarah** who gave you birth. When I called him, he was but one; then I blessed him and multiplied him.

- Romans 4:18-21 Against all hope, Abraham in hope believed and so became the father of many nations, just as he had been told, "So shall your offspring be." Without weakening in his faith, he acknowledged the decrepitness of his body (since he was about a hundred years old) and the lifelessness of **Sarah's** womb. Yet he did not waver through disbelief in the promise of God, but was strengthened in his faith and gave glory to God, being fully persuaded that God was able to do what He had promised. This is why "it was credited to him as righteousness."

- Romans 9:9 For this is what the promise stated: "At the appointed time I will return, and **Sarah** will have a son."

- Hebrews 11:11-12 By faith **Sarah**, even though she was barren and beyond the proper age, was enabled to conceive a child, because she considered Him faithful who had promised. And so from one man, and he as good as dead, came descendants as numerous as the stars in the sky and as countless as the sand on the seashore.

Tamar

GENESIS 38 - WIDOWED DUE TO WICKED WAYS OF HUSBANDS

Susie: This story of the escapades of Judah falls in the middle of the account of Joseph the dreamer, his younger brother.

Susan: When his jealous brothers wanted to kill Joseph, his older brother, Judah, the fourth born son of Jacob intervened on his behalf:

Genesis 37:26-28 Then Judah said to his brothers, "What profit will we gain if we kill our brother and cover up his blood? Come, let us sell him to the Ishmaelites and not lay a hand on him; for he is our brother, our own flesh." And they agreed. So when the Midianite traders passed by, his brothers pulled Joseph out of the pit and sold him for twenty shekels of silver to the Ishmaelites, who took him to Egypt.

Susan: Rather than murder Joseph themselves, they decided to make some money off of this "dreamer" of theirs who had been a thorn in their sides.

Susie: Therefore, they sold him to some Midianites instead. The Midianites then sold him to be a servant of Potiphar, the captain of the Egyptian Pharaoh's guard. Before Joseph's story continues, there is this one-chapter interlude about Judah's escapades.

Susan: The point may be to contrast Judah's unrighteousness and disregard for God's way of doing things with the future righteousness of Joseph. You may remember that when Potiphar's wife propositioned Joseph, he literally ran out of his clothes to flee temptation!

> *Genesis 39:10-12 Although Potiphar's wife spoke to Joseph day after day, he refused to go to bed with her or even be near her. One day, however, Joseph went into the house to attend to his work, and not a single household servant was inside. She grabbed Joseph by his cloak and said, "Sleep with me!" But leaving his cloak in her hand, he escaped and ran outside.*

Susie: But now to the story of Judah and our woman of Christmas, Tamar. Judah was the fourth born son of Jacob (Israel) by his first wife, Leah. However, Judah was in the lineage of Christ. I asked the question, "Why Judah?" We found an answer online:

When he designated Judah as the tribe from which Israel's kings would come, Ja-

cob was speaking a prophecy from God. (Genesis 49:10) It had nothing to do with the rights of the first born, which did accrue to Joseph, but was a sovereign act of God. This prophecy didn't take effect until David became King and was a reward to him for his special relationship with God. (1 Chron. 17:3-14)
https://gracethrufaith.com/ask-a-bible-teacher/why-was-judah-chosen/

Genesis 49:10 The scepter will not depart from Judah, nor the staff from between his feet, until Shiloh comes and the allegiance of the nations is his.

Shiloh is best interpreted as the Messiah. It is the Messiah who has the true right to take the throne and hold the scepter (John 18:36–37; Psalm 2:7–9). It is the Messiah who, at His second coming, will have the people's obedience (Daniel 7:13–14; Isaiah 2:2). It is the Messiah, the Lion of Judah, who will rule the whole world (Revelation 11:15) and preside over a time of unprecedented blessing and peace on earth (Isaiah 11:6–13; Micah 4:1–5).
Read the entire article on "Shiloh" here: https://www.gotquestions.org/shiloh.html

Genesis 49:10 (VOICE) The scepter will not depart from Judah; the ruler's staff will rest securely between his feet. Until the One comes to whom true royalty belongs, all people will honor and obey him.

49:8–12 As strong as a young lion and entrenched as an old lion, to Judah's line belonged national prominence and kingship, including David, Solomon, and their dynasty (640 years after this), as well as "the one to whom the scepter belongs," i.e., Shiloh, the cryptogram for the Messiah, the one also called the "Lion of the Tribe of Judah" (Rev. 5:5). On the march through the wilderness, Judah went first (Num. 10:14) and had the largest population in Moses' census (cf. Num. 1:27; 26:22). This language (vv. 11, 12) describes prosperity so great that people will tie a donkey to a choice vine, letting it eat because there is such abundance; wine will be as plentiful as water and everyone will be healthy. This is likely a millennial prophecy. (19)

Genesis 38:1–2 About that time, Judah left his brothers and settled near a man named Hirah, an Adullamite. There Judah saw the daughter of a Canaanite man named Shua, and he took her as a wife and slept with her.

Susie: Instead of staying with his tribe, with the chosen people, Judah went and lived among Canaanites. He even married the daughter of a Canaanite man named Shua. We are never told the name of the woman Judah married!

Genesis 38:3–5 So she conceived and gave birth to a son, and Judah named him Er. Again she conceived and gave birth to a son, and she named him Onan. Then she gave birth to another son and named him Shelah; it was at Chezib that she gave birth to him.

Susie: She bore him three sons:

Susan: Er which means "watchful," Onan which means "strong," and Shelah which means "request."

Susie: They were still living in a Canaanite village when Shelah was born, living among people who were not Israelites.

Susan: Judah's first mistake was to marry someone who was not an Israelite. Judah was living among people who did not worship the true God, the God of Abraham, Isaac, and his own father, Jacob. Their customs were not in keeping with the ways of the Lord.

Genesis 38:6–7 Now Judah acquired a wife for Er, his firstborn, and her name was Tamar. But Er, Judah's firstborn, was wicked in the sight of the LORD; so the LORD put him to death.

Susie: We surmised that Tamar was a Canaanite since Judah was still living among them instead of back with his father's people, but commentators differ on this point:

> The Bible is silent as to her genealogy. All we know is that she was a Canaanite as her heathen name suggests, and that when widowed the second time, she returned to her father's home, but who he was and where he lived we are not told. (20)

> The text is not clear from whose house Jacob originally took Tamar for his son's wife. Since we are told that Judah's own wife was a Canaanite, had Tamar also been a Canaanite, a similar statement presumably would have been mentioned. Since she was likely not a Canaanite, this introduction shows another point at which the promise to Abraham was in jeopardy. By marrying the daughter of a Canaanite, Judah had realized the worst fears of Abraham (24:3) and Isaac (28:1); so the promise regarding the descendants of Abraham and Isaac was in danger of being unfulfillable. Through Tamar's clever plan, however, the seed of Abraham was preserved by not being allowed to continue through the sons of the Canaanite, the daughter of Shua. The line was continued through Judah and Tamar. The genealogy at the close of the narrative underscores this point. (21)

> *Genesis 24:2-4 So Abraham instructed the chief servant of his household, who managed all he owned, "Place your hand under my thigh, and I will have you swear by the LORD, the God of heaven and the God of earth, that you will not take a wife for my son from the daughters of the Canaanites among whom I am dwelling, but will go to my country and my kindred to take a wife for my son Isaac."…*

> *Genesis 28:1 So Isaac called for Jacob and blessed him. "Do not take a wife from the Canaanite women," he commanded.*

Susan: We do not know specifically what Er's transgression was, but it was so egregious—outstandingly bad, shocking—that God struck him dead.

Susie: Tamar was now a widow which in that era would have made her a beggar and a burden unless she remarried.

Genesis 38:8 Then Judah said to Onan, "Sleep with your brother's wife. Perform your duty as her brother-in-law and raise up offspring for your brother."

Susie: There was a tradition which later would become a part of the law called levirate marriage. We found this note in *Archeological Study Bible*:

> **Genesis 38:8** refers to the social and legal obligation of the levir (Latin for "husband's brother") to marry his widowed sister-in-law in the event his brother had died and left her childless. (22)

Susie: This practice later became a part of the Jewish law.

> *Deuteronomy 25:5-10 When brothers dwell together and one of them dies without a son, the widow must not marry outside the family. Her husband's brother is to take her as his wife and fulfill the duty of a brother-in-law for her. The first son she bears will carry on the name of the dead brother, so that his name will not be blotted out from Israel. But if the man does not want to marry his brother's widow, she is to go to the elders at the city gate and say, "My husband's brother refuses to preserve his brother's name in Israel. He is not willing to perform the duty of a brother-in-law for me." Then the elders of his city shall summon him and speak with him. If he persists and says, "I do not want to marry her," his brother's widow shall go up to him in the presence of the elders, remove his sandal, spit in his face, and declare, "This is what is done to the man who will not maintain his brother's line." And his family name in Israel will be called "The House of the Unsandaled."*

Susie: The first son born to the widow and her brother-in-law would be the heir of her husband who died. This would serve two purposes: 1) the dead man's family line, his legacy, would continue in his name, and 2) the widow would now have children to care for her in her old age instead of being left completely bereft.

Susan: Unless she remarried or was young enough to move back into her father's house, she would be a beggar, dependent on alms if she did not have a son to care for her.

Genesis 38:9 But Onan knew that the offspring would not belong to him; so whenever he would sleep with his brother's wife, he would spill his seed on the ground so that he would not produce offspring for his brother.

Susan: Onan did not want to reduce his own inheritance by having a child in order to carry on his brother's line. His greed won over his responsibility to his brother's widow.

Susie: He knew the first son would be seen as Er's child rather than his own. Thinking only of himself, he slept with Tamar but made sure he did not impregnate her.

Susan: He was deceitful by giving the impression that he was fulfilling his duty to take care of Tamar in this way when he really was not completing the requirements. He was withholding intimacy from her, but more than that he was depriving her of future security. This was disobedience to his father which in that culture was expected even of adult children. His act was incredulously selfish.

Genesis 38:10 What he did was wicked in the sight of the LORD, so He put Onan to death as well.

Susan: God knew of Onan's deceptive heart that led to his "spilling his seed on the ground," and so the Lord caused his death.

Susie: This is now two sons Judah has lost due to their wickedness.

Susan: This story reminds us that God could extinguish evil doers at any time; but in His grace, He often does not. As we read on, we will see that it would have even been right for God kill off the whole family if He so chose, but His grace prevailed.

Genesis 38:11 Then Judah said to his daughter-in-law Tamar, "Live as a widow in your father's house until my son Shelah grows up." For he thought, "He may die too, like his brothers." So Tamar went to live in her father's house.

Susie: Judah pledged to give Shelah to Tamar as a husband when he was old enough. He thought in the back of his mind that Shelah might die like his brothers if he had him marry Tamar.

Susan: Judah was walking in fear instead of faith. However, Tamar respected her father-in-law's wishes, returned to her father's house, and waited for Shelah to be of age. We are not told how old Shelah was when Jacob promised him to Tamar.

Susie: Instead of freeing Tamar to marry someone else, Judah had her live as a widow, unmarried and celibate, awaiting Shelah's coming of age.

Susan: Women could not earn a living reputably in those days, so Tamar had to go back home. Her father assumed responsibility for her once more. Needing to move back home was a major embarrassment and frustration.

Susie: At least in her father's house she would be provided food and shelter. However, she would also be subject to him like a child.

REVIEW QUESTIONS

1. Where did Judah choose to live? Why was this a problem?

2. What were the names of Judah's three sons by his Canaanite wife?

3. What happened to Judah's oldest two sons? Why?

4. Describe "levirate marriage" in your own words.

Ponder This...

We enjoy hearing about and talking about God's love, but we do not often explore His wrath. God is perfect and holy and cannot tolerate wickedness. If He chose to, He could wipe out the world as He did in the days of Noah. This story shows that He can also say to an individual, "I brought you into this world, and I can take you out." Why doesn't He deal with all sinners the way he did with Er and Onan? Mercy and GRACE. Praise the Lord for the grace He has extended to us in the form of His only begotten Son, Jesus, who died in our place on the cross. For those who trust in Jesus, God placed the judgment for their sin on Him. He executed our sin by placing it on Jesus. Praise the Lord!

Tamar

GENESIS 38 - SHE WHO WAS DECEIVED BECOMES THE DECEIVER

Susie: Judah superstitiously thought if he gave Shelah to Tamar, he too would die; therefore, he did *not* keep his promise to give him in marriage.

Susan: He let the superstitions of the Canaanite people infect him rather than remembering that his God is faithful to preserve and protect His chosen people when they behave righteously. He wasn't considering the sovereignty of God.

Genesis 38:12 After a long time Judah's wife, the daughter of Shua, died. When Judah had finished mourning, he and his friend Hirah the Adullamite went up to his sheepshearers at Timnah.

> *Genesis 38:12 (AMP) But quite a while later, Judah's wife, the daughter of Shua, died; and when the time of mourning was ended, he went up to his sheepshearers at Timnah with his friend Hirah the Adullamite.*

Susie: The Amplified version makes it clear that Judah had mourned his wife an appropriate amount of time before attending the sheep shearing. Sheep shearing was a time of celebration and partying often accompanied by licentious—wanton, unrestrained— behavior according to this note in the *MacArthur Study Bible*:

> **38:13 shear his sheep.** Such an event was frequently associated, in the ancient world, with festivity and licentious behavior characteristic of pagan fertility-cult practices. (23)

Susan: Sheep shearing was an event attended by men only. Any women even near it were assumed to be prostitutes.

Genesis 38:13–14 When Tamar was told, "Your father-in-law is going up to Timnah to shear his sheep," she removed her widow's garments, covered her face with a veil to disguise herself, and sat at the entrance to Enaim, which is on the way to Timnah. For she saw that although Shelah had grown up, she had not been given to him as a wife.

Susan: Someone tipped Tamar off to the fact that her father-in-law was attending the sheep shearing. We do not know the motivation of this person or who they were.

Susie: Perhaps they thought she might want to see Judah or confront him about the fact that she was still not married to Shelah.

Susan: Tamar posed as one of the pagan temple prostitutes covering her face with a veil so that Judah would not recognize her. She positioned herself on the path he would have to take to the sheep shearing and back home.

Susie: It speaks to the fact that Judah's character had degraded that Tamar would presume he would proposition a prostitute. Her plan was to lure him into a sexual encounter in order to preserve her husband's lineage and provide herself with a child since Judah had not fulfilled his promise to allow her to marry Shelah. The Hittite culture of the time condoned the practice of having a child with one's father-in-law if the brothers of the deceased husband would not or could not give the woman a child. However, under the future Jewish law, sleeping with her father-in-law would be considered incest.

> *Leviticus 20:12 If a man lies with his daughter-in-law, both must surely be put to death. They have acted perversely; their blood is upon them.*

Susan: Pregnancy was Tamar's end game. She figured she had waited long enough. She may have concluded that desperate situations called for desperate measures.

Genesis 38:15–16 When Judah saw her, he thought she was a prostitute because she had covered her face. Not realizing that she was his daughter-in-law, he went over to her and said, "Come now, let me sleep with you." "What will you give me for sleeping with you?" she inquired.

Susie: Judah's wife had died some time before, and he was now past the time of bereavement; therefore, he sought out who he thought was a pagan temple prostitute. Let us put this conversation between Judah and Tamar in plain language:

Susie: Judah says, "I want to have sex with you."

Susan: Tamar says, "What will you pay me to have sex with you? I'm not giving it away for free!"

Susie: Thus, she purposely deceived Judah into believing she was a prostitute. Her assessment of her father-in-law's lack of respect for God's ways, proved to be correct. She had no intention of truly working as a prostitute. She just wanted a baby from her husband's lineage as she had been promised.

Genesis 38:17 "I will send you a young goat from my flock," Judah answered. But she replied, "Only if you leave me something as a pledge until you send it."

Susie: Judah promised to pay her with a baby goat which would have been a high price to pay and only affordable to someone who owned multiple herds. Since he did not have said goat with him, she asked what he would give her to hold until he sent the goat.

Susan: Tamar demanded a surety deposit.

Genesis 38:18 "What pledge should I give you?" he asked.
She answered, "Your seal and your cord, and the staff in your hand." So he gave them to her and slept with her, and she became pregnant by him.

Susan: She demanded three forms of identification which was a common legal proof in those days.

Susie: She wanted his signet used to seal deals, the bracelet or cord the signet hung from, and his staff which must have been identifiable as being his rather than someone else's. This would be like giving someone your driver's license, social security card, and credit card!

Susan: Judah must have been dense or desperate or both because he gave her what she demanded.

Susie: They had intercourse, and she became pregnant which had been her hope and her plan. Since God is Sovereign, He enabled her to conceive immediately.

Susan: She was using worldly wisdom, the way of the flesh, to accomplish her desire for a child and to carry on the lineage of Er and also of Judah instead of asking God to intervene and waiting on Judah.

Susie: Of course, we must remember Tamar may have come from a pagan culture and may not have totally understood or believed the ways of the Lord. Or even as a Jewish woman she may not have understood the concept of waiting on God's timing. Remember, even Sarah, had been impatient with God's promise of an heir for Abraham.

Susan: Even though the Law had not yet been given to Moses, there would have been oral tradition of morality passed down from generation to generation of Israelites. Tamar seems to have been trying to find a way to honor her husband's lineage even though Judah would not give her Shelah in marriage as promised.

Genesis 38:19 Then Tamar got up and departed. And she removed her veil and put on her widow's garments again.

Susie: After tricking Judah into lying with her in order to conceive, Tamar went back to wearing her widow's clothes and living in her father's house.

Genesis 38:20–23 Now when Judah sent his friend Hirah the Adullamite with the young goat to collect the items he had left with the woman, he could not find her. He asked the men of that place, "Where is the shrine prostitute who was beside the road at Enaim?" "No shrine prostitute has been here," they answered. So Hirah returned to Judah and said, "I could not find her, and furthermore, the men of that place said, 'No shrine prostitute has been here.'" "Let her keep the items," Judah replied. "Otherwise we will become a laughingstock. After all, I did send her this young goat, but you could not find her."

Susie: Judah asked his friend to deliver the promised baby goat to the prostitute.

Susan: But she was nowhere to be found.

Susie: To continue searching for her would bring dishonor to Judah, so he just resigned himself to letting her keep the items he had given her—his signet, its bracelet or cord, and his staff. Big mistake, Judah!

REVIEW QUESTIONS

1. Why did Judah not give Shelah in marriage to Tamar?

2. When Tamar heard through the grapevine that Judah would be going to the sheep shearing, what plan did she hatch?

3. When her plan worked, what surety did she ask Judah to leave since he did not have the promised young goat with him? Why were these items significant?

4. What happened when Judah sent his friend Hirah to take the goat to the "prostitute?"

_____
_____
_____
_____

Ponder This...

Tamar who posed as a prostitute, deceived Judah, and committed incest with her father-in-law, is listed in the lineage of Jesus! It is a brain-twister. Think about it! However, this is a demonstration of both God's sovereignty and grace to His people. Judah's line would have ended had Tamar not deceived the deceiver. The Messiah was to be called "The Lion of Judah," so Judah had to have an heir to carry on his line for there to be a tribe of Judah. Of course, Jacob had not yet blessed Judah and pronounced that prophecy over him. However, God knew the plans He had and made sure Judah would have an heir. When it seems like life is out of control, remember that God knows how He is going to use your present situation in His plans for you.

> *Jeremiah 29:11 For I know the plans I have for you, declares the LORD, plans for welfare and not for evil, to give you a future and a hope.*

In the next lesson, we will see that God's grace prevented Tamar and/or Judah from being put to death for their sin.

Tamar

GENESIS 38: JUDGMENT PRONOUNCED DUE TO UNWED PREGNANCY UNTIL PATERNITY PROVEN

Genesis 38:24 About three months later, Judah was told, "Your daughter-in-law Tamar has prostituted herself, and now she is pregnant." "Bring her out!" Judah replied. "Let her be burned to death!"

Susie: In three months, Tamar began to show. It was obvious she was pregnant. People assumed she had been unfaithful to her promise to wait for Shelah and reported the pregnancy to Judah.

Susan: The people in the village were happy to be gossips and had no regard for Tamar's reputation. Judah was extremely rigid...

Susie: . . . (since he had no idea it had been Tamar posing as the prostitute he used). He did not realize his own culpability in the situation yet.

Susan: Judah acted as judge and jury telling the men to bring her out to be burned to death.

Susie: According to the note in the MacArthur Study Bible, Mosaic law would later proscribe this form of execution in specific cases:

> **38:24 let her be burned!** Double standards prevailed in that Judah, no less guilty than Tamar, commanded her execution for immorality. Later Mosaic legislation would prescribe this form of the death penalty for a priest's daughter who prostituted herself or for those guilty of certain forms of incest (Lev. 20:14; 21:9). (24)

Genesis 38:25 As she was being brought out, Tamar sent a message to her father-in-law: "I am pregnant by the man to whom these items belong." And she added, "Please examine them. Whose seal and cord and staff are these?"

Susie: Tamar then played her trump card.

Susan: She sure did need one! Even though she acted sinfully, God provided her this "get out of jail free card" by giving her the wisdom to ask for these items that would serve as ID cards of Judah.

Susie: Tamar sent the signet, bracelet, and staff that belonged to Judah back to him, saying that she was pregnant by the owner of these things! I am assuming she did this in such a way that the people sent to drag her out to be burned would be witnesses without directly accusing Judah of being the father.

Genesis 38:26 Judah recognized the items and said, "She is more righteous than I, since I did not give her to my son Shelah." And he did not have relations with her again.

Susie: Judah recognized the proof that he was the father *and* acknowledged that fact.

Susan: He finally realized he had been wrong to go back on his word about giving Shelah to Tamar as a husband.

Susie: He took Tamar under his protection as a wife but never had incestuous sexual relations with her again. Her child would be recognized as his. We see the grace of God toward Tamar that she was spared from being executed as an adulteress and instead was taken into Judah's home. Judah may not have realized it, but God was gracious to him in allowing the lineage of Jesus to continue through him directly rather than through his sons whose mother was a Canaanite.

Susan: Unequivocally, without question, God showed grace to Tamar and Judah because He could have slain them as He did Er and Onan. Or he could have allowed the crowd to execute both of them for their sin.

Genesis 38:27–28 When the time came for Tamar to give birth, there were twins in her womb. And as she was giving birth, one of them put out his hand; so the midwife took a scarlet thread and tied it around his wrist. "This one came out first," she announced.

Susie: Birth order was extremely important since a greater share of property passed to the first-born son. Therefore, the midwife tied a scarlet thread on the hand that pushed out of the womb first. But that baby withdrew his arm.

Genesis 38:29 But when he pulled his hand back and his brother came out, she said, "You have broken out first!" So he was named Perez.

Susan: Pharez (Perez) means "breach, breaking forth," so the baby that traded places with the one with scarlet thread and broke out of the womb first was thus named.

Susie: Tamar preserved the line of Judah by bearing Perez, and ultimately, he would be in the lineage of the Messiah, Jesus.

Genesis 38:30 Then his brother came out with the scarlet thread around his wrist, and he was named Zerah.

Susan: The second baby to be born, the one with the scarlet thread around his wrist, was named Zerah, meaning "a rising of light."

Susie: Much later, in the book of Ruth, when the people find out that Boaz is serving as kinsman-redeemer to marry Ruth and produce offspring for her late husband (another levirate marriage), they bless him in the following way:

> *Ruth 4:11-12 "We are witnesses," said the elders and all the people at the gate. "May the LORD make the woman entering your home like Rachel and Leah, who together built up the house of Israel. May you be prosperous in Ephrathah and famous in Bethlehem. And may your house become like the house of Perez, whom Tamar bore to Judah, because of the offspring the LORD will give you by this young woman."*

Susie: And HIS story continued: Boaz and Ruth had Obed who fathered Jesse, the father of David. The promised Messiah would be a descendant of David. Therefore, Ruth as well as Tamar was in the lineage of the Redeemer God had promised to Eve as found in Matthew chapter one:

> *Matthew 1:3-6 Judah was the father of Perez and Zerah by **Tamar**, Perez the father of Hezron, and Hezron the father of Ram. Ram was the father of Amminadab, Amminadab the father of Nahshon, and Nahshon the father of Salmon. Salmon was the father of Boaz by **Rahab**, Boaz the father of Obed by **Ruth**, Obed the father of Jesse, and Jesse the father of David the king.*

Susan: Thus, by the sovereign grace of God, Tamar played an important role as a Woman of Christmas! Her story became a part of HIStory. It is only by the grace of God that any of us humans are included in His plan! However, God designed the earth for human beings and created us in His own image for His own pleasure and glory.

Susie: Like us, you may still be wondering, "Why Judah??? Why would God choose to carry on the promise through him?"

Susan: He just seems like a scalawag until . . .

Susie: . . . the 44th chapter of Genesis. Let me set the scene. The brothers (Israel's sons) go up to Egypt to try to buy food during the famine. Unbeknownst to them, their brother Joseph whom they had sold into slavery was now second only to Pharoah in power in Egypt. His wisdom was the reason Egypt had food. Joseph recognizes them but does not reveal himself to them. He asks nosy questions about their father and family and demands that they bring their youngest brother, Benjamin, back with them. They do so. After treating them to a feast, he fills their bags with grain and sends them back to their father. He has his servant stash his golden goblet in Benjamin's bag. He lets them leave but sends the servant to discover the "stolen" goblet. The men had agreed that the guilty party would become a slave in Egypt. The goblet is "discovered" in Benjamin's bag. They return to Joseph who tells them Benjamin will be his slave. This is when Judah offers himself as a substitute, to sacrifice his own freedom for his brother:

Genesis 44:30-34 So if the boy is not with us when I return to your servant, and if my father, whose life is wrapped up in the boy's life, sees that the boy is not with us, he will die. Then your servants will have brought the gray hair of your servant our father down to Sheol in sorrow. Indeed, your servant guaranteed the boy's safety to my father, saying, 'If I do not return him to you, I will bear the guilt before you, my father, all my life.' Now please let your servant stay here as my lord's slave in place of the boy. Let him return with his brothers. For how can I go back to my father without the boy? I could not bear to see the misery that would overwhelm him."

Susan: In this passage, we see Judah as a "type" of Christ. He was willing to lay down his life for another, to redeem Benjamin from slavery.

Susan: We won't leave you with a cliff hanger: Joseph finally reveals his true identity and tells them to bring their father and their families and live in Egypt. After their father, Israel, dies, the brothers are afraid Joseph will no longer protect them. They come before him volunteering to be his slaves if he will spare them. Then Joseph makes his famous statement:

Genesis 50:20-21 "As for you, what you intended against me for evil, God intended for good, in order to accomplish a day like this—to preserve the lives of many people. Therefore do not be afraid. I will provide for you and your little ones." So Joseph reassured his brothers and spoke kindly to them.

REVIEW QUESTIONS

1. How did Judah find out that Tamar was pregnant?

2. What was Judah's reaction to the news?

3. What was Tamar's "get out of jail free card?"

_____
_____
_____
_____

4. When Judah realized he was the father of Tamar's child, what did he do?
_____
_____
_____
_____

5. Which of Tamar's sons is listed in the lineage of Jesus?
_____
_____
_____

Ponder This...

Do you ever feel you are too bad, or not smart enough, too "rough around the edges," to be used by God? Think again! Adam and Eve brought sin into the world, but God sacrificed animals to clothe their nakedness. Sarah and Abraham were as old as dirt, but God opened Sarah's womb and gave her the strength to give birth to Isaac. Judah lacked integrity, and Tamar slept with her father-in-law; but instead of condemning them to death, God allowed their son to be in the lineage of the Messiah. God graciously used each of these couples, each of these women, to tell His story and to continue the lineage that would produce the Savior, Jesus Christ, GOD'S ONLY BEGOTTEN SON! God can use even people who do not believe in Him, but He wants to not only use you for His purpose but to bless you when you surrender all you are to His control. God's glory can be revealed to others even through YOU!

WORSHIP OPPORTUNITY

Jesus is the Lion of the tribe of Judah as well as the Lamb that was slain (Revelation 5:5, 12). Worship Him along with the Gaither Vocal Band singing, "You're the Lion of Judah":
https://www.youtube.com/watch?v=bcN55lOHaRw

Tamar

WOMAN WHO ENSURED JUDAH'S LINE CONTINUED

- Genesis 38:6-10 Now Judah acquired a wife for Er, his firstborn, and her name was **Tamar**. But Er, Judah's firstborn, was wicked in the sight of the LORD; so the LORD put him to death. Then Judah said to Onan, "Sleep with your **brother's wife**. Perform your duty as her brother-in-law and raise up offspring for your brother." But Onan knew that the offspring would not belong to him; so whenever he would sleep with his **brother's wife**, he would spill his seed on the ground so that he would not produce offspring for his brother. What he did was wicked in the sight of the LORD, so He put Onan to death as well.

- Genesis 38:11 Then Judah said to his daughter-in-law **Tamar**, "Live as a widow in your father's house until my son Shelah grows up." For he thought, "He may die too, like his brothers." So **Tamar** went to live in her father's house.

- Genesis 38:13-14 When **Tamar** was told, "Your father-in-law is going up to Timnah to shear his sheep," **she** removed her widow's garments, covered **her** face with a veil to disguise herself, and sat at the entrance to Enaim, which is on the way to Timnah. For she saw that although Shelah had grown up, **she** had not been given to him as a wife.

- Genesis 38:24 About three months later, Judah was told, "Your daughter-in-law **Tamar** has prostituted herself, and now she is pregnant." "Bring her out!" Judah replied. "Let her be burned to death!"

- Genesis 38:25 As she was being brought out, **Tamar** sent a message to her father-in-law: "I am pregnant by the man to whom these items belong." And **she** added, "Please examine them. Whose seal and cord and staff are these?"
Judah recognized the items and said, "**She** is more righteous than I, since I did not give her to my son Shelah." And he did not have relations with her again.

- Genesis 38:27-29 When the time came for **Tamar** to give birth, there were twins in her womb. And as she was giving birth, one of them put out his hand; so the midwife took a scarlet thread and tied it around his wrist. "This one came out first," she announced. But when he pulled his hand back and his brother came out, she said, "You have broken out first!" So he was named **Perez**. Then his brother came out with the scarlet thread around his wrist, and he was named Zerah.

- Genesis 49:9a & **Judah is a young lion**... The scepter will not depart from **Judah**, nor the staff from between his feet, until **Shiloh** comes and the allegiance of the nations is his.

- Ruth 4:12 And may your house become like the house of **Perez**, whom **Tamar** bore to **Judah**, because of the offspring the LORD will give you by this young woman."

- Matthew 1:3 Judah was the father of Perez and Zerah by **Tamar**, Perez the father of Hezron, and Hezron the father of Ram.

- Revelation 5:5 Then one of the elders said to me, "Do not weep! Behold, the **Lion of the tribe of Judah**, the Root of David, has triumphed to open the scroll and its seven seals."

Rahab

JOSHUA 2 - HARLOT HELPS AND HIDES SPIES

Joshua 2:1 Then Joshua son of Nun secretly sent two spies from Shittim, saying, "Go, inspect the land, especially Jericho." So they went and entered the house of a prostitute named Rahab and stayed there.

Susie: Moses died, and the Lord passed the torch of leadership to his aide, his right-hand man, Joshua. After forty years of wandering in the wilderness, the Israelites were once again on the verge of entering the promised land. In order to do so, they needed to conquer the fortified city of Jericho. Joshua sent in two trusted men to spy out the situation there and report back to him.

Susan: Joshua sent the spies "secretly" without telling the entire nation of Israel in order to avoid what had happened when he himself had been one of the twelve spies sent out by Moses.

Susie: The congregation had trusted the negative report of the ten instead of trusting God and the positive report of Joshua and Caleb. As a consequence of their unbelief, God had the Israelites wander through the wilderness for 40 years until all those who had seen the parting of the Red Sea died, all except Joshua and Caleb. You can read their story in Numbers chapter 14.

Susan: The Israelites failed to see that any number of people (large or small) and GOD create a majority.

Susie: In fact, God by Himself is a majority! But back to the story at hand. Joshua is poised to lead the children of the Israelites who died in the wilderness into the promised land.

Susan: In God's providence, the spies sent out by Joshua stayed in an inn owned by Rahab the harlot in order to go in under the radar, incognito. She may have been working as a prostitute at the time or possibly this was her former profession and had marred her name forever in Jericho.

> It may seem strange that the spies found refuge in the house of a prostitute—what were they, people of God, doing there? The answer may be quite simple. To state the obvious, perhaps the spies were seeking the services of a prostitute. There is another possible explanation, however. The house of a harlot was probably a good place to avoid detection—a couple of travelers entering such a house would probably not arouse much suspicion. The spies, seeking anonymity, figured a house of prostitution would be a good place to find it. Also, Rahab's house was situated on the city wall (Joshua 2:15), providing an escape route. As it turned out, the spies' choice of a hiding place was God-ordained.

You can read the entire article here:
https://www.gotquestions.org/spies-Rahab.html

Susie: As two strangers in town, the hope was that this would make them blend in instead of sticking out as Israelites. Also, it would be a place to hear men talking about the city, about the army of Israelites amassing nearby, and ascertain whether they were seen as a threat or not.

Susan: We see God's sovereignty in leading them to the house of Rahab who, as we will see, believed in the one true God.

Joshua 2:2–3 And it was reported to the king of Jericho: "Behold, some men of Israel have come here tonight to spy out the land." So the king of Jericho sent to Rahab and said, "Bring out the men who came to you and entered your house, for they have come to spy out the whole land."

Susan: The two spies got made! Someone recognized them as Israelites, put two and two together that they were spies, and reported this news to the king. In those days, peoples were often warring over territory, so men were hyper-vigilant about suspicious men in their cities. They must have also overheard that the men went into Rahab's house.

Susie: So, the king sent word to Rahab to bring the men in to be interrogated as he was certain they were spies.

Joshua 2:4–5 But the woman had taken the two men and hidden them. So she said, "Yes, the men did come to me, but I did not know where they had come from. At dusk, when the gate was about to close, the men went out, and I do not know which way they went. Pursue them quickly, and you may catch them!"

Susie: Rahab lied. She claimed she had not known where the men were from and that they had left after dark, just before the city gates were closed for the night; but she didn't know where they were going. She urged the king's men to pursue them immediately in order to catch up to them.

Susan: She lied in order to protect the two spies.

Susie: We will see that Rahab knew the God of the Israelites to be powerful; but at this point, she did not know Him well enough to wait on him in the situation. So, she did the best she knew to take care of the situation herself by covering for the spies with a lie. John MacArthur gives insight into the fact that Rahab was honored for her faith, not for lying:

> **2:4, 5 Cf. vv. 9–11.** Lying is sin to God (Ex. 20:16), for He cannot lie (Titus 1:2). God commended her faith (Heb. 11:31; James 2:25) as expressed in vv. 9–16, not her lie. He never condones any sin, yet none are without some sin (cf. Rom. 3:23), thus the need for forgiveness. But He also honors true faith, small as it is, and im-

parts saving grace (Ex. 34:7). (25)

Joshua 2:6 (But Rahab had taken them up to the roof and hidden them among the stalks of flax that she had laid out there.)

Susan: Rahab hid the spies beneath a blanket of flax she had drying on her roof to weave linen.

Susie: It was a good thing they were not allergic to it. A sneeze would have revealed their whereabouts for sure!

Joshua 2:7 So the king's men set out in pursuit of the spies along the road to the fords of the Jordan, and as soon as they had gone out, the gate was shut.

Susie: Rahab had successfully diverted the king's men to leave the city in pursuit of the two spies. All the while, the two men were lying under the flax on her roof. The king's men had locked the city gate behind them so no one could easily go in or out.

Susan: This would block the spies' escape, or so they thought!

Joshua 2:8–10 Before the spies lay down for the night, Rahab went up on the roof and said to them, "I know that the LORD has given you this land and that the fear of you has fallen on us, so that all who dwell in the land are melting in fear of you. For we have heard how the LORD dried up the waters of the Red Sea before you when you came out of Egypt, and what you did to Sihon and Og, the two kings of the Amorites across the Jordan, whom you devoted to destruction.

Susan: Rahab explained to the spies that the reputation of their God and His people had preceded them. Everyone feared them because of the reports they had heard about the parting of the Red Sea, the conquering of other kings, and the utter destruction of cities that opposed them.

Susie: She expressed her belief that God was going to enable them to conquer Jericho and all of the promised land.

Joshua 2:11 When we heard this, our hearts melted and everyone's courage failed because of you, for the LORD your God is God in the heavens above and on the earth below.

Susie: Rahab declared her belief in the one true God as the God of everything.

Susan: Her allegiance to this God she had only heard about by word of mouth was stronger than her allegiance to her king or city. Her loyalty was to the Almighty Invisible God rather than to the authority over Jericho.

Susie: This was partly out of fear, but I believe she also knew this God had power to protect her.

Joshua 2:12–13 Now therefore, please swear to me by the LORD that you will indeed show kindness to my family, because I showed kindness to you. Give me a sure sign that you will spare the lives of my father and mother, my brothers and sisters, and all who belong to them, and that you will deliver us from death."

Susan: Rahab made a request of the men and asked them to make an oath in the name of the Lord to carry it out.

Susie: She begged the spies to protect her, her family, and all they owned when they came back to destroy the city. She knew the Israelites' reputation for completely wiping out a people and begged to be spared since she had protected the two spies.

Joshua 2:14 "Our lives for your lives!" the men agreed. "If you do not report our mission, we will show you kindness and faithfulness when the LORD gives us the land."

Susan: They told her that as long as she could "zip it," she had their word that they would do as she asked. They swore an oath to fulfill this promise.

Joshua 2:15–16 Then Rahab let them down by a rope through the window, since the house where she lived was built into the wall of the city. "Go to the hill country," she said, "so that your pursuers will not find you. Hide yourselves there for three days until they have returned; then go on your way."

Susie: Rahab found a way for the spies to escape despite the locked city gate.

Susan: She used the Rapunzel method, but instead of her hair she gave them a rope.

Susie: She advised them to hide in the mountains for three days until the search party gave up and returned to the city.

Susan: The fact that they were to hide for three days reminds me of the fact that Jesus was in the tomb for three days.

Susie: And Jonah was in the belly of the fish for three days. I'm sensing a pattern here.

Joshua 2:17–18 The men said to her, "We will not be bound by this oath you made us swear unless, when we enter the land, you have tied this scarlet cord in the window through which you let us down, and unless you have brought your father and mother and brothers and all your family into your house.

Susie: The two spies gave Rahab instructions as well. She was to hang a scarlet thread or cord from her window to identify her house as the one to spare.

Susan: Their instructions were precise and specific. The scarlet thread reminds us of the blood of Christ that saves us from sin.

Susie: Dr. W.A. Criswell preached a great sermon titled "The Scarlet Thread Through the Bible" which was later printed as a booklet. You can read the sermon on this website: https://wacriswell.com/sermons/1995/the-scarlet-thread-through-the-bible/. The thread and the blood are reminiscent of the blood of the Passover lamb that protected the Israelites from death during the final plague back in Egypt. Jesus was our final, perfect Passover Lamb.

Susan: Jesus is the only sacrifice needed for those who believe and trust in Him.

Joshua 2:19 If anyone goes out the door of your house into the street, his blood will be on his own head, and we will be innocent. But if a hand is laid on anyone with you in the house, his blood will be on our heads.

Susie: Just as during the Passover in Egypt, the Israelites had to stay within the house with the blood of the lamb on the doorpost, Rahab's family needed to stay within the house with the scarlet thread in the window in order to be saved.

Susan: They needed to stay within the protective barrier that scarlet thread represented.

Susie: The men explained that they could not be held responsible for any of her family that wandered outside the safety of the house. And they promised protection for those within the house.

Joshua 2:20 . . . And if you report our mission, we will be released from the oath you made us swear."

Susie: If Rahab did not keep their secret, if she blabbed about their whereabouts…

Susan: …their oath would become null and void.

Joshua 2:21 "Let it be as you say," she replied, and she sent them away. And when they had gone, she tied the scarlet cord in the window.

Susie: Rahab agreed to their terms.

Susan: Their word was their bond.

Susie: She followed their instructions by faith in their integrity and faith in the power of their God and tied the scarlet cord so that it hung out the window.

Joshua 2:22 So the spies went out into the hill country and stayed there three days, until their pursuers had returned without finding them, having searched all along the road.

Susie: The two men trusted Rahab and followed her advice, hiding in the mountains until the danger of discovery had passed.

Joshua 2:23–24 Then the two men started back, came down from the hill country, and crossed the river. So they came to Joshua son of Nun and reported all that had happened to them. "The LORD has surely delivered the entire land into our hands," they said to Joshua. "Indeed, all who dwell in the land are melting in fear of us."

Susan: The two spies gave Joshua a full account, including their precarious adventure.

Susie: They told him confidently that the people of Jericho were shaking in their sandals with fear.

Susan: That would be like Texans shaking in their boots.

Susie: They assured Joshua that the Lord would give Jericho to them, that they would be able, in His power, to conquer the city.

Susan: The Lord had their backs in Jericho by using Rahab to protect them. Rahab believed the Lord was able not only to conquer but to save. She wanted to be on the winning side of the battle she knew was to come.

REVIEW QUESTIONS

1. Was Rahab Jewish by nationality? _____
_____

2. Where did Rahab hide the two spies sent out by Joshua? _____
_____
_____

3. Why did Rahab hide the spies instead of handing them over to the king's men?
_____
_____
_____
_____

Ponder This...

"God is our refuge and strength, a very present help in trouble," Psalm 46:1. However, He sometimes provides that help in unusual ways. The spies found refuge in the house of a harlot, and she hid them from their enemies. God's work in our lives is sometimes "mysterious," but we can count on His provision in our times of need. Have you ever had an experience in which you were convinced God had worked on your behalf in mysterious or unusual ways? Susie had longed for children her entire life, but at 39 years old was divorced, not dating, not knowing whether she would ever marry again. She did not relish the idea of giving birth after the age of 40 even if she could conceive which was iffy according to her doctor. However, she prayed believing that God was still going to bless her according to a verse she had memorized in her twenties when first told she might not be able to conceive:

> *Psalm 113:9 He settles the barren woman in her home as a joyful mother to her children. Hallelujah!*

Within three weeks of praying expressing her trust that the Lord would still give her children, she met a man who had four children, three of whom still lived with him. He hired her to keep an eye on his three teenagers when he had to work out of country. Gradually, they became her children! Praise the Lord!

Rahab

JOSHUA 6 – PEOPLE YELLED, WALLS FELL

Susie: After the two spies (who are never called by name) gave a good report to Joshua, the Lord provided the battle plan. It involved marching around Jericho for seven consecutive days following specific instructions. You can read the details in Joshua 6:1-14. We are going to skip ahead to the continuation of Rahab's story.

Joshua 6:15–16 Then on the seventh day, they got up at dawn and marched around the city seven times in the same manner. That was the only day they circled the city seven times. After the seventh time around, the priests blew the horns, and Joshua commanded the people, "Shout! For the LORD has given you the city!

Susan: According to Hebraic understanding, seven is the number of perfection and completion. The first six days, the seven priests carrying seven ram's horns (shofars) were to sound their horns as the troops and the people marched around the city, but Joshua gave strict orders that no one was to shout a battle cry. They were to march in complete silence other than the ram's horns and the sound of marching feet.

> *Joshua 6:10 (MSG) Joshua had given orders to the people, "Don't shout. In fact, don't even speak—not so much as a whisper until you hear me say, 'Shout!'—then shout away!"*

Susan: The shout was a declaration of victory even though it was yet to occur. This reminds me of "Never Lost" going into "Don't Have to Wait 'Til the Battle's Over" by CeCe Winans: https://www.youtube.com/watch?v=Cl8EzTovAcs . Their faith in God was evident in this victory cry and their obedience to wage war in this unconventional way, marching around the city to claim it even while the walls still stood.

Joshua 6:17 Now the city and everything in it must be devoted[H2764] to the LORD for destruction. Only Rahab the prostitute and all those with her in her house will live, because she hid the spies we sent.

Joshua 6:17 (KJV) And the city shall be accursed[H2764], even it, and all that are therein, to the LORD: only Rahab the harlot shall live, she and all that are with her in the house, because she hid the messengers that we sent.

> H2764 chêrem, khay'-rem; or (Zechariah 14:11) cherem; from H2763; physical (as shutting in) a net (either literally or figuratively); usually a doomed object; ab-

stractly extermination:—(ac-) curse(-d, -d thing), dedicated thing, things which should have been utterly destroyed, (appointed to) utter destruction, devoted (thing), net. (26)

Forms of the Hebrew cherem refer to the giving over of things or persons to the LORD, either by destroying them or by giving them as an offering; also in verses 18 and 21. (27)

Susan: God said the city would be under His curse except for Rahab and the inhabitants of her house. Remember, the two spies had instructed her to gather her extended family into her house and remain there with the scarlet thread hanging out of the window.

Susie: God extended mercy and grace to Rahab and her family because of her protection of the two spies.

Susan: Rahab knew of God but did not yet know Him for herself. However, she still did what she thought He would have wanted by hiding and protecting the Israelite spies against her own King and his men.

Joshua 6:18 But keep away from the things devoted to destruction, lest you yourself be set apart for destruction. If you take any of these, you will set apart the camp of Israel for destruction and bring disaster upon it.

Susie: In other words, Joshua was warning them not to take spoils for themselves lest they bring a curse upon their nation, Israel. God had made similar commands after other battles as well.

Joshua 6:19 . . . For all the silver and gold and all the articles of bronze and iron are holy to the LORD; they must go into His treasury."

Susan: They were allowed to collect spoils, treasures, for the Lord only rather than for themselves.

Susie: They were to seize only the specified items and turn them over to the Lord's treasury.

Joshua 6:20 So when the rams' horns sounded, the people shouted. When they heard the blast of the horn, the people gave a great shout, and the wall collapsed. Then all the people charged straight into the city and captured it.

Susie: No battering rams were employed, no catapults, no tools to tear down the great wall. When the priests blew the trumpets, and the people yelled their victory cry, the walls simply fell down!

Susan: If a certain pitch can break glass, perhaps the power of tens of thousands of voices shouting at the same time (possibly joined by the Holy Spirit's thunderous voice) could crumble stone.

Susie: Joshua's men swarmed like locusts over the rubble to conquer Jericho!

Joshua 6:21 At the edge of the sword they devoted to destruction everything in the city—man and woman, young and old, oxen, sheep, and donkeys.

Susan: The army was obedient to the Lord's command. They left no people or animals alive…

Susie: …not even women and children. This seems harsh or barbaric to us.

Susan: But the all-encompassing judgment of God on Jericho and other Canaanite cities was due to their worship of idols and to protect and preserve Israel, His chosen people, those who worshipped the one true God, Yahweh.

> When one realizes the moral perversity of the Canaanites, it is easy to see why God ordered the complete destruction of life within Jericho. Rather than criticize the Lord for administering deserved judgment to the wicked, we should marvel at His grace which preserved Rahab and her family from the same. (28)

Joshua 6:22 Meanwhile, Joshua told the two men who had spied out the land, "Go into the house of the prostitute and bring out the woman and all who are with her, just as you promised her."

Susan: Joshua ordered the two men who had been sent in as spies to go into the city and fulfill their vow to Rahab.

Susie: My question is, "How was Rahab's house still standing with the people inside unharmed if the walls of Jericho fell?" We found a good explanation for this in the *Believer's Bible Commentary:*

> **6:22–27** The faith that brought the walls down (Heb. 11:30) also brought … Rahab and her relatives out (Heb. 11:31). The grace of God not only made provision for her safety but also elevated her to a place in the ancestry of David and ultimately of the Lord Jesus Christ (Matt. 1:5, 6). Grace not only saves us from destruction but also guarantees our exaltation (Rom. 8:29, 30). Faith is the hand that takes hold of grace. (29)

Hebrews 11:30-31 By faith the walls of Jericho fell, after the people had marched around them for seven days. By faith the prostitute Rahab, because she welcomed the spies in peace, did not perish with those who were disobedient.

Susan: Rahab and her family were kept safe because of her belief in the God of the Israelites. He miraculously surrounded her house and kept them safe when the walls crumbled.

Joshua 6:23 So the young spies went in and brought out Rahab, her father and mother and brothers, and all who belonged to her. They brought out her whole family and settled them outside the camp of Israel.

Susan: The two spies were a special task force sent in to extract their benefactor.

Susie: They brought Rahab and her family safely back to the outskirts of the camp of the Israelites. Why were they not accepted into the camp of the Israelites? We found the answer in the *Expositor's Bible Commentary*:

> **22-23** Evidently the part of the wall where Rahab's house was located was miraculously preserved. Rahab and her family were put in "a place outside the camp" as a kind of ritual quarantine. The camp of Israel was holy, and nothing unclean could be allowed to enter (cf. Lev 13:46; Nu 5:3; 31:19; Dt 23:3, 14). After the passage of time and the observance of appropriate rituals, they were received into the congregation (see v.25). (30)

Joshua 6:24 Then the Israelites burned up the city and everything in it. However, they put the silver and gold and articles of bronze and iron into the treasury of the LORD's house.

Susan: Jericho was burned to the ground except for the specific items designated for the Lord's treasury.

Joshua 6:25 And Joshua spared Rahab the prostitute, with her father's household and all who belonged to her, because she hid the men Joshua had sent to spy out Jericho. So she has lived among the Israelites to this day.

Susie: Joshua allowed Rahab and her family to live as the spies had promised because of the kindness and faith she had shown in hiding them. She continued to live in Israel and must have converted to Judaism as she married Salmon.

Susan: Salmon means "clothing."

Susie: By marrying Rahab, Salmon would have provided her continued protection among the Israelites as if covering her with his mantle, clothing her. We have been clothed in the righteousness of Jesus.

Ponder This...

Rahab had covered the two spies with the drying flax. Rahab was "covered" in many ways. The promise made to her by the two spies protected her from being slaughtered. The scarlet cord served as a covering by designating the house affording protection to Rahab and her kin. God's grace covered Rahab's house so it did not crumble along with the walls of Jericho. Salmon covered Rahab by taking her as his wife, making her a member of the community. Those of us who are believers, no matter how undeserving we are, are graciously covered with the robe of Jesus' righteousness. We are protected from the wrath of the Father because we are covered and purchased with the blood of Jesus. Praise the Lord for covering you!

Susie: Rahab stuck her neck out for those two spies Joshua sent to Jericho. She could have been executed for harboring the enemy if someone had discovered that she orchestrated their escape. Although she had once been a harlot, by God's grace she was listed in the lineage of Jesus found in Matthew's gospel.

Susan: God changed Rahab from harlot to a heroine in "HISstory!"

> *Matthew 1:5 Salmon was the father of Boaz by* **Rahab**, *Boaz the father of Obed by* **Ruth**, *Obed the father of Jesse . . .*

Susie: You probably know the next "begat" – Jesse was the father of King David. The Messiah was prophesied to be a descendant of David, and Matthew and Luke both present a lineage of Jesus that shows He was that promised One.

> *Hebrews 11:30-31 By faith the walls of Jericho fell, after the people had marched around them for seven days. By faith the prostitute Rahab, because she welcomed the spies in peace, did not perish with those who were disobedient.*

Susan: Rahab believed that the Israelites were the people of the true God who preserved them. She had not known a god who preserved and protected until she heard of the God of the Israelites.

Susie: The god of her people in Jericho demanded that children be killed as a sacrifice to him. This verse in the Hebrews Hall of Faith indicates that Rahab put her trust in the Lord, the Creator and Sustainer of the universe, the only true God.

> *James 2:25 In the same way, was not even Rahab the prostitute justified by her actions when she welcomed the spies and sent them off on another route?*

Susie: Rahab's works proved her trust in God. It was not her action of protecting the spies that saved her. It was her faith, not her works.

Susan: Her works were *evidence* of her faith.

REVIEW QUESTIONS

1. Why did God tell Joshua to destroy everyone and everything in Jericho except Rahab and her family?

2. What sign was Rahab to hang outside her window to ensure her protection when the city was attacked? What could that cord represent?

3. Compare the signal Rahab used to the sign that caused God to spare the Israelites' firstborn during the plague in Egypt.

4. What attribute of Rahab was praised in Hebrews 11?

5. What evidence is there that Rahab converted to Judaism?

Ponder This...

Why would God include a harlot who lied in the lineage of Christ? Was it only because she hid the spies or was it due to her faith in Him that made her bold enough to protect them? Bottom line is that once again we see the grace of God. There is no way any of us can earn the distinction of being a child of God by our works. We are made His children when by His grace, He calls us and gives us faith to trust in Jesus' finished work on the cross.

WORSHIP OPPORTUNITY

Rahab and her family were spared by the grace of God even though the walls of Jericho came "tumbling down." God protected Rahab's home that was IN THE WALL! Have fun listening to The Martins singing "Joshua Fit the Battle of Jericho" on one of the Gaither videos. If you haven't guessed it already, we subscribe to Gaither TV™.
https://www.youtube.com/watch?v=FoeSdDcS1LA

Susan Slade and Susie Hale

Rahab

Prostitute Who Protected Spies

- Joshua 2:1-2 Then Joshua son of Nun secretly sent two spies from Shittim, saying, "Go, inspect the land, especially Jericho." So they went and entered the house of a **prostitute named Rahab** and stayed there. And it was reported to the king of Jericho: "Behold, some men of Israel have come here tonight to spy out the land."

- Joshua 2:3 So the king of Jericho sent to **Rahab** and said, "Bring out the men who came to you and entered your house, for they have come to spy out the whole land."

- Joshua 2:4-6 But the woman had taken the two men and hidden them. So **she** said, "Yes, the men did come to me, but I did not know where they had come from. At dusk, when the gate was about to close, the men went out, and I do not know which way they went. Pursue them quickly, and you may catch them!" (But **Rahab** had taken them up to the roof and hidden them among the stalks of flax that she had laid out there.)

- Joshua 2:8-9 Before the spies lay down for the night, **Rahab** went up on the roof and said to them, "I know that the LORD has given you this land and that the fear of you has fallen on us, so that all who dwell in the land are melting in fear of you.

- Joshua 2:12-13 Now therefore, please swear to **me** by the LORD that you will indeed show kindness to my family, because **I** showed kindness to you. Give me a sure sign that you will spare the lives of my father and mother, my brothers and sisters, and all who belong to them, and that you will deliver us from death."

- Joshua 2:15-16 Then **Rahab** let them down by a rope through the window, since the house where she lived was built into the wall of the city. "Go to the hill country," she said, "so that your pursuers will not find you. Hide yourselves there for three days until they have returned; then go on your way."

- Joshua 2:17-18, 21 The men said to her, "We will not be bound by this oath you made us swear unless, when we enter the land, you have tied this **scarlet cord** in the window through which you let us down, and unless you have brought your father and mother and brothers and all your family into your house . . . "Let it be as you say," **she** replied, and **she** sent them away. And when they had gone, **she** tied the **scarlet cord** in the window.

- Joshua 6:16-17 After the seventh time around, the priests blew the horns, and Joshua commanded the people, "Shout! For the LORD has given you the city! Now the city and everything in it must be devoted to the LORD for destruction. Only **Rahab** the prostitute and all those with her in her house will live, because she hid the spies we sent.

- Joshua 6:22-23 Meanwhile, Joshua told the two men who had spied out the land, "Go into the house of **the prostitute** and bring out the woman and all who are with her, just as you promised her." So the young spies went in and brought out **Rahab**, her father and mother and brothers, and all who belonged to her. They brought out her whole family and settled them outside the camp of Israel.

- Joshua 6:25 And Joshua spared **Rahab the prostitute**, with her father's household and all who belonged to her, because she hid the men Joshua had sent to spy out Jericho. So **she** has lived among the Israelites to this day.

- Matthew 1:5 Salmon was the father of Boaz by **Rahab**, Boaz the father of Obed by Ruth, Obed the father of Jesse,

- Hebrews 1:30-31 By faith the walls of Jericho fell, after the people had marched around them for seven days. By faith **the prostitute Rahab**, because she welcomed the spies in peace, did not perish with those who were disobedient.

- James 2:25-26 In the same way, was not even **Rahab the prostitute** justified by her actions when she welcomed the spies and sent them off on another route? As the body without the spirit is dead, so faith without deeds is dead.

INTRODUCTION

The book of Ruth itself names no author, but Jewish tradition holds that Samuel was the earthly author. John MacArthur included the following information in his commentary:

> Goethe reportedly labeled this piece of anonymous but unexcelled literature as "the loveliest, complete work on a small scale." What Venus is to statuary and the Mona Lisa is to paintings, Ruth is to literature. (31)

The setting is the time of the Judges, a time when Israel repeatedly turned away from the true God to idols, cried out to God, and had to be rescued by a judge. Ruth, in contrast to the book of Judges, is a story of Ruth's faithful, committed love to her husband, her mother-in-law, the true God, and then Boaz and God's providential provision for those who follow Him. The book may have been written during the reign of David since he is mentioned as a descendent of Ruth and Boaz, and Solomon is not.

The themes of faithfulness, redemption, and restoration of joy are prominent. Ruth demonstrates that women are equal co-heirs of grace and that redemption extends to Gentiles as well as Jews. Once again John MacArthur brings out a great point:

> Ruth describes God's sovereign and providential care of seemingly unimportant people at apparently insignificant times which later prove to be monumentally crucial to accomplishing God's will. (32)

Ruth and Naomi were not mighty leaders like Deborah, the Judge. They did not experience miracle pregnancies like Sarah, Elizabeth, and Mary. They may seem insignificant, but God was at work in their lives just as profoundly. Ruth was an "ordinary" instrument through whom God accomplished His sovereign will. The only other mention of Ruth in the Bible is found in Matthew's genealogy of Jesus. However, the book of Ruth is read as a part of the Jewish celebration of Pentecost since it was set at harvest time, the time of the Feast of Weeks or Pentecost. This festival commemorated the giving of the Law to Moses on Mt. Sinai. In the New Testament book of Acts, we learn that the Holy Spirit fell upon the apostles and other believers gathered with them at the time of Pentecost. In the Old Testament, the Holy Spirit would fall upon a prophet to deliver a specific message. At Pentecost, when the disciples of Jesus were gathered in an upper room, the Holy Spirit came in a new way, to indwell each believer from then on. The difference is that now the Spirit works not just with us on occasion but in and through us continually! With the indwelling of the Holy Spirit, the Lord writes His law on our hearts. We are no longer held prisoner by the fact that we could never keep the Law perfectly because Jesus died as our

Redeemer, the one who paid the price for our sin. Ruth is the story of a Kinsman-Redeemer, a foreshadowing or "type" of the Messiah, Jesus.

Susan Slade and Susie Hale

RUTH 1:1-13 – TRAGEDY STRIKES NAOMI

Ruth 1:1–2 In the days when the judges ruled, there was a famine in the land. And a certain man from Bethlehem in Judah, with his wife and two sons, went to reside in the land of Moab. The man's name was Elimelech, his wife's name was Naomi, and the names of his two sons were Mahlon and Chilion. They were Ephrathites from Bethlehem in Judah, and they entered the land of Moab and settled there.

Susan: Elimelech means "my God is king" and Naomi means "pleasant." Their sons were Mahlon which means "sick" and Chilion which means "pining."

Susie: Perhaps they were sickly at birth or cried a lot. Sometimes names were given for specific reasons such as Isaac (laughter) because Abraham and Sarah laughed.

Susan: Maybe Mahlon and Chilion were colicky babies!

Susie: Did you notice where Elimelech was from before he moved his family temporarily to Moab?

Susan: He and Naomi were from Bethlehem where eventually the Messiah would be born. Bethlehem means "House of Bread" in Hebrew.

Susie: And it would ultimately be the birthplace of The Bread of Life. Later in the story, the writer brings out the fact that Elimelech and Naomi had moved to Moab due to a famine in the land of Bethlehem.

> *John 6:35 Jesus answered, "I am the bread of life. Whoever comes to Me will never hunger, and whoever believes in Me will never thirst."*

Susie: Moab was named after the son conceived of an incestuous relationship between Lot—Abraham's nephew—and his daughter who slept with him after getting him drunk (Genesis 19:30-38). In Numbers 22-25, we read that the King of Moab tried to pay Balaam, a prophet for hire, to curse the Israelites. Therefore, God cursed the Moabites and the Ammonites "to the tenth generation." More on this later. The Moabites were enemies of the Israelites. A good article on this subject can be found at: https://www.gty.org/resources/pdf/sermons/80-238

Ruth 1:3-4 Then Naomi's husband Elimelech died, and she was left with her two sons, who took Moabite women as their wives, one named Orpah and the other named Ruth. And after they had lived in Moab about ten years, both Mahlon and Chilion also died, and Naomi was left without her two sons and without her husband.

Susie: After they moved to Moab, Elimelech died. Nothing is said of the manner of his death. Naomi became a widow with two grown sons. At least she still had sons to take care of her in a society where widows often became destitute.

Susan: After their father's death, Naomi's sons decided to marry and settle down in Moab. It is not clear whether they intended to stay or to return to Bethlehem when things were better there. Perhaps they had forgotten that Moabites were their enemies.

Susie: Or it could be that Orpah and Ruth agreed to convert to Judaism in order to marry them.

Susan: The Word really does not make this clear, but these are some hypotheses.

Susan: Orpah means "stubborn," and Ruth means "friendship."

Susie: We do not know if Orpah's name was prophetic of her character, but Ruth was certainly suitably named. Naomi's time in Moab lasted at least a decade. Naomi lost her husband, and now her two sons died as well. We are not given the reason for their deaths or how they came to die—illness or accidents.

Susan: Now Naomi was all alone. Deep in her heart she must have felt forsaken and full of despair. She must have wondered why God would allow so much grief to befall her.

Susie: Who would take care of her and her sons' widows? Neither daughter-in-law had children at the time of their husbands' deaths.

Ruth 1:6–7 When Naomi heard in Moab that the LORD had attended to His people by providing them with food, she and her daughters-in-law prepared to leave the land of Moab. Accompanied by her two daughters-in-law, she left the place where she had been living and set out on the road leading back to the land of Judah.

Susie: Word reached Naomi that the Lord had relieved Judah of the famine by sending much needed rain. God was still providentially caring for His chosen people and Naomi in particular, although she could not yet see His plan.

Susan: She did not perceive the Lord's watchful care over her yet. Naomi decided to go back home and began the journey to Bethlehem with both daughters-in-law. She wanted to return to the city where she had friends and family for moral support. Naomi was still grieving deeply and may not have been the easiest person for her daughters-in-law to travel or live with. She had what we call "smaditude" which is a sad attitude with a pinch of being mad or angry. This was how Naomi was feeling toward God rather than trusting that He would take care of her.

Susie: At this point, she does not mention or seem to remember the possibility of a kinsman redeemer for one of her daughters-in-law.

Susan: Naomi was somewhat blinded by her grief and not seeing a hopeful future.

Ruth 1:8–9a Then Naomi said to her two daughters-in-law, "Go back, each of you to your mother's home. May the LORD show you loving devotion, as you have shown to your dead and to me. May the LORD enable each of you to find rest in the home of your new husband."

Susie: Naomi urged her daughters-in-law to go back home, find new husbands, and live happily ever after.

Susan: She was releasing them from any obligation as daughters-in-law. Orpha and Ruth had been faithful, attentive wives to Naomi's sons and kind, loving daughters-in-law.

Susie: Naomi pronounced a blessing upon them asking the Lord to help them remarry. When she kissed them good-bye both daughters-in-law wept.

Ruth 1:9b-10 And she kissed them as they wept aloud and said, "Surely we will return with you to your people."

Susie: Initially, both Ruth and Orpah intended to return to Bethlehem with Naomi.

Susan: This speaks to the depth of their devotion to their husbands and their mother-in-law.

Ruth 1:11–13 But Naomi replied, "Return home, my daughters. Why would you go with me? Are there still sons in my womb to become your husbands? Return home, my daughters. Go on, for I am too old to have another husband. Even if I thought there was hope for me to have a husband tonight and to bear sons, would you wait for them to grow up? Would you refrain from having husbands? No, my daughters, it grieves me very much for your sakes that the hand of the LORD has gone out against me."

Susan: Naomi points out that it is not feasible for them to continue with her. If she were to remarry immediately, even if she were carrying a baby at that moment, it would not be in their best interest to wait for that boy to grow up.

Susie: She may have even been past the age of menopause because she implies there are no more sons in her womb.

Susan: Even if they were willing to wait for Naomi's future sons to grow up, Orpah and Ruth would then possibly be past the age of childbearing.

Susie: So, she urges them to go back home to Moab where they at least have the hope of a "normal" life.

Susan: Naomi felt that the Lord was against her because her husband and two sons had all died. She felt cursed. She wasn't, but she felt that way.

Susie: She could not see the future, the beautiful intervention of the Lord that makes up the rest of the story. To be continued…

REVIEW QUESTIONS

1. Where were Naomi and her husband, Elimelech, originally from?

2. Why was Moab an odd choice for their new home?

3. What tragedies occurred that caused Naomi to return to Judah?

4. Why did Naomi encourage her daughters-in-law to return to Moab?

Ponder This…

Have you ever felt forsaken, like God has left you high and dry? I (Susie) know that feeling. The night my husband left me, I cried out to God that it wasn't fair! Divorce is never a good thing, but

God used my husband's leaving to direct me to a church where I would be discipled and my walk with Him strengthened. Naomi could not see the future, and neither can we. However, we can trust that our God is in control and using even our worst experiences for our good, for making us more like Jesus! Can you think of a time in your own life that seemed terrible but when you look back on it, you can see how God was using that time for your eventual good?

RUTH 1:14-22 – DEVOTED DAUGHTER-IN-LOVE DETERMINED TO DWELL WITH NAOMI

Ruth 1:14 Again they wept aloud, and Orpah kissed her mother-in-law goodbye, but Ruth clung to her.

Susie: The Voice translation paints this picture vividly with words:

Ruth 1:14 (VOICE) At this Orpah and Ruth wailed and wept again. Then Orpah kissed Naomi, said goodbye, and returned the way she had come. Yet Ruth refused to let go of Naomi.

Susie: Orpah made the decision to return to Moab and hope to remarry, so she kissed her mother-in-law goodbye.

Susan: Ruth held on to her mother-in-law tightly.

Susie: She was like a child clinging to her mother, fearing abandonment at the door to school.

Susan: Ruth did not want to be without Naomi because not only had she come to love her mother-in-law but probably saw much in Naomi's life she wanted to emulate. She wanted to continue under Naomi's guidance and strength even though at this time, Naomi was broken-hearted. Naomi had an intimacy with her God that Ruth had never experienced with the gods of Moab.

Ruth 1:15 "Look," said Naomi, "your sister-in-law has gone back to her people and her gods; follow her back home."

Susie: Naomi pointed out that Orpah had taken her advice and returned to her people **and her gods.** The Moabites worshipped Chemosh who required child sacrifices (2 Kings 3:27). Even if Orpah had worshiped God with her husband, she must not have truly, wholeheartedly converted to Judaism since she returned to her gods.

> *2 Kings 3:27 When the king of Moab saw that the battle was too fierce for him, he took with him seven hundred swordsmen to break through to the king of Edom, but they could not prevail. So he took his firstborn son, who was to succeed him, and offered him as a burnt offering on the city wall. And there was great fury against the Israelites, so they withdrew and returned to their own land.*

Susan: Orpah may have gone through the motions of conversion but had not truly given the one true God her heart. Surely, she was not grounded in the Jewish faith of her husband, or she would not have returned to worshipping Chemosh.

Susie: Naomi once again encouraged Ruth to go back to Moab and do the same.

Ruth 1:16–17 But Ruth replied: "Do not urge me to leave you or to turn from following you. For wherever you go, I will go, and wherever you live, I will live; your people will be my people, and your God will be my God. Where you die, I will die, and there I will be buried. May the LORD punish me, and ever so severely, if anything but death separates you and me."

Susie: Ruth's famous speech to Naomi is often read or sung at weddings. It is a beautiful testimony of commitment to her husband's mother.

Susan: Ruth begged Naomi to stop insisting that she leave her. Ruth did not want to go back to Moab and her old way of life. She wanted to stay with Naomi whom she had come to love as her own mother.

Susie: A wise, older friend of mine (she was 99 at the time) named Beula once corrected me when I called my son's wife my "daughter-in-law." She said, "No, dear. She is your daughter-in-LOVE." Ruth was Naomi's daughter in covenant love, the covenant she had made in marriage to Naomi's son and the covenant she made in trusting the one true God, the God of the Jews. Ruth declared that she would travel wherever Naomi did and live wherever she lived.

Susan: Ruth pledged to devote herself not only to Naomi, but to her people, her family, her relatives. She set herself in covenant with the Israelites rather than with the Moabites. She set aside her family and heritage for the heritage of Israel and the worship of the one, true God.

Susie: She testified that Naomi's God would now be her God. She left Chemosh and other false gods behind and chose to follow the God of the Israelites.

Susan: Two things most of us have are our choices and our voices. Ruth was aligning both with the God of Israel, professing Him with her mouth.

Susie: Jesus had not yet been born, but Ruth (without knowing it) was following what Paul spoke about by confessing her trust in God. She expressed her faith in what she knew of God. Jesus had not yet been born as a man, so her confession of the God of Jews sufficed.

> *Romans 10:8-9 But what does it say? "The word is near you; it is in your mouth and in your heart," that is, the word of faith we are proclaiming: that if you confess with your mouth, "Jesus is Lord," and believe in your heart that God raised Him from the dead, you will be saved.*

Susie: Ruth asserted that she was with Naomi for life, that only death could part them. In fact, she vowed that if she let anything come between them, the Lord could slay her.

Susan: She bonded herself to Naomi with her word and a vow before the Lord.

Ruth 1:18 When Naomi saw that Ruth was determined to go with her, she stopped trying to persuade her.

Susan: When Naomi saw Ruth's tenacious determination to stay with her, she finally conceded and stopped trying to talk Ruth into going back to Moab.

Susie: She had no idea how important that decision would be to her own and her daughter-in-love's futures!

Ruth 1:19 So Naomi and Ruth traveled until they came to Bethlehem. When they entered Bethlehem, the whole city was stirred because of them, and the women of the city exclaimed, "Can this be Naomi?"

> 1:19 they came to Bethlehem. A trip from Moab (at least 60–75 mi.) would have taken about 7–10 days. Having descended about 4,500 ft. from Moab into the Jordan Valley, they then ascended 3,750 ft. through the hills of Judea. (33)

Susie: After the long and strenuous journey, Naomi and Ruth arrived in Bethlehem. The people may have been moved by the devotion of Ruth to travel so far from her homeland to take care of her mother-in-law even after her husband's death. They were probably also moved by the changes they saw in Naomi.

Susan: Naomi's friends and other people who knew her in Bethlehem almost didn't recognize her because her countenance had been so drastically altered by her hardships.

Susie: Being widowed and having both her sons die as well had taken a toll on her.

Ruth 1:20–21 "Do not call me Naomi," she replied. "Call me Mara, because the Almighty has dealt quite bitterly with me. I went away full, but the LORD has brought me back empty. Why call me Naomi? After all, the LORD has testified against me, and the Almighty has afflicted me."

Susan: Naomi told them not to call her by her name which means "pleasant" but to call her Mara which means "bitter or discontented." She was bitterly discontented with God because she thought He had dealt bitterly with her. She felt God had forgotten or abandoned her in her greatest time of need.

Susie: She blamed God for her empty feeling due to the loss of her husband and sons. She felt He had afflicted her rather than seeing the deaths as a normal course of life on a fallen earth. She was right that God is in control of everything but was failing to trust that same Sovereign Lord for the next chapter of her life.

Ruth 1:22 So Naomi returned from the land of Moab with her daughter-in-law Ruth the Moabitess. And they arrived in Bethlehem at the beginning of the barley harvest.

Susie: Naomi and Ruth settled into Bethlehem. Their journey back to the land of Judah was complete, but their story was really just beginning. The providence of God had brought them back to Bethlehem just in time for the barley harvest and gleaning. We will see how important that is in the next segment.

REVIEW QUESTIONS

1. What promises did Ruth make to Naomi?

2. How did the people of Bethlehem react when they saw Naomi returning from Moab to settle in Bethlehem?

3. What did Naomi tell her friends to call her? Why?

Ponder This...

We live in a society with the attitude that if things don't work out, you can always leave. Commitment is not valued as it once was. Ruth remained committed to Naomi even when the death of Mahlon and Naomi releasing her would have made that commitment seem unnecessary. Biblical, covenant love expects commitment in our marriages, our friendships, and most importantly to our Lord. Ruth's devotion serves as a reminder to us to remain steadfast in our commitment to God and our relationships with the people He brings into our lives.

Ruth 2 - RUTH GLEANS AND MEETS A MAN OF MEANS

Ruth 2:1 Now Naomi had a relative on her husband's side, a prominent man of noble character from the clan of Elimelech, whose name was Boaz.

Susie: Boaz may have been Elimelech's brother or cousin. We will see, also, that Boaz was the son of Rahab the harlot!

Susan: Boaz means "in him is strength."

Susie: Great name! As we will see later, his relationship to Elimelech qualifies him to be a kinsman-redeemer. You may remember that Tamar's desperation sprang from the fact that Judah would not give her Shelah as a kinsman-redeemer.

> The kinsman-redeemer is a male relative who, according to various laws of the Pentateuch, had the privilege or responsibility to act on behalf of a relative who was in trouble, danger, or need. The Hebrew term (go el) for kinsman-redeemer designates one who delivers or rescues (Genesis 48:16; Exodus 6:6) or redeems property or person (Leviticus 27:9–25, 25:47–55). The kinsman who redeems or vindicates a relative is illustrated most clearly in the book of Ruth, where the kinsman-redeemer is Boaz.
> https://gotquestions.org/kinsman-redeemer.html

Ruth 2:2 And Ruth the Moabitess said to Naomi, "Please let me go into the fields and glean heads of grain after someone in whose sight I may find favor." "Go ahead, my daughter," Naomi replied.

Susie: Naomi addresses Ruth as "my daughter" demonstrating the close bond the two women have formed.

Susan: With Naomi's blessing, Ruth went out to pick up the stalks of barley that the harvesters dropped which is known as gleaning. According to Leviticus 19:9-10, the corners of the field and the stalks that were dropped along the way were left for the needy to pick up, especially widows like Ruth, orphans, and strangers.

Leviticus 19:9-10 When you reap the harvest of your land, you are not to reap to the very edges of your field or gather the gleanings of your harvest. You must not strip your vineyard bare or gather its fallen grapes. Leave them for the poor and the foreigner. I am the LORD your God.

Susie: Ruth volunteered to do this, and Naomi allowed her to go. This was one way Ruth could take care of her mother-in-love since in that culture, women did not leave the home to work a regular job.

Ruth 2:3 So Ruth departed and went out into the field and gleaned after the harvesters. And she happened to come to the part of the field belonging to Boaz, who was from the clan of Elimelech.

Susan: From man's point of view, Ruth just "happened" to end up in Boaz's field; but it is obvious her gleaning there was the providence of our gracious, sovereign God.

Susie: This is the turning point of the story—the part where boy meets girl.

Susan: This is the moment when redeeming love first begins.

Ruth 2:4 Just then Boaz arrived from Bethlehem and said to the harvesters, "The LORD be with you." "The LORD bless you," they replied.

Susie: The way Boaz and his workers greeted one another shows his godliness...

Susan: ...and the excellent relationship he had with them as their employer.

Ruth 2:5 And Boaz asked the foreman of his harvesters, "Whose young woman is this?"

Susie: For some reason, Boaz noticed Ruth among all the reapers.

Susan: She probably had a countenance and a diligence in her work that struck him.

Susie: Perhaps she was beautiful outside as well as inside. He inquired to whom Ruth belonged, probably thinking of her as a maidservant or a daughter of a poor person.

Ruth 2:6–7 The foreman answered, "She is the Moabitess who returned with Naomi from the land of Moab. She has said, 'Please let me glean and gather among the sheaves after the harvesters.' So she came out and has continued from morning until now, except that she rested a short time in the shelter."

Susie: The worker informed Boaz that she was the Moabitess, Naomi's daughter-in-law...

Susan: ...and that she had been working continually and fervently since the morning.

Susie: She only took brief breaks in the shelter set up for the workers.

Ruth 2:8–9 Then Boaz said to Ruth, "Listen, my daughter. Do not go and glean in another field, and do not go away from this place, but stay here close to my servant girls. Let your eyes be on the field they are harvesting, and follow along after these girls. Indeed, I have ordered the young men not to touch you. And when you are thirsty, go and drink from the jars the young men have filled."

Susie: Boaz addressed Ruth as "daughter" because he was probably closer in age to Naomi and Elimelech, and she would have been much younger than him. Boaz invited Ruth to glean exclusively in his fields. He told her to follow the young women who tied up the sheaves for the harvesters. Perhaps he took care of Ruth because she was the daughter-in-law of his near relative, Elimelech.

Susan: He promised the young male workers would leave her alone and would not hassle her or behave in any inappropriate manner. He told her she would not have to draw her own water when she was thirsty but could drink from that provided for his workers. Boaz demonstrated himself to be a kind man.

Susie: These verses let us know that Boaz was a man of means since he had several servant girls as well as paid workers.

Ruth 2:10 At this, she fell on her face, bowing low to the ground, and said to him, "Why have I found such favor in your eyes that you should take notice of me, even though I am a foreigner?"

Susan: Ruth was shocked that Boaz would pay this kind of positive attention to her since she was from Moab. She would have expected enmity from a Hebrew man due to their deep-seated cultural history, and instead he extended an unexpected welcome.

Susie: We must remember that the Lord had cursed Moab, so it was perfectly natural that Ruth would be surprised by Boaz's kindness.

Susie: She bowed to the ground to show respect and gratitude to him and was flabbergasted at his overwhelming graciousness and generosity.

Ruth 2:11 Boaz replied, "I have been made fully aware of all you have done for your mother-in-law since the death of your husband, how you left your father and mother and the land of your birth, and how you came to a people you did not know   before . . .

Susan: Boaz praised Ruth for leaving everyone and everything she knew behind and choosing to look after Naomi, her deceased husband's mother.

Susie: He recognized her possible discomfort in being among a people who were not her own, had different customs, and were even prejudiced against her as a Moabitess. News had traveled fast in Bethlehem, so he knew a great deal about Ruth's exceptional character.

Ruth 2:12 . . . May the LORD repay your work, and may you receive a rich reward from the LORD, the God of Israel, under whose wings you have taken refuge."

Susan: Boaz prayed on Ruth's behalf that the Lord would reward her in light of her selflessness. This was a blessing he pronounced on her.

Susie: He makes the statement that Ruth has come to trust the Lord and is under his wings. Ruth had converted to Judaism, possibly when she married Mahlon but definitely when she told Naomi, "Your God will be my God." The idea here is that of a mother hen gathering her chicks under her wings to hide and protect them from predators. The Lord is the covering for those who place their trust in Him.

> *Psalm 91:4 He will cover you with His feathers; under His wings you will find refuge; His faithfulness is a shield and rampart.*

Ruth 2:13 "My lord," she said, "may I continue to find favor in your eyes, for you have comforted and spoken kindly to your maidservant, though I am not like one of your servant girls."

Susan: Ruth was grateful that Boaz had taken her under his protection even though she was not an Israelite. Ruth was under Naomi's care like a daughter. Now Boaz is taking special interest in her, but ultimately, it is the Lord who is protecting and guiding her.

Susie: She humbly thanked Boaz for his kindness, calling him "lord" which would be in recognition of his social status as a landowner and her elder.

Ruth 2:14 At mealtime Boaz said to her, "Come over here; have some bread and dip it into the vinegar sauce." So she sat down beside the harvesters, and he offered her roasted grain, and she ate and was satisfied and had some left over.

Susie: Boaz invited Ruth to stay and eat some of the lunch he provided for his own workers. She ate until her hunger was satisfied and rose up to go back to gleaning. But this is just the beginning of the relationship between Ruth and Boaz. At this point, neither of them knew what the Lord had in store for them.

REVIEW QUESTIONS

1. Define "gleaning" in your own words.

2. Did Ruth seek out the fields of Boaz on purpose? Explain.

3. How does the fact that Ruth ended up harvesting in the field of Boaz demonstrate the sovereignty of God?

4. How did Boaz react to the fact that Naomi's daughter-in-law was gleaning in his fields?

5. How did Ruth respond to Boaz's generosity?

Ponder This...

Susan's Grannie often told her "Pretty is as pretty does." We definitely see this in the account of Boaz meeting Ruth for the first time. What he praises in her is not her outward beauty. In fact, she was probably hot and sweaty while working in the field. He praises her excellent character qualities and her loving commitment to Naomi. When people look past our outward appearance, what do they see? Our hope and our goal should be that they see the Lord Jesus shining out of our lives.

RUTH 2:15-23 - NAOMI'S FAITH REKINDLED

Ruth 2:15–16 When Ruth got up to glean, Boaz ordered his young men, "Even if she gathers among the sheaves, do not insult her. Rather, pull out for her some stalks from the bundles and leave them for her to gather. Do not rebuke her."

Susie: Boaz went farther than the law commanded.

Susan: He told his reapers to drop some stalks of grain on purpose, so that Ruth would have an abundance to pick up.

Susie: He told them not to run her off or scold her for gleaning or even taking wheat out of the sheaves that had already been tied in bundles but instead to take care of her.

Susan: He told them to make her gleaning easier and more successful. He knew she was gathering food not only for herself but for Naomi. He told the workers to take care of her in such a way that her dignity remained intact.

Ruth 2:17–18 So Ruth gathered grain in the field until evening. And when she beat out what she had gleaned, it was about an ephah of barley. She picked up the grain and went into the town, where her mother-in-law saw what she had gleaned. And she brought out what she had saved from her meal and gave it to Naomi.

    2:17 ephah. Over one-half bushel, weighing about 30 to 40 lbs. (34)

Susan: Ruth had worked hard and fast all day and then continued working by beating out the edible grain from that which she had gleaned. Ruth did not have an idle bone in her body. Even in her work, Naomi was always at the forefront of her thoughts.

Susie: She not only brought Naomi the barley she had beaten out, but she had saved some of the lunch Boaz provided his workers for her mother-in-love.

Ruth 2:19 Then her mother-in-law asked her, "Where did you glean today, and where did you work? Blessed be the man who noticed you." So she told her mother-in-law where she had worked. "The name of the man I worked with today is Boaz," she said.

Susie: Naomi must have realized that Ruth brought home far more than expected from a day's gleaning and asked whose field she worked in. She pronounced a blessing on whatever man had taken an interested in their plight.

Susan: The observant and compassionate man who had noticed Ruth in his field.

Susie: Ruth told her the man who owned the field was named Boaz.

Ruth 2:20 Then Naomi said to her daughter-in-law, "May he be blessed by the LORD, who has not withdrawn His kindness[H2617] from the living or the dead." Naomi continued, "The man is a close relative. He is one of our kinsman-redeemers."

Susan: "Kindness" in this verse is the Hebrew word cheçed meaning "loving-kindness, merciful kindness."

> H2617 cheçed, kheh'-sed; from H2616; kindness; by implication (towards God) piety; rarely (by opposition) reproof, or (subjectively) beauty:—favour, good deed(-liness, -ness), kindly, (loving-) kindness, merciful (kindness), mercy, pity, reproach, wicked thing. (35)

Susie: Boaz was demonstrating the love of God through his actions. Naomi again pronounces a blessing on Boaz for remembering her husband and sons by being kind to their widows. She brings up the possibility that Boaz could be a kinsman-redeemer, one who would care for the widow of a near relative.

> Naomi began to understand God's sovereign working, covenant loyalty, lovingkindness, and mercy toward her because Ruth, without human direction (2:3), found the near relative Boaz. (36)

Susie: God's providence had led Ruth to Boaz just as the spies in Joshua chapter 2 were led to the house of Rahab. We keep seeing the sovereignty of our Lord in the stories behind the Women of Christmas!

Ruth 2:21 Then Ruth the Moabitess said, "He also told me, 'Stay with my young men until they have finished gathering all my harvest.'"

Susie: Ruth told Naomi how Boaz had instructed her to glean only in his fields. He had the resources to provide extra for her and had his reapers make sure she gleaned plenty of grain for her and Naomi.

Susan: He was also offering her protection that she might not find elsewhere since she was from Moab.

Ruth 2:22 And Naomi said to her daughter-in-law Ruth, "My daughter, it is good for you to work with his young women, so that nothing will happen to you in another field."

Susie: Naomi encouraged Ruth to do as Boaz had instructed.

Susan: She was saying to stay with Boaz' reapers lest she be assaulted by the men in someone else's fields because she was a foreigner from an enemy country. She was already under the protection of Boaz.

Ruth 2:23 So Ruth stayed close to the servant girls of Boaz to glean grain until the barley and wheat harvests were finished. And she lived with her mother-in-law.

Susie: The two harvests lasted approximately two months from the middle of April until the middle of June. Ruth continued to glean behind Boaz's workers that entire time.

Susan: Ruth was guaranteed work and was able to provide food for Naomi as well as herself due to the kindness and generosity of Boaz.

REVIEW QUESTIONS

1. What did Boaz instruct his workers concerning Ruth?

   _____
   _____
   _____
   _____
   _____
   _____
   _____
   _____

   What amount of grain did Ruth bring home to Naomi? Was this a typical amount to glean from the leftovers in a field?

   _____
   _____
   _____
   _____
   _____
   _____

2. What did Naomi realize when Ruth told her the name of the owner of the fields she gleaned in?

   _____
   _____
   _____
   _____
   _____
   _____

3. How did God use Boaz to protect Ruth?

_____
_____
_____
_____
_____

Ponder This...

Naomi had felt abandoned by God due to the loss of her husband and sons. She was in a crisis of faith but still recognized and worshiped Him as her Lord. When she saw God's provision by directing Ruth to the field of a near kinsman, that spark of faith began to be a flicker of faith, then once again became a flame within her, and she had hope. Have you lost hope because you cannot see how God is working in your life? Continue to trust Him, continue to obey, continue to worship, and wait expectantly to see what He will do. If you have trusted in Jesus, His sovereignty is always at work. Even though at times it is difficult to perceive exactly how or when God will move, we can trust that He WILL move. This makes me think of the songs "Praise You in This Storm" by Casting Crowns and "You're Still God" by Phillips, Craig, and Dean. You can listen to them on YouTube™.

Susan Slade and Susie Hale

Ruth 3:1-7 - INTRIGUING INSTRUCTIONS

Ruth 3:1–2 One day Ruth's mother-in-law Naomi said to her, "My daughter, should I not seek a resting place for you, that it may be well with you? Now is not Boaz, with whose servant girls you have been working, a relative of ours? In fact, tonight he is winnowing barley on the threshing floor.

Susan: Naomi sees a way she might help Ruth to have a secure future.

Susie: Naomi does not seem to even think about the fact that this would secure her own future as well.

Susan: Her focus was no longer on her own personal pity party but on the needs of Ruth, beginning to prioritize the needs of others above her own. She continues to feel responsible for Ruth's welfare as she did when she urged her to go back to Moab and find a husband because she had no more sons to offer her. Ruth has been taking care of Naomi by gleaning for food, but Naomi is also taking care of Ruth. The Lord had begun to change Naomi's heart condition from bitterness to hope.

Susie: Naomi points out that Boaz will most likely be spending the night on the threshing floor protecting his grain from being stolen. In the next few verses, she gives Ruth intriguing instructions that will benefit not only Ruth, but Naomi as well.

Susan: Naomi is going to tell Ruth how to be at the right place, at the right time and exactly what to do.

Ruth 3:3 Therefore wash yourself, put on perfume, and wear your best clothes. Go down to the threshing floor, but do not let the man know you are there until he has finished eating and drinking.

Susan: Naomi told her to bathe, put on oils or lotions, and don her best clothes. This night might turn out to be the most important of her life!

Susie: Naomi told Ruth to hide until Boaz had finished his meal and drink and had laid down to sleep.

Ruth 3:4 When he lies down, note the place where he lies. Then go in and uncover his feet, and lie down, and he will explain to you what you should do."

Susie: Naomi was instructing Ruth in an ancient Near Eastern custom which was a proper way for a woman to propose to a man. It sounds very strange to us, but there was no impropriety or sexual overtone to her actions.

Susan: She told Ruth to uncover his feet and lay down by them until he woke up. Then he would tell her what to do next.

Susie: Boaz would be familiar with this custom and recognize what Ruth was doing.

Ruth 3:5 "I will do everything you say," Ruth answered.

Susie: I guess Naomi had explained the custom to Ruth. Whether she understood it or not, Ruth demonstrated great respect and trust in her mother-in-love.

Susan: She was also courageous and trusting of Boaz's character to meet with him alone in this manner after dark.

Ruth 3:6–7 So she went down to the threshing floor and did everything her mother-in-law had instructed her to do. After Boaz had finished eating and drinking and was in good spirits, he went to lie down at the end of the heap of grain. Then Ruth went in secretly, uncovered his feet, and lay down.

Susie: Ruth did everything Naomi had told her to do.

Susan: After supper, Boaz was merry and had a sense of well-being. He was probably incredibly thankful to God for the good harvest after years of famine. His heart was full of gratitude for the rain and sun God had provided to bless his hard work with a plentiful crop.

Susie: While he was contentedly sleeping, Ruth sneaked up on him, uncovered his feet, and laid down to wait for the instructions Naomi had promised that Boaz would give her.

REVIEW QUESTIONS

1. What did Naomi mean by "seek a resting place for you?"
   _____
   _____
   _____
   _____
   _____

2. What were Naomi's exact instructions to Ruth concerning her actions on the threshing floor?

_____
_____
_____
_____
_____
_____
_____
_____
_____

3. How was Boaz feeling after his meal?

_____
_____
_____
_____

4. What did Ruth do after Boaz had fallen asleep?

_____
_____
_____
_____

Ponder This...

There is no direct application here. At least *I'm* not planning on lying down at a man's feet any time soon. However, sometimes the Lord's instructions may seem odd to us—such as giving an offering even though we do not have much to give. However, obeying the Lord leads to security and blessing. He has told us to love our enemies—that's a hard one as well; but if we obey Him, He will reward us. OBEDIENCE is most important:

> *1 Samuel 15:22 (VOICE) Samuel: Does the Eternal One delight in sacrifices and burnt offerings as much as in perfect obedience to His voice? Be certain of this: that obedience is better than sacrifice; to heed His voice is better than offering the fat of rams.*

RUTH 3:8-18 - RUTH PROPOSES TO BOAZ BUT RUNS INTO A SNAG

Ruth 3:8 At midnight, Boaz was startled, turned over, and there lying at his feet was a woman!

Susie: Feeling something at his feet, Boaz was startled.

Susan: He may not have been sure whether it was a human or a beast.

Susie: So, he turned where he could see and discovered a woman lying there but could not clearly see who she was in the dark. That must have been a shock!

Ruth 3:9 "Who are you?" he asked. "I am your servant Ruth," she replied. "Spread the corner of your garment over me, for you are a kinsman-redeemer."

Susie: By asking Boaz to literally cover her, she is figuratively asking him to marry her. She is saying, "Cover me like the Lord covers us under His wings" (Psalm 91:4). The kinsman-redeemer could provide protection and a family for a widow by agreeing to a levirate marriage—a man taking his dead brother or near relative's wife as his own in order to continue the family line of the deceased. He also had the right to redeem any land belonging to the deceased as belonging to the wife.

Ruth 3:10 Then Boaz said, "May the LORD bless you, my daughter. You have shown more kindness now than before, because you have not run after the younger men, whether rich or poor.

Susie: Boaz asked the Lord to bless Ruth, whom he continues to address as daughter, and praises her for following the law in seeking a kinsman-redeemer to continue her husband's line. She was still young and could have pursued younger men than Boaz who was probably a generation older than her.

Susan: But she followed her heart of love for her husband's memory and her love for his mother and sought Boaz instead as Naomi had instructed her. His previous kindness to her may have helped her to readily obey Naomi's unusual counsel.

Ruth 3:11 And now do not be afraid, my daughter. I will do for you whatever you request, since all my fellow townspeople know that you are a woman of noble character.

Susie: Boaz pledges to fulfill the requirements of a kinsman-redeemer, including levirate marriage.

Susan: In the short time Ruth had lived in Bethlehem, her pleasant countenance, excellent character, and loving care of Naomi had broken down the cultural barrier between the Israelites and Moabites that had existed for generations.

Susie: Her behavior and willingness to follow the law proved her to be a true convert to Judaism...

Susan: ...in the eyes of Boaz and possibly all of Bethlehem. He was confident others saw in her, as he did, noble character.

Ruth 3:12 Yes, it is true that I am a kinsman-redeemer, but there is a redeemer nearer than I.

Susie: Major snag—there is another man more qualified to be the kinsman-redeemer! We are not told why this man was more qualified. He may have been a brother to Elimelech and Boaz only a cousin, or relative age may have played a part. We are not told.

Ruth 3:13 Stay here tonight, and in the morning, if he wants to redeem you, good. Let him redeem you. But if he does not want to redeem you, as surely as the LORD lives, I will. Now lie here until morning."

Susie: Boaz declares that he will speak to this other kinsman-redeemer on Ruth's behalf since widows truly had no rights. He may not have wanted her to have to humble herself before another man after having lain at his feet like a servant.

Susan: We found this interesting tidbit in *Matthew Henry's Commentary:*

> The Hebrew word for a widow signifies one that is dumb. Boaz will therefore open his mouth for the dumb (Prov. 31:8) and will say that for this widow which she knew not how to say for herself. (37)

Proverbs 31:8 (CJB) Speak up for those who can't speak for themselves, for the rights of all who need an advocate.

Susie: The position of kinsman redeemer is a picture of Jesus redeeming the church. However, in Matthew Henry's note, I see that Boaz also acted as an advocate for Ruth much as Jesus advocates for us at the throne of God.

1 John 2:1 My dear children, I write this to you so that you will not sin. But if anybody does sin, we have an advocate with the Father—Jesus Christ, the Righteous One.

Ruth 3:14 So she lay down at his feet until morning, but she got up before anyone else could recognize her. Then Boaz said, "Do not let it be known that a woman came to the threshing floor."

Susie: The next morning, they got up early enough that she would not be recognized as it was still dark.

Susan: This way no one could accuse them of impropriety.

Susie: Her character would not be tarnished by possible gossip.

Susan: Boaz had her leave early as a protective measure for her reputation.

Ruth 3:15 And he told her, "Bring the shawl you are wearing and hold it out." When she did so, he shoveled six measures of barley into her shawl. Then he went into the city.

> Ephah / Bath (10 omers, sometimes translated "bushel," "peck," "deal, "part," "measure," or "6 or 7 pints"): 22 L or 3/5 bsh
> https://www.gotquestions.org/biblical-weights-and-measures.html
>
> **six measures:** Possibly six seahs (two ephahs), or approximately 39.6 dry quarts or 43.8 liters (about 58 pounds or 26.3 kilograms of barley). (38)

Susie: Ruth must have been a strong girl because Boaz gave her a large quantity of barley, possibly as much as almost 60 pounds! He wrapped it in her shawl and laid it on her back to carry. Strange engagement gift! This might even be seen as a "bride price" paid to Naomi as her guardian.

Ruth 3:16 When Ruth returned to her mother-in-law, Naomi asked her, "How did it go, my daughter?" Then Ruth told her all that Boaz had done for her.

Susie: Naomi inquired, "How'd it go?" Ruth gave her a detailed account.

Ruth 3:17 And she said, "He gave me these six measures of barley, for he said, 'Do not go back to your mother-in-law empty-handed.'"

Susie: With this gift, Naomi knew that Boaz intended to change their poor estate.

Ruth 3:18 "Wait, my daughter," said Naomi, "until you find out how things go, for he will not rest unless he has resolved the matter today."

Susie: Naomi was confident that Boaz would do all in his power to settle things quickly since he had shown such loving-kindness to them already. More anticipation for Ruth as they awaited word from Boaz.

REVIEW QUESTIONS

1. Ruth asked Boaz to cover her. What did this symbolize?
   _____
   _____
   _____
   _____
   _____

2. What were the possible reasons that another man might be a "closer" kinsman-redeemer?
   _____
   _____
   _____
   _____
   _____
   _____
   _____

3. In what two ways does Boaz as Ruth's kinsman-redeemer picture the work of Jesus on our behalf?
   _____
   _____
   _____
   _____
   _____

4. How much barley did Boaz pour into Ruth's shawl for her to take back to Naomi?
   _____
   _____
   _____
   _____
   _____
   _____

Ponder This...

Jesus is our Kinsman-redeemer. We were in bondage to our sin nature, and He took our punishment on Himself in order to redeem us to be His bride. To be His bride, we had to humble ourselves to realize we could not take care of our problem ourselves and must accept the gift He offers freely to us that cost Him everything on the cross. As Ruth lay at the feet of Boaz, we must lay ourselves down at the foot of the cross, a position of total submission and trust. Have you trusted Jesus as your Redeemer. If not, now is the time to do so.

2 Corinthians 6:2 (NLT) For God says, "At just the right time, I heard you. On the day of salvation, I helped you." Indeed, the "right time" is now. Today is the day of salvation.

RUTH 4:1-8—LET'S MAKE A DEAL

Ruth 4:1 Meanwhile, Boaz went to the gate and sat down there. Soon the kinsman-redeemer of whom he had spoken came along, and Boaz said, "Come over here, my friend, and sit down." So he went over and sat down.

Susan: The city gate during those times was where business deals were struck and witnessed by the men of the city.

Susie: Boaz sat down and waited for the other kinsman-redeemer to pass by.

Susan: When Boaz saw him, he said, "Hey! So-and-so, come and sit down," because he had business to transact with him. He had a proposition for him.

Susie: The Bible does not name this man saying "such a man" or "such-and-such," so we put that purposeful omission in our own vernacular. So the man did as his relative, Boaz, asked him.

Ruth 4:2 Then Boaz took ten of the elders of the city and said, "Sit here," and they did so.

> **4:2 ten men**. This number apparently comprised a quorum to officially transact business, although only two or three witnesses were needed for judicial proceedings (cf. Deut. 17:6; 19:15). (39)

Susan: Boaz was a man of clout and influence in Bethlehem.

Susie: Therefore, when he asked some of the elders to join in as witnesses to the deal, they did so. Transactions of this nature required witnesses to validate the deal. Reminds me of when I signed my will. We had to have two witnesses and a notary public to make it official.

Ruth 4:3–4 And he said to the kinsman-redeemer, "Naomi, who has returned from the land of Moab, is selling the piece of land that belonged to our brother Elimelech. I thought I should inform you that you may buy it back in the presence of those seated here and in the presence of the elders of my people. If you want to redeem it, do so. But if you will not redeem it, tell me so I may know, because there is no one but you to redeem it, and I am next after you." "I will redeem it," he replied.

Susie: Boaz explained that Naomi's husband Elimelech had owned some land near Bethlehem, and since this other kinsman was first in line to redeem it, he was offering him the first chance to buy it. Boaz did ask that he let him know his intentions since he was second in line for the property. He indicated that Naomi would need to sell the property in order to live. He wisely omitted the fact that the land and Ruth were a package deal. The man said he would redeem it, buy it. Uh oh!

Ruth 4:5 Then Boaz said, "On the day you buy the land from Naomi and also from Ruth the Moabitess, you must also acquire the widow of the deceased in order to raise up the name of the deceased on his inheritance."

Susan: Boaz points out that the way of integrity would be to also marry Ruth when he redeemed the land in order to provide children for their deceased relative. In other words, engage in a levirate marriage with the widow.

Susie: This was certainly Boaz's intention if he were allowed to redeem it.

Ruth 4:6 The kinsman-redeemer replied, "I cannot redeem it myself, or I would jeopardize my own inheritance. Take my right of redemption, because I cannot redeem it."

Susan: The relative back-pedaled really fast at that time because it would interfere with the inheritance of his own children since he was already married. He wasn't willing to help Naomi and Ruth at the expense of his own family's established inheritance.

Susie: Therefore, he encouraged Boaz to redeem it for himself. He abdicated his right to the land and the hand of Ruth, which we believe was Boaz's sincere hope from the beginning.

Ruth 4:7–8 Now in former times in Israel, concerning the redemption or exchange of property, to make any matter legally binding a man would remove his sandal and give it to the other party, and this was a confirmation in Israel. So the kinsman-redeemer removed his sandal and said to Boaz, "Buy it for yourself."

Susan: To seal the deal, the man took off his shoe according to their custom as a testimony before the witnesses that the transaction was agreed upon. In their culture, a shoe in the hand sealed the deal.

Susie: In our culture, a handshake used to be as good as our word. However, these days, a contract would have to be drawn up, signed, and notarized.

REVIEW QUESTIONS

1. Why did Boaz sit at the city gate the next morning?
   _____
   _____
   _____

2. How many elders of the city did Boaz gather? Why?

3. Boaz omitted what crucial bit of information in his first proposal to the other kinsman-redeemer?

4. Why was the other kinsman-redeemer not willing to purchase the land after Boaz filled in the detail about marrying the widow?

5. What was the unusual symbolic custom for sealing the deal?

Ponder This...

Boaz was a man of the utmost integrity and kept his word to Ruth to approach the nearer relative on her behalf. How seriously do we take giving our word? Are we known as people of integrity in our workplaces, churches, and most importantly, our own homes?

RUTH 4:9-12 - IT'S A DONE DEAL

Ruth 4:9 At this, Boaz said to the elders and all the people, "You are witnesses today that I am buying from Naomi all that belonged to Elimelech, Chilion, and Mahlon.

Susan: Boaz bought everything that was for sale...

Susie: ...that which was redeemable by the near kinsman under the law. This included the land belonging to Naomi's sons as well as her husband Elimelech's total inheritance.

Susan: Boaz cleaned out the estate sale in order to have the estate remain in the family.

Ruth 4:10 Moreover, I have acquired Ruth the Moabitess, Mahlon's widow, as my wife, to raise up the name of the deceased through his inheritance, so that his name will not disappear from among his brothers or from the gate of his home. You are witnesses today."

Susie: In addition, he was going to engage in Levirate marriage to redeem the name of Mahlon by having children with his widow. He was asking the elders to witness his right to do this in accordance with the Law of Moses.

> *Deuteronomy 25:5-6 When brothers dwell together and one of them dies without a son, the widow must not marry outside the family. Her husband's brother is to take her as his wife and fulfill the duty of a brother-in-law for her. The first son she bears will carry on the name of the dead brother, so that his name will not be blotted out from Israel.*

Susan: Boaz was rescuing both Naomi and Ruth from the certain destitution which befell most childless widows. Ruth's firstborn son would be the heir to all the property that formerly belonged to Elimelech and his sons.

Ruth 4:11 "We are witnesses," said the elders and all the people at the gate. "May the LORD make the woman entering your home like Rachel and Leah, who together built up the house of Israel. May you be prosperous in Ephrathah and famous in Bethlehem.

Susie: The men in the gate verified that they were witnesses to Boaz's right to redeem the property and marry Ruth.

Susan: They gave their blessing on the marriage and prayed Ruth would be like Rachel and

Leah, the wives of Jacob, the mothers of who would become the heads of the twelve tribes of Israel. Boaz was kinsman-redeemer and rescuer. He redeemed the property belonging to Elimelech and rescued the two widows from poverty.

Susie: The elders prayed he would make a good name for himself in Bethlehem, and that the Lord would bless them with a great family.

Ruth 4:12 "And may your house become like the house of Perez, whom Tamar bore to Judah, because of the offspring the LORD will give you by this young woman."

Susan: Pharez (Perez) was the ancestor of the Ephrathites and Bethlehemites and was the firstborn twin of Tamar who you may remember had incestuous relations with her father-in-law Judah who subsequently legitimized her sons by joining with her in levirate marriage.

Susan: However, the fact that she deceived Judah into impregnating her enabled his family line to continue and earned her a place in the lineage of Jesus, the Messiah. Perez would have also been a great, great, etc. grandfather of Boaz.

> Perez – (breach). The "children of Perez," or Pharez, the son of Judah, appear to have been a family of importance for many centuries. (1 Chronicles 27:3; Nehemiah 11:4,6) (40)

> *1 Chronicles 27:2-3 Jashobeam son of Zabdiel was in charge of the first division, which was assigned the first month. There were 24,000 men in his division. He was a descendant of Perez and chief of all the army commanders for the first month.*

> *Nehemiah 11:3-6 These are the heads of the provinces who settled in Jerusalem. (In the villages of Judah, however, each lived on his own property in their towns—the Israelites, priests, Levites, temple servants, and descendants of Solomon's servants—while some of the descendants of Judah and Benjamin settled in Jerusalem.) From the descendants of Judah: Athaiah son of Uzziah, the son of Zechariah, the son of Amariah, the son of Shephatiah, the son of Mahalalel, a descendant of Perez; and Maaseiah son of Baruch, the son of Col-hozeh, the son of Hazaiah, the son of Adaiah, the son of Joiarib, the son of Zechariah, a descendant of Shelah. The descendants of Perez who settled in Jerusalem totaled 468 men of valor.*

Susie: They prayed that not only would Ruth conceive, but that her children would be noteworthy citizens in Israel. The elders and the other people in the city gate not only witnessed the transaction but heartily approved.

Susan: Their approval may have been due to the integrity of both Boaz and Ruth and Naomi's respected position in the town.

REVIEW QUESTIONS

1. Whose property was included in the land Boaz purchased?

2. What reason did Boaz give for marrying Ruth?

3. What blessing did the elders pronounce on Ruth?

4. What other "Woman of Christmas" that we have studied did they mention in their blessing on the house of Boaz?

Ponder This...

Blessings. The people blessed Boaz in response to his commitment to redeem Naomi and Ruth's land and marry Ruth. Do we ever pronounce blessings on our family and friends today? Why or why not? It seems to be a practice that needs to be revived. You may want to pray for and write out a blessing for each of your children.

RUTH 4:13-22 AND MATTHEW 1:5
NAOMI'S ARMS EMPTY NO MORE

Ruth 4:13 So Boaz took Ruth, and she became his wife. And when he had relations with her, the LORD enabled her to conceive, and she gave birth to a son.

Susan: It sounds like as soon as the marriage was consummated, they conceived by the grace and power of God.

Susie: God blessed them not only with each other but with a son.

> *Psalm 127:3 (NASB) Behold, children are a gift of the Lord, The fruit of the womb is a reward.*

Ruth 4:14 Then the women said to Naomi, "Blessed be the LORD, who has not left you this day without a kinsman-redeemer. May his name become famous in Israel . . .

Susie: The son born to Ruth and Boaz would now serve as Naomi's kinsman. Since he was seen as Mahlon's son rather than Boaz's, he would be Naomi's grandson and would care for her in her golden years. They prayed the blessing on Boaz that his name would become famous in Israel. You cannot get more famous than to be in the lineage of the Messiah!

Ruth 4:15 . . . He will renew your life and sustain you in your old age. For your daughter-in-law, who loves you and is better to you than seven sons, has given him birth."

Susie: There is nothing like the birth of your first grandchild to rejuvenate you (even though you may say it makes you feel old). Holding that precious baby revitalizes a grandparent.

Susan: Naomi had declared herself to be empty, but now her arms and her heart were filled with life and love.

Susie: It could be said of Ruth, "Many daughters have done noble things, but you surpass them all!" just as the woman in Proverbs 31:29. Some commentators even speculate that Ruth may have been the model for the woman described in the 31st chapter of Proverbs.

Susan: Ruth was God's definition of the perfect family for Naomi.

4:15 better...than seven sons. Seven represented the number of perfection and thus 7 sons would make the complete family (cf. 1 Sam. 2:5). However, Ruth exceeded this standard all by herself. (41)

Ruth 4:16 And Naomi took the child, placed him on her lap, and became a nurse to him.

Susan: Naomi was similar to a nanny but even closer.

Susie: She would help to raise the baby as if he were her own son.

Susan: Ruth loved Naomi and was glad to fill her arms again. She would have been happy to see the relationship blossom between the baby and his grandmother.

Ruth 4:17 The neighbor women said, "A son has been born to Naomi," and they named him Obed. He became the father of Jesse, the father of David.

Susie: This is the only time recorded in the Old Testament that someone was named by a person not in the family.

Susan: Obed means "servant." *The Cambridge Bible for Schools and Colleges* notes that Obed is an abbreviated form of Obadiah which means "servant of the Lord." He would serve Naomi as was expected of a grandchild to his grandmother.

Susie: He is counted as being the son of Naomi because he would restore the line of her husband Elimelech by being the child of her son Mahlon. From Obed, God's servant, came the kingly line of David and ultimately, the Messiah.

Ruth 4:18–22 Now these are the generations of Perez: Perez was the father of Hezron, Hezron was the father of Ram, Ram was the father of Amminadab, Amminadab was the father of Nahshon, Nahshon was the father of Salmon, Salmon was the father of Boaz, Boaz was the father of Obed, Obed was the father of Jesse,
and Jesse was the father of David.

Susie: Here we see how the tribe of Judah through his son Perez were David's ancestors and eventually the "Lion of the tribe of Judah,"—Jesus—descended from them. Therefore, Ruth the Moabitess is included in Matthew's genealogy of Jesus Christ.

> *Matthew 1:5–6 Salmon was the father of Boaz by Rahab, Boaz the father of Obed by Ruth, Obed the father of Jesse, and Jesse the father of David the king. David was the father of Solomon by Uriah's wife.*
>
> The story of Ruth and Naomi is an important one, not just because of the loyalty modeled by Ruth but because of the way it reveals the sovereignty of God. In Beth-

lehem, the Lord allowed Ruth to remarry and give birth to a son named Obed, who became grandfather to King David. Despite Ruth's non-Jewish, outsider status, God worked through her life to change the history of the world.
https://www.gotquestions.org/Ruth-and-Naomi.html

Susie: We will stop here for now because "Uriah's wife" is Bathsheba, our next Woman of Christmas!

REVIEW QUESTIONS

1. Ruth's firstborn son would be considered the son of what man?

2. In the opinion of the women of Bethlehem, Ruth was better to Naomi than what?

3. Why did the neighbor women say, "A son has been born to Naomi?"

4. What is the meaning of the name "Obed?"

Ponder This...

So far in this study of the "Ten Women of Christmas," we have studied Eve who was deceived, Sarah who laughed, Tamar who pretended prostitution, Rahab who *was* a harlot, and Ruth who came from the wrong side of the camel path, Moab. If you think you are so bad God could never save you or even if He did, He could never use you for His glory, THINK AGAIN. God's grace and power can extend even to you when you put your trust in Jesus and surrender your will to His. After my husband divorced me (Susie), I thought I was rendered useless as far as service to the Lord. However, after some time of healing, the Lord placed me in a Christian school as a teacher, then curriculum coordinator. Now He has brought Susan into my life and helped us begin Precious Jewels Ministries, Inc. and author several books together, including this first Bible study curriculum. God is in the business of turning things around for His glory and our good!

Moabitess Ruth Redeemed to be Great Grandmother of King David

- Ruth 1:1-5 In the days when the judges ruled, there was a famine in the land. And a certain man from Bethlehem in Judah, with his wife and two sons, went to reside in the land of Moab. The man's name was Elimelech, his wife's name was Naomi, and the names of his two sons were Mahlon and Chilion. They were Ephrathites from Bethlehem in Judah, and they entered the land of Moab and settled there. Then Naomi's husband Elimelech died, and she was left with her two sons, who took Moabite women as their wives, one named Orpah and the other named **Ruth**. And after they had lived in Moab about ten years, both Mahlon and Chilion also died, and Naomi was left without her two sons and without her husband.

- Ruth 1:11 & 14 But Naomi replied, "Return home, my daughters. Why would you go with me? Are there still sons in my womb to become your husbands? . . . Again they wept aloud, and Orpah kissed her mother-in-law goodbye, but **Ruth** clung to her.

- Ruth 1:16-17 But **Ruth** replied: "Do not urge me to leave you or to turn from following you. For wherever you go, I will go, and wherever you live, I will live; your people will be my people, and your God will be my God. Where you die, I will die, and there I will be buried. May the LORD punish me, and ever so severely, if anything but death separates you and me."

- Ruth 1:18 When Naomi saw that **Ruth** was determined to go with her, she stopped trying to persuade her.

- Ruth 1:22 So Naomi returned from the land of Moab with her daughter-in-law **Ruth the Moabitess**. And they arrived in Bethlehem at the beginning of the barley harvest.

- Ruth 2:2 And **Ruth the Moabitess** said to Naomi, "Please let me go into the fields and glean heads of grain after someone in whose sight I may find favor."

- Ruth 2:3 So **Ruth** departed and went out into the field and gleaned after the harvesters. And she happened to come to the part of the field belonging to Boaz, who was from the clan of Elimelech.

- Ruth 2:5-6 And Boaz asked the foreman of his harvesters, "Whose **young woman** is this?" The foreman answered, "She is **the Moabitess** who returned with Naomi from the land of Moab.

- Ruth 2:8 Then Boaz said to **Ruth**, "Listen, my daughter. Do not go and glean in another field, and do not go away from this place, but stay here close to my servant girls.

- Ruth 2:15 When **Ruth** got up to glean, Boaz ordered his young men, "Even if she gathers among the sheaves, do not insult her. Rather, pull out for her some stalks from the bundles and leave them for her to gather. Do not rebuke her."

- Ruth 2:17 So **Ruth** gathered grain in the field until evening. And when she beat out what she had gleaned, it was about an ephah of barley. She picked up the grain and went into the town, where her mother-in-law saw what she had gleaned. And she brought out what she had saved from her meal and gave it to Naomi.

- Ruth 2:19 Then her mother-in-law asked her, "Where did you glean today, and where did you work? Blessed be the man who noticed you." So **she** told her mother-in-law where she had worked. "The name of the man I worked with today is Boaz," she said.

- Ruth 2:20 Then Naomi said to her **daughter-in-law**, "May he be blessed by the LORD, who has not withdrawn His kindness from the living or the dead." Naomi continued, "The man is a close relative. He is one of our kinsman-redeemers."

- Ruth 2:21-23 Then **Ruth the Moabitess** said, "He also told me, 'Stay with my young men until they have finished gathering all my harvest.'" And Naomi said to her **daughter-in-law Ruth**, "My daughter, it is good for you to work with his young women, so that nothing will happen to you in another field." So **Ruth** stayed close to the servant girls of Boaz to glean grain until the barley and wheat harvests were finished. And she lived with her mother-in-law.

- Ruth 3:1-2 One day **Ruth's** mother-in-law Naomi said to her, "My daughter, should I not seek a resting place for you, that it may be well with you? Now is not Boaz, with whose servant girls you have been working, a relative of ours? In fact, tonight he is winnowing barley on the threshing floor.

- Ruth 3:5-7 "I will do everything you say," **Ruth** answered. So **she** went down to the threshing floor and did everything her mother-in-law had instructed her to do. After Boaz had finished eating and drinking and was in good spirits, he went to lie down at the end of the heap of grain. Then **Ruth** went in secretly, uncovered his feet, and lay down.

- Ruth 3:8-9 At midnight, Boaz was startled, turned over, and there lying at his feet was a **woman**! "Who are you?" he asked. "I am your servant **Ruth**," she replied. "Spread the corner of your garment over me, for you are a kinsman-redeemer."

- Ruth 3:11 And now do not be afraid, **my daughter**. I will do for you whatever you request, since all my fellow townspeople know that you are a **woman of noble character**.

- Ruth 3:16-18 When **Ruth** returned to her mother-in-law, Naomi asked her, "How did it go, **my daughter**?" Then **Ruth** told her all that Boaz had done for her. And she said, "He gave me these six measures of barley, for he said, 'Do not go back to your mother-in-law empty-handed.' " "Wait, **my daughter**," said Naomi, "until you find out how things go, for he will not rest unless he has resolved the matter today."

- Ruth 4:5 Then Boaz said, "On the day you buy the land from Naomi and also from **Ruth the Moabitess**, you must also acquire the **widow** of the deceased in order to raise up the name of the deceased on his inheritance."

- Ruth 4:9-10 At this, Boaz said to the elders and all the people, "You are witnesses today that I am buying from Naomi all that belonged to Elimelech, Chilion, and Mahlon. Moreover, I have acquired **Ruth the Moabitess**, Mahlon's widow, as my wife, to raise up the name of the deceased through his inheritance, so that his name will not disappear from among his brothers or from the gate of his home. You are witnesses today."

- Ruth 4:11-12 "We are witnesses," said the elders and all the people at the gate. "May the LORD make the **woman** entering your home like Rachel and Leah, who together built up the house of Israel. May you be prosperous in Ephrathah and famous in Bethlehem. And may your house become like the house of Perez, whom Tamar bore to Judah, because of the offspring the LORD will give you by this **young woman**."

- Ruth 4:13 So Boaz took **Ruth**, and she became his wife. And when he had relations with her, the LORD enabled her to conceive, and she gave birth to a son.

- Ruth 4:14-17 Then the women said to Naomi, "Blessed be the LORD, who has not left you this day without a kinsman-redeemer. May his name become famous in Israel. He will renew your life and sustain you in your old age. For your **daughter-in-law**, who loves you and is better to you than seven sons, has given him birth." And Naomi took the child, placed him on her lap, and became a nurse to him. The neighbor women said, "A son has been born to Naomi," and they named him Obed. He became the father of Jesse, the father of David.

- Matthew 1:5-6 Salmon was the father of Boaz by Rahab, Boaz the father of Obed by **Ruth**, Obed the father of Jesse, and Jesse the father of David the king.

Bathsheba

2 SAMUEL 11 – BATHSHEBA'S BATH LEADS DAVID DOWN SIN'S PATH

We have studied Eve who was the first to whom the promise of redemption was given, Sarah who gave birth to the son of the covenant in her old age, Tamar who deceived her father-in-law but bore Judah a son to carry on his name and head the tribe from whom the redeemer would come, Rahab the harlot who hid Joshua's spies and gave birth to Boaz, and Ruth who married the kinsman-redeemer, Boaz, who was a picture of the Redeemer to come and gave birth to King David's grandfather, Obed. Now we will learn about the next Woman of Christmas who was one of the five women mentioned in Matthew's genealogy of Jesus.

2 Samuel 11:1 In the spring, at the time when kings march out to war, David sent out Joab and his servants with the whole army of Israel. They destroyed the Ammonites and besieged Rabbah, but David remained in Jerusalem.

Susie: The time when kings went to battle would have been spring when there was ample food supply along the way, and the weather was better.

Susan: David's first mistake was not being at his post, leading his army as most kings would and as he usually did.

Susie: This point is emphasized perhaps as a criticism of David's lack of leadership. Rabbah was the capital city of the Ammonites to which they had retreated during the previous year's battle. The Ammonites were descended from the incestuous relationship between Lot and his younger daughter and were the enemies of the Israelites along with the tribe descended from Lot's older daughter, the Moabites (Remember: Ruth was a Moabitess). Now Joab and David's army were laying siege to that walled city.

> *Genesis 19:36–38 Thus both of Lot's daughters became pregnant by their father. The older daughter gave birth to a son and named him Moab. He is the father of the Moabites of today. The younger daughter also gave birth to a son, and she named him Ben-ammi. He is the father of the Ammonites of today.*

2 Samuel 11:2 One evening David got up from his bed and strolled around on the roof of the palace. And from the roof he saw a woman bathing—a very beautiful woman.

Susan: If David had been at battle as he should have been, he would not have been home to see the woman. Being in the wrong place at the wrong time set him up for trouble.

Susie: Looking out over the city from the vantage point of the palace roof, his eyes fell on a gorgeous woman bathing at her house below, perhaps in a courtyard. He should have looked away immediately. Instead, he asked the servants who she was.

2 Samuel 11:3 So David sent and inquired about the woman, and he was told, "This is Bathsheba, the daughter of Eliam and the wife of Uriah the Hittite."

Susan: David asked who the woman was, and someone told him she was named Bathsheba which means "daughter of an oath" and was the daughter of Eliam and wife of Uriah. He should have never inquired, but then he should have stopped right there when he heard the names of her father and husband!

Susie: The important thing to know about these two men is that both of them served as part of David's famous Mighty Men.

Susan: David's A-team. They were loyal to him and trustworthy. Uriah was a Hittite but must have converted to Judaism as his is a Hebrew name meaning "the Lord is my light."

Susie: So, David should have stopped right there! But he didn't. He succumbed to the lust of the eyes and the flesh.

> *1 John 2:16 (NIV) For everything in the world—the lust of the flesh, the lust of the eyes, and the pride of life—comes not from the Father but from the world.*

Susan: He should have exercised the same loyalty those two warriors had given him, but He betrayed their trust completely!

2 Samuel 11:4–5 Then David sent messengers to get her, and when she came to him, he slept with her. (Now she had just purified herself from her uncleanness.) Then she returned home. And the woman conceived and sent word to David, saying, "I am pregnant."

Susan: David sent for her, and she came. This was not rape, because "she came in unto him" in the King James Version indicates willing participation in sexual union. Something that had totally flown over my head because of the delicate way most translations put it was that Bathsheba had just finished her cycle and her bath was the ritual purifying cleansing. Therefore, there is no way she could have already been carrying a child by Uriah. The baby conceived was definitely David's.

Susie: 2 Samuel 11:6–10 summary: David sent for Uriah under the guise of asking how the siege was going and encouraged him to take a day or two of rest in his own home. He was hoping he would have relations with Bathsheba so everyone would think the baby was his. However, Uriah would not go to his home.

2 Samuel 11:11 Uriah answered, "The ark and Israel and Judah are dwelling in tents, and my master Joab and his soldiers are camped in the open field. How can I go to my house to eat and drink and sleep with my wife? As surely as you live, and as your soul lives, I will not do such a thing!"

Susan: Uriah's integrity would not allow him to engage in leisure activities while the rest of the army was still in harm's way, and he certainly would not sleep with his wife while others were camping in a field.

Susie: This was the very attitude the king was lacking! Let us reiterate that David should have been with his fighting men.

2 Samuel 11:12–13 "Stay here one more day," David said to Uriah, "and tomorrow I will send you back." So Uriah stayed in Jerusalem that day and the next. Then David invited Uriah to eat and drink with him, and he got Uriah drunk. And in the evening Uriah went out to lie down on his cot with his master's servants, but he did not go home.

Susie: David even resorted to getting Uriah drunk, but Uriah still held on to his conviction that he should not take pleasure in his wife while others were still at the front.

Susan: He would not taste the delights of home while his men and his leaders were still engaged in battle with the Ammonites. In this case, Uriah was the better man than David.

2 Samuel 11:14-15 The next morning David wrote a letter to Joab and sent it with Uriah. In the letter he wrote: "Put Uriah at the front of the fiercest battle; then withdraw from him, so that he may be struck down and killed."

Susie: David sent Uriah back to the battle and to Joab carrying a letter. I'm sure it was sealed, but David was confident Uriah would not look in it even if it were not because Uriah was one of his inner circle—his mighty men who would lay down their lives for him. Uriah's loyalty could never have been questioned. In the letter, David instructed Joab to put Uriah in the hottest area of battle where the enemy's best soldiers fought. Then Joab was to pull the rest of the men back, leaving Uriah to certain death! Talk about cold blooded! David had Uriah carry his own death warrant to Joab!

Susan: Had Uriah returned from battle and found his wife to be pregnant, he would have had every right under the law to have Bathsheba and whoever had impregnated her stoned to death, even king David. David was intent on saving his own skin rather than concerned for Bathsheba's welfare.

Susie: In 2 Samuel 11:16-25, we read that Joab loyally obeyed his king, then sent a messenger to

David. He instructed the messenger to give David details of the battle and the fact that many men close to the wall were lost but to emphasize the point that Uriah the Hittite was killed as well. Joab is covering himself from being blamed for the loss of men too close to the wall by having the messenger add that Uriah was one of the men lost in the battle.

Susan: This seems worse than a scene from the modern movie "The Godfather" as David had said, "Let me know when the deed is done." David just added the sin of pre-meditated murder to the sin of adultery!

Susie: One act of deceit leads to another. Sin is a slippery slope.

Susan: David was burying himself deeper and deeper in iniquity, pre-meditated sin.

2 Samuel 11:26–27 When Uriah's wife heard that her husband was dead, she mourned for him. And when the time of mourning was over, David had her brought to his house, and she became his wife and bore him a son. But the thing that David had done was evil in the sight of the LORD.

Susan: I believe Bathsheba had love for Uriah, but she lusted after the king.

Susie: She mourned Uriah's death. Nothing is said about David mourning his death. David seemed to have no remorse for having Uriah killed.

> **11:26, 27** her mourning was over. The customary period of mourning was probably 7 days (Gen. 50:10; 1 Sam. 31:13). Significantly, the text makes no mention of mourning by David. (42)

Susie: After Bathsheba mourned the required seven days, David took her into his home as his wife. They probably thought they had gotten away with their sin since it was so early in her pregnancy that people might not have suspected that she was pregnant before David married her. However, as Susan's granddad, B.J., used to say, "The Lord knows." God saw what they thought they could hide. The last sentence of this chapter seems to be an understatement. David's behavior was abhorrent to the Lord, but God still loved him, a testimony to the grace of God.

> *1 Kings 15:5 (VOICE) David did what was good in the eyes of the Eternal, for he did not abandon the commands of the Eternal during his lifetime, with the exception of the incident with Uriah the Hittite.*

REVIEW QUESTIONS

1. Where should King David have been on the evening that he saw Bathsheba on the rooftop?

2. What were the names of Bathsheba's father and husband? Who were they to David?

   What did David try to trick Uriah into doing when he had him come home from the frontline of the battle? How did Uriah respond?

3. When Uriah would not sleep with his wife, what plan did David devise? Who did he use as a messenger to carry that plan to Joab?

4. David thought he had covered his and Bathsheba's sin by marrying her as soon as she finished mourning Uriah. Who could they never hide from?

_____
_____
_____
_____

Ponder This...

Have you ever felt that you have blown it so badly that God could never use you again? David broke several of the Ten Commandments in this one incident:

1. He coveted his neighbor's wife.
2. He committed adultery.
3. He lied to Uriah by trying to trick him into sleeping with Bathsheba.
4. He committed pre-meditated murder.

However, the Lord still referred to David as "a man after my own heart," and established David's line as the one from which the Messiah would be born to reign as King forever.

> *Acts 13:22-23 After removing Saul, He raised up David as their king and testified about him: 'I have found David son of Jesse a man after My own heart; he will carry out My will in its entirety.' From the descendants of this man, God has brought to Israel the Savior Jesus, as He promised....*

Bathsheba

2 SAMUEL 12 – DAVID, YOU ARE THE MAN!

2 Samuel 12:1–3 Then the LORD sent Nathan to David, and when he arrived, he said, "There were two men in a certain city, one rich and the other poor. The rich man had a great number of sheep and cattle, but the poor man had nothing except one small ewe lamb that he had bought. He raised it, and it grew up with him and his children. It shared his food and drank from his cup; it slept in his arms and was like a daughter to him.

Susie: Nathan the prophet was sent by God to point out David's sin. He did so by telling the parable above about a poor man with a sweet, little pet female lamb, and a rich man who had plenty of sheep.

Susan: The pet lamb would have never been slaughtered by the family of the poor man because they had grown to love it as a member of their family.

2 Samuel 12:4 Now a traveler came to the rich man, who refrained from taking one of his own sheep or cattle to prepare for the traveler who had come to him. Instead, he took the poor man's lamb and prepared it for his guest."

Susan: Wait a minute! Why would the rich man steal the poor man's lamb when he has plenty of his own to kill and serve to the traveler. That makes no sense except that the rich man is a miser and selfish, only looking out for number one.

Susie: The rich man had no regard for the poor family and abused his power to take what was theirs never giving thought to how it would impact the family.

2 Samuel 12:5–6 David burned with anger against the man and said to Nathan: "As surely as the LORD lives, the man who did this deserves to die! Because he has done this thing and has shown no pity, he must pay for the lamb four times over."

Susie: The law called for restoring a stolen, slaughtered lamb fourfold, but David initially said the heartless man should die. The penalty for both adultery and murder was death under the law. In the story, the lamb represents Bathsheba and the man represents Uriah whom David, the rich man, had murdered.

2 Samuel 12:7a Then Nathan said to David, "You are that man! . . .

Susie: Uh oh! David had pronounced what should have been his punishment—death for the sins of adultery and murder. Ultimately, he did lose fourfold of what he had stolen as four of his sons were killed.

> **12:6** fourfold. Exodus 22:1 demanded a 4-fold restitution for the stealing of sheep. There is an allusion here to the subsequent death of 4 of David's sons: Bathsheba's first son (v. 18), Amnon (13:28, 29), Absalom (16:14, 15), and Adonijah (1 Kin. 2:25). (43)

2 Samuel 12:7b–8 . . . This is what the LORD, the God of Israel, says: 'I anointed you king over Israel, and I delivered you from the hand of Saul. I gave your master's house to you and your master's wives into your arms. I gave you the house of Israel and Judah, and if that was not enough, I would have given you even more.

Susan: Nathan recounted the goodness of God to David, blessing by blessing by blessing. God used Nathan to remind David of all the blessings he seemed to have forgotten, how good God had been to him.

2 Samuel 12:9 Why then have you despised the command of the LORD by doing evil in His sight? You put Uriah the Hittite to the sword and took his wife as your own, for you have slain him with the sword of the Ammonites.

Susan: Basically, Nathan told David he had despised God's word and His precepts even to the point of stealing Uriah's wife and murdering one of his loyal, mighty men.

Susie: God had informed Nathan the prophet of all of David's sinful actions.

2 Samuel 12:10–12 Now, therefore, the sword will never depart from your house, because you have despised Me and have taken the wife of Uriah the Hittite to be your own.' This is what the LORD says: 'I will raise up adversity against you from your own house. Before your very eyes I will take your wives and give them to another, and he will lie with them in broad daylight. You have acted in secret, but I will do this thing in broad daylight before all Israel.'"

Susan: God, through Nathan, predicted that chaos would reign in the midst of David's own household because of his choice to take Bathsheba, to choose his way instead of God's way.

Susie: His own sons would rebel against him. One of them even slept with David's concubines on the roof of the palace for all the people to see! David had sinned in secret, but the results of that sin would be public knowledge.

> **12:11** adversity...from your own house. David had done evil to another man's family (11:27). Therefore, he would receive evil in his own family, such as Amnon's rape of Tamar (13:1–14), Absalom's murder of Amnon (13:28, 29), and Absalom's rebellion against David (15:1–12). **lie with your wives in the sight of this sun.**

This prediction was fulfilled by Absalom's public appropriation of David's royal concubines during his rebellion (16:21, 22). (44)

2 Samuel 2:13–14 Then David said to Nathan, "I have sinned against the LORD." "The LORD has taken away your sin," Nathan replied. "You will not die. Nevertheless, because by this deed you have shown utter contempt for the word of the LORD, the son born to you will surely die."

Susan: David does the first right thing in this entire account of the "Uriah the Hittite Incident." He confesses that he has sinned against his God and Lord.

Susie: David confessed more completely in Psalms 32 and 51. He never attempted to justify his sin. Nathan tells him that God has "taken away" which means forgiven his sin. Despite David's heinous behavior, God graciously redeemed him.

Susan: However, the sin would still have consequences. One immediate consequence would be the death of the baby Bathsheba conceived during their adulterous encounter.

Susie: This was not cruel to the baby who would be with the Lord upon death.

Susan: In God's mercy, he would not live to possibly be taunted and gossiped about because of being the product of adultery.

Susie: Summary of 2 Samuel 2:15–23: The Lord caused the son of Bathsheba and David to become deathly ill. David fasted and prayed, lying on the floor, and his most loyal servants could not coax him to eat. He prayed the Lord in His mercy might decide to spare the child.

Susan: But the newborn died after seven days which as noted before may have actually been a merciful act on God's part by sparing the child the notoriety that would come from his conception if the truth was ever made known. As far as we know this child was never given a name by his parents. I would like to hypothesize that the Lord chose to name him Himself, so that the child's identity would be in God and not associated with the sin of his parents.

Susie: This is Susan's hypothesis, but it sounds logical. God's word does not tell us whether the child was named, and if not, why not. After the child died, David bathed, anointed with fragrant oils, and had a meal. There was no more reason to fast and plead with God. David told his servants that someday he would be reunited with his son. This demonstrates his faith that God had forgiven him, and that the child, being before an age of accountability, would be immediately with the Lord.

2 Samuel 12:24a Then David comforted his wife Bathsheba, and he went to her and lay with her. So she gave birth to a son, and they named him Solomon.

Susie: We are not given the details of Bathsheba's mourning her firstborn baby, just the fact that David comforted her and had relations with her again.

Susan: They conceived again and named the baby boy Solomon which means "Peace." It is interesting that David named the boy "Peace." David was a warrior who desired peace but would not have it even in his own family, but during Solomon's reign, there was peace.

Susie: God loved Solomon and eventually made sure Solomon would be the next king on David's throne.

Susan: (For further research on the children of David, read 1 Chronicles chapter 3).

2 Samuel 2:24b-25 Now the LORD loved the child and sent word through Nathan the prophet to name him Jedidiah because the LORD loved him.

Susan: The Lord through Nathan named the baby Jedidiah which means "Beloved of the Lord."

Susie: God's grace is seen throughout this portion of Israel's history. Solomon was born after David and Bathsheba were husband and wife, but their union still originated from adultery. However, God was gracious and blessed Bathsheba's son, Solomon, by making him the one to inherit the throne and thus be in the lineage of Jesus. The specifics of how the Lord orchestrated the succession to the throne **not** going to David's firstborn of his first wife will be told in the next lesson.

REVIEW QUESTIONS

1. Summarize the story Nathan the prophet told David about a poor man's lamb.

   _____
   _____
   _____
   _____
   _____
   _____
   _____
   _____
   _____

2. How did David react to the story and what judgment did he pronounce against the rich man?

   _____
   _____
   _____
   _____
   _____

3. Why did Nathan say to David, "You are that man?"

4. In what way did David pay four-fold for his sin?

List the consequences the Lord gave David for his sins of adultery and murder.

5. What happened to the baby Bathsheba conceived during their act of adultery?

6. What is the meaning of the name David gave to the second son born to him and Bathsheba? What is the meaning of that name?

7. What name did God give to Solomon, and what does it mean?

Ponder This...

God forgave David for committing both adultery and murder, but there were still consequences related to his sin. Sometimes people think the Lord's forgiveness means they can live as they please and ask forgiveness later. This is a bad plan because even though the Lord in His mercy and grace forgives us our sins, there are still natural consequences that result from our sinful actions. When considering any action, we must weigh the consequences, good or bad. Living according to God's commands results in joy whereas the opposite results in strife. Choose obedience and joy today!

Bathsheba

1 KINGS 1 – BATHSHEBA'S SON TO BE NUMBER ONE

A little background: David had multiple sons by multiple wives and concubines (1 Chronicles 3). Usually, a kingship would pass to the firstborn son. However, Amnon, David's firstborn was killed by his half-brother Absalom after he raped Absalom's full sister, Tamar (2 Samuel 13:32). The second born son, Kileab or Daniel (1 Chronicles 3:1), probably died at a young age since there is no record of his adult life. Absalom, the third born, was killed by David's general Joab when he mounted a rebellion against his aging father (2 Samuel 18:14). That brings us to Adonijah, the fourth son, who naturally considered himself to be next in line to the throne and jumped the gun by setting himself up as king before David drew his last breath.

1 Kings 1:11–12 Then Nathan said to Bathsheba the mother of Solomon, "Have you not heard that Adonijah son of Haggith has become king, and our lord David does not know it? Now please, come and let me advise you. Save your own life and the life of your son Solomon.

Susan: Adonijah was mounting a deceitful coup, an underhanded overthrow, while he knew his father, David, could not put up a physical fight.

Susie: It was typical in those days for a new king to slaughter the family of the old king in order to have no opposition to his claim to the throne, even if those men where his half-brothers.

Susan: Nathan came in to give Bathsheba the news that she and her son Solomon would be on Adonijah's "most wanted" list, his "hit list."

Susie: Nathan, being a prophet, knew it was not the will of God for Adonijah to sit on David's throne.

Susan: Adonijah means "worshipper," but he seemed to be a worshipper of himself rather than the Lord God. He did not seem to live up to the honor and privilege of his name.

1 Kings 1:13 Go at once to King David and say, 'My lord the king, did you not swear to your maidservant, "Surely your son Solomon will reign after me, and he will sit on my throne"? Why then has Adonijah become king?'

Susie: Nathan instructed Bathsheba to remind David that Solomon had been chosen to reign after him and to inform him that Adonijah had already set himself up as king.

Susan: If I were David, that would have made me livid! God chose Solomon just like He chose David.

> *1 Chronicles 28:5 And of all my sons—for the LORD has given me many sons—He has chosen Solomon my son to sit on the throne of the kingdom of the LORD over Israel.*

1 Kings 1:14 Then, while you are still there speaking with the king, I will come in after you and confirm your words."

Susan: Nathan planned to come in a few minutes later to validate what Bathsheba told David.

Susie: Perhaps Nathan thought David would believe it better coming from his wife rather than himself.

1 Kings 1:15–19 So Bathsheba went to see the king in his bedroom. Since the king was very old, Abishag the Shunammite was serving him. And Bathsheba bowed down in homage to the king, who asked, "What is your desire?" "My lord," she replied, "you yourself swore to your maidservant by the LORD your God: 'Surely your son Solomon will reign after me, and he will sit on my throne.' But now, behold, Adonijah has become king, and you, my lord the king, did not know it. And he has sacrificed an abundance of oxen, fattened calves, and sheep, and has invited all the other sons of the king, as well as Abiathar the priest and Joab the commander of the army. But he did not invite your servant Solomon.

Susie: Bathsheba followed Nathan's instructions.

Susan: She said that Adonijah had usurped the throne that King David had promised to Solomon.

Susie: Adonijah had called key people into a presumptuous counsel but had excluded Solomon since he was the rightful heir to the throne.

1 Kings 1:20–21 And as for you, my lord the king, the eyes of all Israel are upon you to tell them who will sit on the throne of my lord the king after him. Otherwise, when my lord the king rests with his fathers, I and my son Solomon will be counted as criminals."

Susan: Bathsheba urged David to officially declare his successor lest she and Solomon be seen as enemies of the kingdom by Adonijah and be executed.

1 Kings 1:22–27 And just then, while Bathsheba was still speaking with the king, Nathan the prophet arrived. So the king was told, "Nathan the prophet is here." And Nathan went in and bowed facedown before the king. "My lord the king," said Nathan, "did you say, 'Adonijah will reign after me, and he will sit on my throne'? For today he has gone down and sacrificed an abundance of oxen, fattened calves, and sheep, and has invited all the sons of the king, the commanders of the army, and Abiathar the priest. And behold, they are eating and drinking before him, saying, 'Long live King Adonijah!' But me your servant he did not invite, nor Zadok the priest, nor Benaiah son of Jehoiada, nor your servant Solomon. Has my lord the king let this happen without informing your servant who should sit on the throne after my lord the king?"

Susie: Nathan told him the same thing Bathsheba had just declared to give validity to her words.

Susan: Adonijah was hosting a coronation party and leaving out the king's chief advisors and the priest because he knew he was in the wrong. Adonijah had purposely left out those whose conscience would not allow them to support his overthrow of David's kingdom, those who knew Solomon was the chosen heir. Adonijah had apparently been plotting this act of treason for some time. He had his eyes on the prize of the throne instead of on the Lord's plan for Israel.

Susie: Nathan asked if it was true that David wanted Adonijah to take over the kingdom. He was asking whether David had authorized this takeover without consulting with him even though he already knew the answer was that he did not.

1 Kings 1:28–30 Then King David said, "Call in Bathsheba for me." So she came into the king's presence and stood before him. And the king swore an oath, saying, "As surely as the LORD lives, who has redeemed my life from all distress, I will carry out this very day exactly what I swore to you by the LORD, the God of Israel: Surely your son Solomon will reign after me, and he will sit on my throne in my place."

Susie: David called Bathsheba back into his room and swore to fulfill his promise to make Solomon the next king that very day.

Susan: He assured her his word was true and certain, and He would make sure her son sat upon the throne of Israel by abdicating in favor of Solomon immediately.

1 Kings 1:31 Bathsheba bowed facedown in homage to the king and said, "May my lord King David live forever!"

Susan: Bathsheba graciously bowed before the king to show gratitude for this proclamation.

1 Kings 1:32–35 Then King David said, "Call in for me Zadok the priest, Nathan the prophet, and Benaiah son of Jehoiada." So they came before the king. "Take my servants with you," said the king. "Set my son Solomon on my own mule and take him down to Gihon. There Zadok the priest and Nathan the prophet are to anoint him king over Israel. You are to blow the ram's horn and declare, 'Long live King Solomon!' Then you shall go up with him, and he is to come and sit on my throne and reign in my place. For I have appointed him ruler over Israel and Judah."

Susan: From his bed, David instructed Nathan and the priests in the ceremonial protocol to follow in order to declare Solomon as the rightful king. Even from his deathbed, David was still "large and in charge" as both Nathan and Bathsheba acknowledged.

1 Kings 1:36–37 "Amen," replied Benaiah son of Jehoiada. "May the LORD, the God of my lord the king, so declare it. Just as the LORD was with my lord the king, so may He be with Solomon and make his throne even greater than that of my lord King David."

Susie: Benaiah affirmed that this was the will of God and pronounced a blessing on Solomon's future reign.

> **1:8** Benaiah the son of Jehoiada. Benaiah was the commander of the Cherethites and Pelethites, mercenary forces who functioned in large measure as David's royal guard (2 Sam. 8:18; 20:7; 23:20; 1 Chr. 18:17). (45)

1 Kings 1:38–40 Then Zadok the priest, Nathan the prophet, and Benaiah son of Jehoiada, along with the Cherethites and Pelethites, went down and set Solomon on King David's mule, and they escorted him to Gihon. Zadok the priest took the horn of oil from the tabernacle and anointed Solomon. Then they blew the ram's horn, and all the people proclaimed, "Long live King Solomon!" All the people followed him, playing flutes and rejoicing with such a great joy that the earth was split by the sound.

Susie: Nathan, Benaiah, Zadok and the others with them did just as David had said. They anointed Solomon as king…

Susan: …and had a boisterous celebration with trumpets so loud that they shook the earth with their blast!

Susie: No one in Jerusalem could miss the commotion to proclaim Solomon king.

1 Kings 1:41–48 Now Adonijah and all his guests were finishing their feast when they heard the sound of the ram's horn. "Why is the city in such a loud uproar?" asked Joab. As he was speaking, suddenly Jonathan the son of Abiathar the priest arrived. "Come in," said Adonijah, "for you are a man of valor. You must be bringing good news." "Not at all," Jonathan replied. "Our lord King David has made Solomon king. And with Solomon, the king has sent Zadok the priest, Nathan the prophet, and Benaiah son of Jehoiada, along with the Cherethites and Pelethites, and they have set him on the king's mule. Zadok the priest and Nathan the prophet have anointed him king at Gihon, and they have gone up from there with rejoicing that rings out in the city. That is the noise you hear. Moreover, Solomon has taken his seat on the royal throne. The king's servants have also gone to congratulate our lord King David, saying, 'May your God make the name of Solomon more famous than your own name, and may He make his throne greater than your throne.' And the king has bowed in worship on his bed, saying, 'Blessed be the LORD, the God of Israel! Today He has provided one to sit on my throne, and my eyes have seen it.'"*

Susan: King David had proved that even a bed can be a place of power when the Lord God is on your side.

Susie: Adonijah thought all the hubbub was about him and a messenger was bringing him good news. WRONG.

Susan: The messenger took the wind right out of his sails as he explained that Solomon had been officially anointed king. David's last official act as king was to honor God's choice of his successor by insuring Solomon's possession of the kingdom.

1 Kings 1:49–50 At this, all the guests of Adonijah arose in terror and scattered. But Adonijah, in fear of Solomon, got up and went to take hold of the horns of the altar.

Susan: The partygoers celebrating Adonijah fled and hid. Adonijah sought refuge by taking hold of the horns of the altar…

Susie: …(symbolic of asking God's protection)…

Susan: …as he feared for his life believing that Solomon would now have him summarily executed.

1 Kings 1:51–53 It was reported to Solomon: "Behold, Adonijah fears King Solomon, and he has taken hold of the horns of the altar, saying, 'Let King Solomon first swear to me not to put his servant to the sword.'" And Solomon replied, "If he is a man of character, not a single hair of his will fall to the ground. But if evil is found in him, he will die." So King Solomon summoned Adonijah down from the altar, and he came and bowed down before King Solomon, who said to him, "Go to your home."

Susan: Solomon mercifully gave Adonijah a break saying he would not slay him as a usurper as long as his conduct thereafter was good. However, in (1 Kings 2:13-25), we see Adonijah trying to lay claim to the throne by marrying one of David's concubines (or so he thought), the girl who was his nurse in his last days. Solomon recognized this as another ploy to take the throne and had him executed.

Susie: We included all that to show that Bathsheba was named in the lineage of Jesus because the Lord chose her son Solomon to be king after David. Note that Matthew refers to her as "Uriah's wife." Although the Lord forgave the sin of adultery between David and Bathsheba, the consequent notoriety never left her.

Matthew 1:5-6 Salmon was the father of Boaz by Rahab, Boaz the father of Obed by Ruth, Obed the father of Jesse, and Jesse the father of David the king. Next: David was the father of Solomon by Uriah's wife, . . .

REVIEW QUESTIONS

1. Name David's son who mounted a coup while David lay on his deathbed. What did his name mean?

2. Who told Bathsheba that one of David's sons was trying to steal the throne David had promised to her son, Solomon?

3. Bathsheba followed his instructions by doing what?

4. After Nathan confirmed what Bathsheba had told him, what did David instruct Zadock, Nathan, and Benaiah to do?

5. What did Adonijah do when the noise of Solomon's coronation parade interrupted his own party?

6. Solomon did not kill Adonijah immediately. However, what did Adonijah eventually do that caused Solomon to have him executed?
   _____
   _____
   _____

7. How did Matthew refer to Bathsheba in his genealogy of Jesus?
   _____
   _____
   _____

Ponder This...

Bathsheba did nothing to earn or deserve such a prominent place in history, being included as an ancestor of the Messiah. In fact, her notoriety comes from committing adultery with King David. However, God in His grace, chose her son Solomon to be David's successor and, therefore, in the lineage of Jesus. We do not know what her personal relationship with the Lord was like. God is sovereign and can choose whomever He desires to choose. If you have trusted Jesus as your Savior, give thanks to God the Father who in His grace chose you to be His son or daughter. David confessed and repented for his sins of adultery and murder, and God graciously forgave him. Ask the Lord to reveal anything in your life that you need to repent (turn away) from? Confess it (agree with God) and ask Him to forgive you and make you clean.

> *1 John 1:9 If we confess our sins, He is faithful and just to forgive us our sins and to cleanse us from all unrighteousness.*

WORSHIP OPPORTUNITY

Even after the sins of adultery and murder, David was forgiven and referred to as a man after God's own heart. Worship along with Stephen Curtis Chapman singing "Man After Your Own Heart": https://www.youtube.com/watch?v=_WlcxDf1lvs

Susan Slade and Susie Hale

Bathsheba

MOTHER OF KING SOLOMON

- 2 Samuel 11:2-3 One evening David got up from his bed and strolled around on the roof of the palace. And from the roof he saw a woman bathing—a very beautiful woman. So David sent and inquired about the woman, and he was told, "This is **Bathsheba**, the daughter of Eliam and the wife of Uriah the Hittite."

- 2 Samuel 11:4-5 Then David sent messengers to **get her**, and when she came to him, he slept with her. (Now she had just purified herself from her uncleanness.) Then she returned home. And **the woman** conceived and sent word to David, saying, "I am pregnant."

- 2 Samuel 11:11 Uriah answered, "The ark and Israel and Judah are dwelling in tents, and my master Joab and his soldiers are camped in the open field. How can I go to my house to eat and drink and sleep with **my wife**? As surely as you live, and as your soul lives, I will not do such a thing!"

- 2 Samuel 11:26-27 When **Uriah's wife** heard that her husband was dead, she mourned for him. And when the time of mourning was over, David had her brought to his house, and **she became his wife** and bore him a son. But the thing that David had done was evil in the sight of the LORD.

- 2 Samuel 12:7-10 Then Nathan said to David, "You are that man! This is what the LORD, the God of Israel, says: 'I anointed you king over Israel, and I delivered you from the hand of Saul. I gave your master's house to you and your master's wives into your arms. I gave you the house of Israel and Judah, and if that was not enough, I would have given you even more. Why then have you despised the command of the LORD by doing evil in His sight? You put Uriah the Hittite to the sword and **took his wife** as your own, for you have slain him with the sword of the Ammonites. Now, therefore, the sword will never depart from your house, because you have despised Me and have taken the **wife of Uriah the Hittite** to be your own.'

- 2 Samuel 12:15 After Nathan had gone home, the LORD struck the child that **Uriah's wife** had borne to David, and he became ill.

- 2 Samuel 2:24-25 Then David comforted his wife **Bathsheba**, and he went to her and lay with her. So she gave birth to a son, and they named him Solomon. Now the LORD loved the child and sent word through Nathan the prophet to name him Jedidiah because the

LORD loved him.

☐ 1 Kings 1:11 Then Nathan said to **Bathsheba the mother of Solomon,** "Have you not heard that Adonijah son of Haggith has become king, and our lord David does not know it?

☐ 1 Kings 1:15-18 So **Bathsheba** went to see the king in his bedroom. Since the king was very old, Abishag the Shunammite was serving him. And **Bathsheba** bowed down in homage to the king, who asked, "What is your desire?" "My lord," **she** replied, "you yourself swore to your maidservant by the LORD your God: 'Surely your son Solomon will reign after me, and he will sit on my throne.' But now, behold, Adonijah has become king, and you, my lord the king, did not know it.

☐ 1 Kings 1:22 And just then, while **Bathsheba** was still speaking with the king, Nathan the prophet arrived.

☐ 1 Kings 1:28-31 Then King David said, "Call in **Bathsheba** for me." So she came into the king's presence and stood before him. And the king swore an oath, saying, "As surely as the LORD lives, who has redeemed my life from all distress, I will carry out this very day exactly what I swore to you by the LORD, the God of Israel: Surely your son Solomon will reign after me, and he will sit on my throne in my place." **Bathsheba** bowed facedown in homage to the king and said, "May my lord King David live forever!"

☐ Matthew 1:6 . . . and Jesse the father of David the king. Next: David was the father of Solomon by **Uriah's wife**

ESTHER 1 - QUEEN VASHTI BANISHED

Susie: You may or may not be familiar with the story of Hadassah, better known as Esther. The entire book of Esther is not that long if you wanted to give it read through. We will cover much of it; but in some places, we will just give the highlights.

Susan: Hadassah was the Jewish name of our Woman of Christmas. It means "myrtle tree."

Susie: Myrtles are extremely resilient which certainly applies to our heroine.

Susan: Esther, her Persian name, means "star," and she certainly is a star in Jewish history! The following commentary from Matthew Henry sets the scene for the book of Esther:

> Several things in this chapter itself are very instructive and of great use; but the design of recording the story of it is to show how way was made for Esther to the crown, in order to her being instrumental to defeat Haman's plot, and this long before the plot was laid, that we may observe and admire the foresight and vast reaches of Providence...This shows how God serves his own purposes even by the sins and follies of men, which he would not permit if he know not how to bring good out of them. (46)

Susie: Another good introduction for this book comes from Max Lucado's book *You Were Made for This Moment: Courage for Today and Hope for Tomorrow*:

> Might you be open to a gold nugget that lies in the substratum of the Esther story? Quiet providence. *Providence* is the two-dollar term theologians use to describe God's continuous control over history. He not only spoke the universe into being, but he governs it by his authority. He is "sustaining all things by his powerful word" (Heb. 1:3). He is regal, royal, and—this is essential—he is *right here*. He is not preoccupied with the plight of Pluto at the expense of your problems and pain. (47)

Susan: God knew He would use the king's folly for the purpose of moving Esther into the right place at the right time for His sovereign providence to prevail.

Esther 1:1-4 This is what happened in the days of Xerxes, who reigned over 127 provinces from India to Cush. In those days King Xerxes sat on his royal throne in the citadel of Susa. In the third year of his reign, Xerxes held a feast for all his officials and servants. The military leaders of Persia and Media were there, along with the nobles and princes of the provinces. And for a full 180 days he displayed the glorious riches of his kingdom and the magnificent splendor of his greatness.

> Kings in general, and Persian kings in particular, enjoy throwing lavish feasts and banquets for honored guests. It is their best opportunity to show off their wealth and power. Occasions like this are useful for impressing and intimidating foreign agents, making treaties and deals, maintaining the illusion of greatness, making the powerless feel especially helpless, and even bullying would-be troublemakers. It is during these occasions that much of the business of ruling is accomplished. But only men are allowed at this party. (48)

Susie: Imagine throwing a party that lasted SIX MONTHS! The king was flagrantly showing off his wealth and power.

Susan: Culturally, the women of Persia were not of import as far as running the kingdom but were more like decorative property. However, it was also against their code of dignity and modesty for women to be present at a party . . .

Susie: . . . with a bunch of drunken men!

Esther 1:5-8 At the end of this time, in the garden court of the royal palace, the king held a seven-day feast for all the people in the citadel of Susa, from the least to the greatest. Hangings of white and blue linen were fastened with cords of fine white and purple material to silver rings on the marble pillars. Gold and silver couches were arranged on a mosaic pavement of porphyry, marble, mother-of-pearl, and other costly stones. Beverages were served in an array of goblets of gold, each with a different design, and the royal wine flowed freely, according to the king's bounty. By order of the king, no limit was placed on the drinking, and every official of his household was to serve each man whatever he desired.

> *Esther 1:8 (VOICE) But no one was required to drink. The king merely ordered his servants to let his guests do as they wished.*

Susie: The six-month party ended with a seven-day royal picnic, allowing every man in the kingdom—even the poor—to celebrate together in the splendor of the royal gardens. The king was extremely generous to allow even commoners to drink fine wine from golden goblets. "No one was required to drink" is an interesting notation because many kings enforced drinking or at least made people feel they must get drunk. He allowed his guests to drink or not drink as they chose.

Susan: However, most likely the majority chose to drink to excess.

Esther 1:9 Queen Vashti also gave a banquet for the women in the royal palace of King Xerxes.

Susie: According to custom, the queen threw her own separate, extravagant celebration for women only.

Susan: This way their modesty was intact as women were usually sequestered and their beauty reserved for their husband's eyes only.

Esther 1:10-12 On the seventh day, when the king's heart was merry with wine, he ordered the seven eunuchs who served him—Mehuman, Biztha, Harbona, Bigtha, Abagtha, Zethar, and Carkas—to bring Queen Vashti before him, wearing her royal crown, to display her beauty to the people and officials. For she was beautiful to behold. Queen Vashti, however, refused to come at the king's command brought by his eunuchs. And the king became furious, and his anger burned within him.

Susan: The king was feeling his wine and wanted to show off his queen in the same manner he had displayed his other possessions.

Susie: This was totally against proprieties of the day especially since commoners were attending as well as those of more noble birth. Women were supposed to stay separate from men.

Susan: Vashti kept her dignity and self-respect even to the point of losing her status in the kingdom by refusing to appear. She always seems to get a bad rap because of her disobedience to her husband. However, she should be applauded for her reverence of her own body . . .

Susie: . . . and commitment to modesty.

Susan: The king is rarely if ever chastised from the pulpit for his disrespect for the treasure that God gave him. Pastors and teachers never seem to call him to account for exploiting his wife. Is this not a double standard? Until I read the following commentary, I had always denigrated Vashti for her disobedience and cheered Esther. I am embarrassed to admit that.

Susie: I guess I had never even given Vashti a second thought. I had never questioned WHY she would disobey. The part about him being drunk and demanding had flown right over my head. Note that Ahasuerus is another name for Xerxes.

Vashti
The Woman Who Exalted Modesty
The book contains a genuine strain of human interest, but it is also heavy with the air of divine providence. Although the story of Vashti only covers a few paragraphs in the book, yet in the setting of oriental grandeur we have the elements of imperishable drama. While the bulk of the book revolves around Esther, from our point of view the shining character in the story is the queenly Vashti, who was driven out because she refused to display her lovely face and figure before the lustful eyes of

a drunken court.

The Demand Had the king been sober he would not have considered such a breach of custom, for he knew that Eastern women lived in seclusion and that such a request as he made in his drunken condition amounted to a gross insult. "For Vashti to appear in the banquet hall, though dressed in her royal robes and crowned, would be almost as degrading as for a modern woman of our modern world to go naked into a man's party." What Ahasuerus demanded was a surrender of womanly honor, and Vashti, who was neither vain nor wanton, was unwilling to comply. Plutarch reminds us that it was the habit of a Persian king to have his queen beside him at a banquet, but when he wished to riot and drink, he sent his queen away and called in the wives of inferior rank—his concubines. Perhaps that is the historic clue to Vashti's indignant refusal for she knew only too well that Persian custom dictated that a queen be secluded during the feasts where rare wines flowed freely. (49)

Allow us to summarize what happened next in Esther 1:13-18. The king responds to Vashti's refusal to come at his bidding by asking his advisors what the laws and customs of the day say that he should do. The king is looking for a way to punish the queen's disobedience within the law, so that he is covered. He is still not thinking about WHY she may have disobeyed. He is not thinking about his wife but only of himself and how it hurt his ego. Perhaps he is afraid he will appear weak if he does not "control" his wife or respond decisively to her actions. An advisor named Memucan puts forth the idea that Vashti must be dealt with harshly. Memucan was being a drama queen. He was jumping to the conclusion that this would set a precedent for women disobeying their husbands. Still, no one had searched out the reason for the disobedience of Vashti. On the one hand, she should not be disobedient; but on the other, her husband should NOT have asked such a vile thing of her. Memucan proposed that a law be made that Queen Vashti could never be in the presence of the king again, that she be banished, and another Queen be chosen to replace her.

Esther 1:19-22 So if it pleases the king, let him issue a royal decree, and let it be recorded in the laws of Persia and Media so that it cannot be repealed, that Vashti shall never again enter the presence of King Xerxes, and that her royal position shall be given to a woman better than she. The edict the king issues will be heard throughout his vast kingdom—and so all women, from the least to the greatest, will honor their husbands." The king and his princes were pleased with this counsel; so the king did as Memucan had advised. He sent letters to all the provinces of the kingdom, to each province in its own script and to each people in their own language, proclaiming that every man should be master of his own household.

Susan: Memucan's counsel would make King Xerxes come out smelling like rose. This seems a drastic course of action to modern readers.

Susie: However, keep in mind, the king could have someone executed just for entering his presence uninvited. Once this idea of banishing Vashti was made into official law, it could never be repealed. She could never be reinstated, even after he sobered up. He would be bound by law to choose a new queen.

Susan: I wonder how many important decisions were made during these drunken parties? How many of these decisions were not the best for the long term of the kingdom?

Susie: The king made this decree in his passion but with the advice of his counselors. We do not know the entire exchange that may have occurred between the king and the queen or the attitude or tone of Vashti. However, God had a plan to save the Israelites, and He used this to advance His choice for queen to the throne.

Susan: The important thing to take away from this is that no matter the follies of men, God's sovereignty prevails.

REVIEW QUESTIONS

1. How long had King Xerxes been feasting with the nobles and princes of the provinces? How long was the picnic he hosted for the common men?

   _____
   _____
   _____
   _____

2. What was the king's command concerning Queen Vashti on the seventh day of the party that included the commoners? Was this according to Persian custom? Do you think the king's judgment was impaired?

   _____
   _____
   _____
   _____
   _____
   _____
   _____

3. Why would Queen Vashti refuse to obey the king's order?

   _____
   _____
   _____
   _____
   _____
   _____

4. What were the consequences of the queen's disobedience?

   _____
   _____
   _____
   _____
   _____
   _____

5. Do you believe God orchestrates circumstances to bring about His will? Can you think of an example of this in your own life?

   _____
   _____
   _____
   _____
   _____
   _____
   _____
   _____

Ponder This...

1. If you are able to take a little time before making an important decision, do! Seek the Lord in His word, seek counsel from godly friends (choose your counselors wisely), and do not do anything drastic in the heat of the moment.

2. Take time to consider the other person's side of the story, and the long term effects of your potential actions.

3. Trust that even when you make wrong choices, by surrendering to the Lord, He can create a message out of your mess.

Esther

ESTHER 2: ESTHER MADE QUEEN

Esther 2:1-4 Some time later, when the anger of King Xerxes had subsided, he remembered Vashti and what she had done, and what had been decreed against her. Then the king's attendants proposed, "Let a search be made for beautiful young virgins for the king, and let the king appoint commissioners in each province of his kingdom to assemble all the beautiful young women into the harem at the citadel of Susa. Let them be placed under the care of Hegai, the king's eunuch in charge of the women, and let them be given beauty treatments. Then let the young woman who pleases the king become queen in place of Vashti." This suggestion pleased the king, and he acted accordingly.

Susan: When the king was sober and no longer hot with anger, he realized he would need to replace Vashti.

Susie: His attendants proposed a kingdom wide search for suitable virgins for him to choose from.

Susan: Next ensued the quintessential beauty pageant to choose a new queen. Details are given about the months of preparation the young women endured. One of these was Esther, a Jewess, who may have been taken against her will.

Esther 2:5-7 Now there was at the citadel of Susa a Jewish man from the tribe of Benjamin named Mordecai son of Jair, the son of Shimei, the son of Kish. He had been carried into exile from Jerusalem by Nebuchadnezzar king of Babylon among those taken captive with Jeconiah king of Judah. And Mordecai had brought up Hadassah (that is, Esther), the daughter of his uncle, because she did not have a father or mother. The young woman was lovely in form and appearance, and when her father and mother had died, Mordecai had taken her in as his own daughter.

Susie: Esther (aka Hadassah) had been orphaned and was being raised by her cousin, Mordecai. Note that Mordecai was a descendant of Kish, the father of King Saul.

> *1 Samuel 9:1-2 Now there was a Benjamite, a powerful man, whose name was Kish son of Abiel, the son of Zeror, the son of Becorath, the son of Aphiah of Benjamin. And he had a son named Saul, choice and handsome, without equal among the Israelites—a head taller than any of the people.*

Susan: Esther was beautiful inside and out. She was pleasant and precious in character as well as pleasing to the eyes. The *NIV Woman's Study Bible* points out that Esther was known by two names:

> **2:7** Hadassah, meaning "myrtle," is Esther's Hebrew name. The myrtle plant was used metaphorically in the OT to symbolize the Lord's forgiveness and acceptance of his people (see Isa 55:13). Her Babylonian name Esther (lit. "star") may be a form of the name Ishtar, the Babylonian goddess of love and war. (50)

Esther 2:8-9 When the king's command and edict had been proclaimed, many young women gathered at the citadel of Susa under the care of Hegai. Esther was also taken to the palace and placed under the care of Hegai, the custodian of the women. And the young woman pleased him and obtained his favor, so he quickly provided her with beauty treatments and the special diet. He assigned to her seven select maidservants from the palace and transferred her with them to the best place in the harem.

Susan: The king's men had rounded up the loveliest young ladies of the kingdom whether they wanted to participate or not. Esther caught the attention of Hegai in a positive way. Therefore, he gave her preferential treatment including her own maidservants and the best place in the harem.

Esther 2:10-11 Esther did not reveal her people or her lineage, because Mordecai had instructed her not to do so. And every day Mordecai would walk back and forth in front of the court of the harem to learn about Esther's welfare and what was happening to her.

Susie: Mordecai had wisely advised Esther not to divulge the fact that she was Jewish.

Susan: This was of great importance later in her story. The Lord was directing Mordecai whether he was aware of it or not. Once again, we see God's hand on their lives even though He is never mentioned by name in the entire book of Esther.

Susie: Mordecai kept an eye on Esther by hanging out near the court of the harem to find out any news about her welfare.

Esther 2:12-14 In the twelve months before her turn to go to King Xerxes, the harem regulation required each young woman to receive beauty treatments with oil of myrrh for six months, and then with perfumes and cosmetics for another six months. When the young woman would go to the king, she was given whatever she requested to take with her from the harem to the king's palace. She would go there in the evening, and in the morning she would return to a second harem under the care of Shaashgaz, the king's eunuch in charge of the concubines. She would not return to the king unless he delighted in her and summoned her by name.

Susie: After an entire YEAR of beauty treatments, each young woman was given one night to impress the king. Unless she was called back by name, she was sent to the harem of concubines, those not chosen for the special status of Queen.

Esther 2:15 Now Esther was the daughter of Abihail, the uncle from whom Mordecai had adopted her as his own daughter. And when it was her turn to go to the king, she did not ask for anything except what Hegai, the king's trusted official in charge of the harem, had advised. And Esther found favor in the eyes of everyone who saw her.

Susan: Esther wisely listened to the eunuch in charge of the harem when it was her turn to spend a night with the king. God had given her favor with everyone she met.

Esther 2:16-18 She was taken to King Xerxes in the royal palace in the tenth month, the month of Tebeth, in the seventh year of his reign. And the king loved Esther more than all the other women, and she found grace and favor in his sight more than all of the other virgins. So he placed the royal crown upon her head and made her queen in place of Vashti. Then the king held a great banquet, Esther's banquet, for all his officials and servants. He proclaimed a tax holiday in the provinces and gave gifts worthy of the king's bounty.

Susie: The king found Esther to be the most beautiful not only outwardly but in character as well.

Susan: Xerxes is credited with choosing Esther to replace Vashti; but in reality, God in His sovereign providence promoted Esther to be queen of Persia. God used Xerxes as His instrument to place Esther in the right position for the right time.

Susie: Then, of course, Xerxes used the occasion as an excuse to host another party. This banquet was held in Esther's honor. He also gave the people a tax holiday which I am sure everyone was pleased with.

Susan: Whether drunk or sober, Xerxes was the quintessential party animal of his day!

Esther 2:19-20 When the virgins were assembled a second time, Mordecai was sitting at the king's gate. Esther still had not revealed her lineage or her people, just as Mordecai had instructed. She obeyed Mordecai's command, as she had done under his care.

Susie: Even after being chosen as queen, Esther obeyed Mordecai's admonition to not reveal her parentage.

Susan: Her heritage must remain a mystery.

Esther 2:21-23 In those days, while Mordecai was sitting at the king's gate, Bigthane and Teresh, two of the king's eunuchs who guarded the entrance, grew angry and conspired to assassinate King Xerxes. When Mordecai learned of the plot, he reported it to Queen Esther, and she informed the king on Mordecai's behalf. After the report had been investigated and verified, both officials were hanged on the gallows. And all this was recorded in the Book of the

Chronicles in the presence of the king.

Susie: Mordecai overheard two of the king's servants plotting to kill King Xerxes. He passed on this knowledge to Esther who warned the king but made sure Mordecai got the credit.

Susan: The plan was thwarted, and Bigthane and Teresh met their demise by being executed.

Susie: King Xerxes had the incident written in the Chronicles of his reign. Remember this. It's important later.

REVIEW QUESTIONS

1. What was the purpose of the big beauty pageant?

2. What was Esther's Jewish name and what is its significance? What was her Babylonian name and its significance?

3. Who was Mordecai to Esther?

4. When Esther was taken into the king's harem, with whom did she find favor?

5. What instruction did Mordecai give Esther when she was taken to the palace?

6. After Esther became the new queen for King Xerxes, what did Mordecai overhear and share with her?

7. What did King Xerxes command to be written in the Chronicles of his reign?

Ponder This...

The following quote from *Lockyear's All the Women of the Bible* sheds some light on why Mordecai instructed Esther *not* to reveal that she was Jewish:

> The marriage of Ahasuerus to Esther, a Jewess, was against Persian law which held that one of the royal line must marry a wife belonging to the seven great Persian families. (51)

Mordecai may or may not have been familiar with the law prohibiting King Ahasuerus (Xerxes) from marrying outside his race, but God gave him the wisdom to have Esther conceal her heritage. Although God is never referred to in the book of Esther, we continue to see His sovereignty and grace at work to redeem His people, the Jews.

ESTHER 3: HAMAN HATCHES EXTERMINATION PLAN

Susie: Let us start chapter 3 with a little background information on the ancestors of the two key characters, Haman and Mordecai. Haman was called an Agagite which meant he was a descendent of Agag the king of the Amalekites. The Amalekites had opposed Israel as they fled Egypt to return to the Holy Land, so God had placed Amalek under a curse saying that nation would be destroyed by a future generation of Israelites (See Exodus 17:14-16). Fast forward to the time of Israel's first king, Saul the Benjaminite. He is the ancestor of Mordecai, Esther's guardian. God commanded Saul to destroy the Amalekites completely, including their cattle. (See 1 Samuel chapter 15) Israel was to take none of the customary spoils of war. However, Saul and his men kept some of the best cattle, supposedly to sacrifice to the Lord, and took King Agag captive rather than killing him. The Lord God made the prophet Samuel aware of Saul's disobedience. Samuel confronted Saul and then took a sword and addressing King Agag, said, "Just as your sword has taken children from women, so will this sword make your mother a childless woman," (1 Samuel 15:33). Then Samuel took a sword and hacked Agag to pieces! No wonder Haman hated the Jews, and Mordecai had no respect for Haman! Again, Max Lucado, the master storyteller, puts this feud into perspective for us:

> The Amalekites picked off the stragglers: the old, the sick, the widowed, the disabled. They had not the courage to attack from the front. Moses saw the evil people for who they were: instruments of Satan. Lucifer hated the Jews. He knew God's plan was to redeem the world through Jesus, and he made it his aim to annihilate the family tree before it could bear fruit. (52)

Esther 3:1-4 After these events, King Xerxes honored Haman son of Hammedatha, the Agagite, elevating him to a position above all the princes who were with him. All the royal servants at the king's gate bowed down and paid homage to Haman, because the king had commanded that this be done for him. But Mordecai would not bow down or pay homage. Then the royal servants at the king's gate asked Mordecai, "Why do you disobey the command of the king?" Day after day they warned him, but he would not comply. So they reported it to Haman to see whether Mordecai's behavior would be tolerated, since he had told them he was a Jew.

Susan: Mordecai's reason for this civil disobedience was his Jewish heritage and faith. He would bow before no one except the one, true God.

Susie: The Persian officials may or may not have understood his logic.

Susan: The officials probably were not aware of the longstanding historical animosity between the Amalekites and the Jews. Mordecai would bow to no man, but especially not to an Amalekite.

Susie: They went to Haman and asked if Mordecai's reason for not kneeling and bowing down was acceptable.

Esther 3:5-6 When Haman saw that Mordecai would not bow down or pay him homage, he was filled with rage. And when he learned the identity of Mordecai's people, he scorned the notion of laying hands on Mordecai alone. Instead, he sought to destroy all of Mordecai's people, the Jews, throughout the kingdom of Xerxes.

Susan: Haman was due respect according to the king's decree but even more so in his own mind.

Susie: Haman suffered from an extremely inflated ego and narcissism.

Susan: It wasn't enough for Haman to exact retribution against his arch enemy, Mordecai. Haman's desire was to desecrate and annihilate every Jew in Persia and its provinces. Haman wanted the world cleansed of the Jewish race in its entirety.

Susie: Does this remind us of someone in the 20th century?

Susan: That would be Hitler.

Susie: If something did not stop Haman, there would have been no Jews, no tribe of Judah, and therefore, no Messiah in the future!

Esther 3:7 In the twelfth year of King Xerxes, in the first month, the month of Nisan, the Pur (that is, the lot) was cast before Haman to determine a day and month. And the lot fell on the twelfth month, the month of Adar.

Susie: Haman and his cohorts cast lots to determine the best day for the destruction of the Jews. This was a common method for determining dates and times. The date selected was nearly a year away.

Susan: Then he approached the king with his determined, diabolical, dastardly plan.

Esther 3:8-9 Then Haman informed King Xerxes, "There is a certain people scattered and dispersed among the peoples of every province of your kingdom. Their laws are different from everyone else's, and they do not obey the king's laws. So it is not in the king's best interest to tolerate them. If it pleases the king, let a decree be issued to destroy them, and I will deposit ten thousand talents of silver into the royal treasury to pay those who carry it out."

> **3:9** 10,000 talents of silver. This enormous bribe is calculated to have been about two-thirds the annual revenue of the Persian Empire under King Darius. (53)

Susie: The casting of lots to determine the best day to carry out his plans was a superstitious method used in Persia. God providentially controlled this process to give the Jews eleven months before the plot was carried out (Proverbs 16:33). Notice that Haman gave no indication of the nationality of the people he was proposing to be wiped out. This may have been on purpose since Jews were among some of the king's own officials. He told the king he would finance the entire campaign.

> *Proverbs 16:33 The lot is cast into the lap, but its every decision is from the LORD.*

Susan: Haman was so determined to persuade King Xerxes that he was willing to possibly impoverish himself and his family to hire mercenaries to execute his plan.

Esther 3:10 So the king removed the signet ring from his finger and gave it to Haman son of Hammedatha, the Agagite, the enemy of the Jews.

3:10 signet ring. Yet another of the king's impulsive responses authorized Haman to issue royal edicts (cf. Gen. 41:42). The repetition of Haman's full name together with the added phrase, "the enemy of the Jews," underlines the terrible predicament of the Jews at this point. (54)

Susan: The king had been kept in the dark as to whom he would be destroying.

Susie: He had no idea that his own beloved Queen Esther was a member of this people group as well as Mordecai who was one of his officials. The king was unwittingly being manipulated by Haman's venomous hatred of the Jews.

Susan: Once again, King Xerxes was acting with undue haste. The king was reacting to information without verification from sources other than Haman. He should have checked Haman's "facts" for himself before issuing any decree. He failed to do what Susie's supervisor told her when she was promoted to a supervisory position, "Always inspect what you expect."

Esther 3:11 "Keep your money," said the king to Haman. "These people are given to you to do with them as you please."

Susie: The king did not accept Haman's money and gave Haman permission to do what he desired with this "people who did not obey his laws."

Susan: I feel that the king was abdicating his responsibility. Xerxes wore the crown but allowed Haman to make too many crucial, pivotal decisions.

Esther 3:12-15 On the thirteenth day of the first month, the royal scribes were summoned and the order was written exactly as Haman commanded the royal satraps, the governors of each province, and the officials of each people, in the script of each province and the language of every people. It was written in the name of King Xerxes and sealed with the royal signet ring. And the letters were sent by couriers to each of the royal provinces with the order to destroy, kill, and annihilate all the Jews—young and old, women and children—and to plunder their possessions on a single day, the thirteenth day of Adar, the twelfth month. A copy of the text of the edict was to be issued in every province and published to all the people, so that they would be ready on that day. The couriers left, spurred on by the king's command, and the edict was issued in the citadel of Susa. Then the king and Haman sat down to drink, but the city of Susa was in confusion.

Susie: The king gave Haman the power to dictate the order himself and use the king's signet ring to seal it.

Susan: Basically, the king gave Haman the power to decree an order in the name of Xerxes, making it an irreversible law.

Susie: It was translated so that everyone in all the provinces of Persia would understand it.

Susan: The decree stated emphatically that they were to "destroy, kill, and annihilate all of the Jews."

Susie: No one could possibly misunderstand the intent of this decree.

Susan: No one was to be spared. They were to kill even women and children. As the Jews were put to death...

Susie: ...whoever killed them gained the reward of taking their possessions...

Susan: ...the wealth they had accumulated even while living as captives. Haman had the king celebrating this edict with, of course, drinking!

Susie: Meanwhile, the people living in Susa—both Jews and Persians—were trying to make heads or tails of such a proclamation.

Susan: This proclamation made no sense to them. They were thrown into a state of confusion.

Susie: However, it was now law, had to be obeyed, and could not be rescinded or overturned.

REVIEW QUESTIONS

1. What did Mordecai refuse to do even though King Xerxes had ordered it? Why did he refuse?

   _____
   _____
   _____
   _____
   _____
   _____

2. Why did Haman want to destroy not only Mordecai but all the Jews?

3. How did Haman determine the date for the annihilation of the Jews? Who really determined it?

4. Was Haman completely honest in how he approached King Xerxes with his plan? Explain.

5. Was King Xerxes wise to listen to Haman? What should he have done before turning over his signet ring to Haman?

6. Where was the proclamation that Haman dictated sent?

7. What were the king and Haman doing while the city was in upheaval over the proclamation? What does this reveal about King Xerxes' character?

Ponder This...

The Jews had faced many enemies and were at this time technically captives even though they had assimilated into the Persian culture. However, this plot aimed to wipe out the entire nation of Israel! At this point in the story, it seems that God is letting them slip through His fingers; but we know that is not true. God's control is seen in His elevating Esther to be queen, controlling the lot cast to determine the proposed day of destruction, and allowing Mordecai to overhear a plan to kill the king. Stay tuned to see exactly why Esther is one of our "Women of Christmas."

Think about times in your own life that God seemed to be ignoring your situation, when you may have felt abandoned by the Father. Were there Scripture verses or Bible stories that encouraged you? What would you say to someone who is feeling like God does not care about their problems?

ESTHER 4: FOR SUCH A TIME AS THIS

Esther 4:1-2 When Mordecai learned of all that had happened, he tore his clothes, put on sackcloth and ashes, and went out into the middle of the city, wailing loudly and bitterly. But he went only as far as the king's gate, because the law prohibited anyone wearing sackcloth from entering that gate.

Susie: Mordecai went into extreme mourning which may also reflect the idea that he knew his refusal to bow to Haman was at the center of this edict. He tore his clothes, put on the clothing of the poor, and put ashes on his body symbolic of death. He wailed in public! Mordecai was faced with the annihilation of ALL his people.

Susan: More than that, he saw himself as the source of the cloud of anguish that had enveloped them.

Susie: He took his mourning to the place where he had sat as one of the king's officials, the king's gate.

Susan: Mordecai may have been hoping that Esther would hear the cries of his heavy and distraught heart.

Susie: However, he could not enter in his mourning attire. There was a law that you could not appear in such a state in the court. No one could show a sad face in front of the king or disrupt the party spirit of the court. Nehemiah encountered this same rule when he approached the king of his day about returning to Jerusalem to rebuild the wall (Nehemiah 2:1-6).

Esther 4:3 In every province to which the king's command and edict came, there was great mourning among the Jews. They fasted, wept, and lamented, and many lay in sackcloth and ashes.

Susie: Mordecai was not the only Jew responding to the news of their coming destruction in this way. The entire populace of Jews "fasted, wept, and screamed out in misery."

> *Esther 4:3 (VOICE) In the meantime, as word of the king's decree began to spread throughout all of the provinces, terrible distress grew among the Jews. They fasted, wept, and screamed out in misery. Like Mordecai, many put on sackcloth and ashes.*

Susan: What Mordecai and many of the Jews did was a demonstration of the intense helplessness that they felt. They feared they had no advocate to turn to. Once something was set down as a law in Persia, it could not be repealed or revoked. A seemingly hopeless situation—the kind of predicament where God loves to show up.

Susie: Many of them, like Mordecai, were assimilated into the Persian community. No wonder Susa was thrown into confusion. Their Persian neighbors may have been quite distressed by this edict as well. They had become friends with Jews and may have not even realized who among them were of this nationality. Now they were being told on a certain day in the future they were to kill these neighbors and their children!

Esther 4:4 So When Esther's maidens and eunuchs came and told her about Mordecai, the queen was overcome with distress. She sent clothes for Mordecai to wear instead of his sackcloth, but he would not accept them.

Susie: Since Mordecai displayed his grief publicly, the maids and the eunuchs in charge of the king's harem reported his distress to Esther.

Susan: Mordecai knew that Esther could not see him because as queen she was protected. But he also knew her maids and the keepers of the harem would report his seemingly bizarre behavior to Esther. At this time, the queen had no knowledge of what had taken place, she was completely in the dark.

Susie: She must not have seen or heard of the edict, or she would have been able to figure out why Mordecai was mortified. Esther sent nicer clothes to Mordecai. Some proposed that she wanted him to be fit to enter the court so she could speak with him in person and hear his explanation.

Esther 4:5 Then Esther summoned Hathach, one of the king's eunuchs appointed to her, and she dispatched him to Mordecai to learn what was troubling him and why.

Susan: Since Esther did not know about Haman's order, she did not understand Mordecai's refusal to accept the appropriate court attire.

Susie: Esther sent a representative to find out the cause of Mordecai's wailing and wearing sackcloth and ashes. She charged him to report everything he found out to her.

Esther 4:6-8 So Hathach went out to Mordecai in the city square in front of the king's gate, and Mordecai told him all that had happened to him, including the exact amount of money that Haman had promised to pay into the royal treasury in order to destroy the Jews. Mordecai also gave Hathach a copy of the written decree issued in Susa for the destruction of the Jews, to show and explain to Esther, urging her to approach the king, implore his favor, and plead before him for her people.

Susie: Mordecai explained the entire situation to Hathach.

Susan: Mordecai provided evidence in the form of a copy of the edict proclaiming that the Jews were to be annihilated on a certain date.

Susie: He asked the eunuch to relay the story to Esther and be sure she understood the order. Many women of that time did not read or read very little. The edict would have been in legalese, terminology she might not have been used to.

Susan: He wanted Esther to understand the full magnitude and weight of this order written by Haman and approved by the king.

Susie: Mordecai had instructed Hathach to persuade Esther to beg the king for the lives of the Jews and her own life as well.

Esther 4:9-11 So Hathach went back and relayed Mordecai's response to Esther. Then Esther spoke to Hathach and instructed him to tell Mordecai, "All the royal officials and the people of the king's provinces know that one law applies to every man or woman who approaches the king in the inner court without being summoned—that he be put to death. Only if the king extends the gold scepter may that person live. But I have not been summoned to appear before the king for the past thirty days."

Susie: Esther must have trusted Hathach implicitly and sent him back to Mordecai with a reply explaining the difficulty of meeting with the king.

Susan: She had not been called into the king's inner room in a month's time.

Susie: The king had commanded that anyone who entered uninvited was to be put to death unless he held out his scepter to them.

Susan: Esther knew that if the king did not hold out the gold scepter to her, she would be instantly executed. Guards were posted to make sure this order was carried out. However, even though Esther had not been called by King Xerxes, she was about to discover that she had been called by the King of kings.

Esther 4:12-14 When Esther's words were relayed to Mordecai, he sent back to her this reply: "Do not imagine that because you are in the king's palace you alone will escape the fate of all the Jews. For if you remain silent at this time, relief and deliverance for the Jews will arise from another place, but you and your father's house will perish. And who knows if perhaps you have come to the kingdom for such a time as this?"

Susan: *The Voice Bible* comments:

Of all the books in the Bible, Esther is unique because God is never once mentioned explicitly. Still, for those who know God and who know history, God is in the story, behind it, above it, beneath it. He is the main actor in history, even if He is not acknowledged. Here, Mordecai shows great wisdom. The Jews, God's chosen people, will be delivered whether Esther involves herself or not. Divine Providence has ways and means that go beyond human understanding. Still Providence has made Esther queen for a purpose, a purpose she cannot easily escape. (55)

Susan: Mordecai reminded Esther that her position as queen would not spare her from the edict because the order was to kill ALL the Jews.

Susie: Mordecai expressed his faith that God would deliver the Jews with or without Esther's help.

Susan: He told her that the Jews would be saved even if she chose not to be the instrument of deliverance.

Susie: He also prophesied that if she refused, she and her family would NOT be delivered but would die. Then he made the most often quoted statement of the book of Esther:

Esther 4:14b (VOICE) "And who knows? Perhaps you have been made queen for such a time as this".

Susan: God's providence had arranged for her to find favor and be queen for God's specific purpose.

Esther 4:15 Then Esther sent this reply to Mordecai: "Go and assemble all the Jews who can be found in Susa, and fast for me. Do not eat or drink for three days, night or day, and I and my maidens will fast as you do. After that, I will go to the king, even though it is against the law. And if I perish, I perish!"

Susie: Esther sent word to Mordecai to organize a fast on her behalf. Most translations of the Bible do not use the words "and pray" or "intercede". However, prayer always accompanied Jewish fasts in the Old Testament. This was to be longer than the usual one day fast which denotes the gravity of the situation. She and her maids would also fast for three days.

Susan: When Esther would go before the king this time, she definitely would not be donning her fashion face but her fasting face.

Susie: After three days of fasting, she would look tired and weak; and Persian kings wanted healthy women. She determined that after this time of fasting and prayer, she would take the risk of entering the king's presence without being summoned.

Susan: She fearlessly resolved within her heart to obey Mordecai even though that meant disobeying the king and the possibility of her own eminent execution if she did not find favor with the king.

Susie: She courageously stated, "And if I die, then I die!"

Susan: She made this declaration despite her human fear because after fasting, God had strengthened Esther to risk her life to save her people.

Esther 4:17 So Mordecai went and did all that Esther had instructed him.

Susie: When Mordecai received this message from Esther, he left the king's gate to gather the people and immediately do as Esther had instructed him. He was a father figure to her, but this demonstrates their mutual respect.

REVIEW QUESTIONS

1. What did Mordecai do when he heard of Haman's edict?

2. Why might Mordecai feel he had brought this woe upon his people?

3. How did Jews in every province respond to this evil edict?

4. Who did Esther send to Mordecai to find out why he was in mourning?

5. What was Mordecai's reply to Esther?

6. What dilemma did Esther have Hathach explain to Mordecai?

7. What often quoted reply did Mordecai send back to Esther?

8. Esther instructed Mordecai to have the Jews fast for her for three days after which she would risk going before the king. She concluded her statement with what brave words?

Ponder This...

Mordecai was confident that God would deliver the Jews from destruction one way or another but believed Esther was the most probable answer to the dilemma. God's sovereignty and grace has been at work in each of the "Women of Christmas" we have studied, and we certainly see Him working in the life of Esther even though He is never mentioned by name, remaining somewhat incognito in this book of the Bible. Esther asked that the Jews and her handmaidens fast for three days. Have you ever fasted and prayed before making an important decision or facing a daunting task? Have you fasted and prayed on behalf of a family member or friend?

Esther

ESTHER 5 - HAMAN'S EGO STROKED BUT THEN HIS ANGER PROVOKED

Esther 5:1-2 On the third day, Esther put on her royal attire and stood in the inner court of the palace across from the king's quarters. The king was sitting on his royal throne in the royal courtroom, facing the entrance. As soon as the king saw Queen Esther standing in the court, she found favor in his sight. The king extended the gold scepter in his hand toward Esther, and she approached and touched the tip of the scepter.

Susie: After fasting for three days, Esther prepared to do as she had promised Mordecai.

Susan: Obedience to Mordecai and, therefore, to God put her in the precarious position of disobedience to the law of the king in that no one was to approach him unless he called for them. But obedience to the King of kings supersedes obedience to the king of Persia or any other country for that matter.

Susie: She dressed in all her queenly finery. I don't know if this was protocol for a visit to the king's room or if she was dressing for confidence or if she felt the king needed a reminder that she wasn't just any member of his harem but was his chosen wife and queen. The king was facing the entry hall and saw Queen Esther standing there waiting.

Susan: She had already advanced to the place of danger, being inside the court even though the king had not summoned her. The king was pleased when he saw her. According to Proverbs 21:1 (ESV), "The king's heart is a stream of water in the hand of the LORD; he turns it wherever he will." Even though God is not mentioned by name in the book of Esther, we can rest assured that God orchestrated Esther's favor with the king. Xerxes extended the golden scepter allowing her to approach the throne unscathed. Esther could breathe again!

Ponder This...

Why do you think the king who had so hastily punished Vashti for disobeying by failing to appear, accepted Esther when she disobeyed the rules and appeared unsummoned? Why is he so eager to please her? Is it simply deep love, or do you think the truth of Proverbs 21:1 had something to do with these events? God was making certain Esther would live to be a "Woman of Christmas."

Esther 5:3 "What is it, Queen Esther?" the king inquired. "What is your request? Even up to half the kingdom, it will be given to you."

Susie: The king was really asking something akin to "What is troubling you?" Surely she looked gaunt after the fast, or maybe he just realized she would not dare to enter his presence uninvited except under extreme circumstances.

Susan: The thought of Jewish annihilation had to be causing her inner torment. Perhaps that showed in her countenance.

Susie: Would the king literally give Esther half of his kingdom? Probably not, but the exaggeration expressed his desire to completely satisfy his chosen queen.

Susan: On the other hand, this king had the bad habit of saying and doing things in haste. Maybe he would have given her up to half the kingdom feeling he had to honor what he promised in front of witnesses.

Esther 5:4 "If it pleases the king," Esther replied, "may the king and Haman come today to the banquet I have prepared for the king."

Susie: Esther does not immediately present the dilemma that she and the rest of the Jews face due to Haman's evil edict.

Susan: Esther did not tip her hand right away. She was also careful to think before she spoke and began her humble, heart-felt proposal with "If it pleases the king."

Susie: Esther makes the seemingly simple request that the king join her for a banquet and bring his second in command, Haman, with him. She states she has prepared the meal to honor the king.

Susan: She knew this would inflate Haman's narcissistic tendencies; and, therefore, she would be elevated in his good graces.

Esther 5:5 "Hurry," commanded the king, "and bring Haman, so we can do as Esther has requested." So the king and Haman went to the banquet that Esther had prepared.

Susie: The king wasted no time but commanded that Haman be found immediately. He made it clear that he was accepting the queen's invitation.

Susan: The king instructed his servants to make whatever Esther desired happen.

Esther 5:6 And as they drank their wine, the king said to Esther, "What is your petition? It will be given to you. What is your request? Even up to half the kingdom, it will be fulfilled."

Susie: Nothing is said of the dinner conversation between the royal couple and Haman during the main part of the banquet. During the final course of a long meal, the wine course, the king gave Esther another open opportunity to present him her wish list.

Susan: The king was anxious to hear her request, but Esther did not jump in quickly with her demands even with the king pressing her for details. She was wisely cautious.

Esther 5:7-8 Esther replied, "This is my petition and my request: If I have found favor in the sight of the king, and if it pleases the king to grant my petition and fulfill my request, may the king and Haman come tomorrow to the banquet I will prepare for them. Then I will answer the king's question."

Susie: Scripture does not tell us why Esther put off her answer by asking the king and Haman to a second banquet the next day, so we are not sure if this was part of her original plan or if she just felt queasy about what she needed to do and used the second banquet to stall.

Susan: Maybe she used the delay of the second banquet to bolster her courage.

Susie: However, the rest of chapter 5 and chapter 6 shed light on the reason for the delay from the perspective of divine providence. Whatever Esther's reason for the 2nd banquet, God had plans for the intervening time.

Esther 5:9-11 That day Haman went out full of joy and glad of heart. At the king's gate, however, he saw Mordecai, who did not rise or tremble in fear at his presence. And Haman was filled with rage toward Mordecai. Nevertheless, Haman restrained himself and went home. And calling for his friends and his wife Zeresh, Haman recounted to them his glorious wealth, his many sons, and all the ways the king had honored and promoted him over the other officials and servants.

Susan: Only the highest of society were invited to dine with the king and queen, so Haman thought he had arrived beyond all others since he was the only official invited. Therefore, he could consider himself an intimate of the king and queen in his inflated mind.

Susie: However, when he saw Mordecai still sitting at the king's gate, his happiness vanished into thin air.

Susan: Mordecai's lack of fear or any kind of response to Haman's presence caused seething anger to billow up out of Haman as out of a volcano.

Susie: Haman squelched this anger for the moment until he was in the privacy of his own home. He and his wife entertained friends for the evening.

Susan: Haman always needed to stroke his ego, so he engaged in this behavior every chance he had.

Susie: That night he strutted his stuff like a peacock. He bragged on his position, his ten sons, his wealth, and his close relationship with the king.

Esther 5:12-13 "What is more," Haman added, "Queen Esther invited no one but me to join the king at the banquet she prepared, and I am invited back tomorrow along with the king. Yet none of this satisfies me as long as I see Mordecai the Jew sitting at the king's gate."

Susan: Haman is a legend in his own mind. He is under the delusion that Queen Esther prefers him over all the other officials of the court.

Susie: How ironic is that? He brags about the invitation to dine with the king and queen not only once, but again the next day. Then he confessed that there was something robbing him of his happiness.

Susan: His hatred for Mordecai outweighed his pleasure and enjoyment of all the good that had happened to him that day.

Susie: The Lord had hidden the fact that Mordecai had raised Esther from Haman, so he made no connection between them. This was because Esther continued to obey her bonus, adopted father by not revealing her nationality or heritage.

Esther 5:14 His wife Zeresh and all his friends told him, "Have them build a gallows fifty cubits high, and ask the king in the morning to have Mordecai hanged on it. Then go to the banquet with the king and enjoy yourself." The advice pleased Haman, and he had the gallows constructed.

> 50 cubits is approximately 75 feet or 22.9 meters high. (56)
>
> **5:14 pole**. Refers to a pike for impaling victims (see note on 2:23). But in the reliefs from ancient Assyria, such pikes are usually not much larger than the people impaled on them. It is possible that Haman's 75-foot-tall "pole" includes the hill or platform on which the pike stands. (57)

Susan: Zeresh, Haman's wife, was the one who strategized the plot to have Mordecai executed by impalement on a pole.

Susie: The proposed height of this pole would have been about the same as an eight-story building, perhaps even constructed on top of a building to allow for this height. Since Jews were taught that being hung on a tree symbolized being under a curse from the Lord, this would be particularly humiliating.

> *Galatians 3:13 Christ redeemed us from the curse of the law by becoming a curse for us. For it is written: "Cursed is everyone who is hung on a tree."*

Susan: This was exactly Haman's desire at all times, to humiliate Jews, especially Mordecai.

Susie: Zeresh then put forth the idea that after the grizzly demise of his enemy, Haman would be able to eat, drink, and be merry with the king and queen!

Susan: This shows that Zeresh knew that her husband, Haman, was hungry to see Mordecai humiliated and put to death and would have no remorse. Therefore, he could eat and party with the king with no thought of what he had just orchestrated.

Susie: Since this fed Haman's hatred, he thought it was an excellent idea. However, chapter six will prove that God was still in control and had other plans for Mordecai.

REVIEW QUESTIONS

1. What happened when Esther stood in the entrance to the kings' court after three days of fasting?

   _____
   _____
   _____
   _____
   _____

2. Who gave Esther favor with the king? Explain your answer.

   _____
   _____
   _____
   _____
   _____
   _____

3. What was King Xerxes willing to give Queen Esther?

   _____
   _____
   _____

4. What was Queen Esther's humble invitation to the King?

5. How did the king respond to Esther's invitation?

6. After dinner, what did Esther ask of the king?

7. Haman's ego was puffed up at the thought of being invited to a second banquet. What quickly deflated it?

8. What did Haman brag about at the dinner party in his home that night?

9. What did Haman's wife, Zeresh, propose that he do about his nemesis, Mordecai?

Ponder This...

1. God had a purpose for Esther to fulfill and gave her favor with the king. If God has called you to a task, He will enable you to accomplish it. Rely on His power and not your own.

2. When delays and even dilemmas arise in your life, trust that our sovereign Lord is still in control and is using circumstances to mold you into the image of Christ for His glory and your good. Read Proverbs 3:5-6, Matthew 6:33, Isaiah 41:10, Romans 8:28-29.

Esther

ESTHER CHAPTER 6:1-11 - MODECAI HONORED, HAMAN HUMILIATED

Esther 6:1-3 That night sleep escaped the king; so he ordered the Book of Records, the Chronicles, to be brought in and read to him. And there it was found recorded that Mordecai had exposed Bigthana and Teresh, two of the eunuchs who guarded the king's entrance, when they had conspired to assassinate King Xerxes. The king inquired, "What honor or dignity has been bestowed on Mordecai for this act?" "Nothing has been done for him," replied the king's attendants.

Susie: What does a king do when he cannot sleep? He has the record of his reign read to him, so he can relive his glory days. Even sleeplessness can be due to the divine work of our Lord. It had been five years since Mordecai reported the plot against the king's life, and he had never received a reward for this good deed. The king's readers chose the portion of the record that reported that his life was saved by Mordecai. I believe God directed them there. Having been made aware of this incident, the king wanted to know if Mordecai received any kind of thank you. The servants reported that he had not.

Susan: Maybe one of the reasons Haman and King Xerxes got along pretty well is because they were both self-absorbed, two peas in a pod. Perhaps they saw their own reflection, a mirror image when they looked at each other.

Esther 6:4-5 "Who is in the court?" the king asked. Now Haman had just entered the outer court of the palace to ask the king to hang Mordecai on the gallows he had prepared for him. So the king's attendants answered him, "Haman is there, standing in the court." "Bring him in," ordered the king.

Susie: The king asked if there was any official in the outer court. Enter Haman at exactly the wrong time! He was there because he was going to talk to the king about the plan to impale Mordecai on a pole. He had no idea what the king had just read!

Susan: Haman had no clue how close he was to putting his big foot in his self-promoting mouth.

Susie: Since the king had called for him, Haman chose to let the king be the first to open the conversation. This was both good and bad for Haman. Good that he didn't immediately share his plot against someone the king wished to reward. But bad, as you will see, because his frustration with the Jew who would not bow down to him was about to be increased.

Susan: In fact, Haman's hatred of Mordecai was about to be tuned up to a fever pitch!

Esther 6:6 Haman entered, and the king asked him, "What should be done for the man whom the king is delighted to honor?" Now Haman thought to himself, "Whom would the king be delighted to honor more than me?"

Susie: The king asked Haman's advice on how to reward someone. In his vanity, Haman assumed he was the one to be rewarded.

Susan: Isn't it ironic that the king poses such an interesting question to Haman, and Haman had *no* thought of anyone else the king would want to honor other than him. Haman was self-absorbed, egomaniacal, and narcissistic!

Esther 6:7-9 And Haman told the king, "For the man whom the king is delighted to honor, have them bring a royal robe that the king himself has worn and a horse on which the king himself has ridden—one with a royal crest placed on its head. Let the robe and the horse be entrusted to one of the king's most noble princes. Let them array the man the king wants to honor and parade him on the horse through the city square, proclaiming before him, 'This is what is done for the man whom the king is delighted to honor!'"

Susie: Any official could have been in that outer court, but God was working toward not only honoring Mordecai and ultimately saving the Jews, but also putting Haman in his place. Since Haman is cocky and sure that he is to be the one honored, he sets forth his own personal wish list.

Susan: His idea is a lavish, extravagant plan to display the man's prominence in the eyes of the king for all the kingdom to see.

Susie: Since I know the rest of the story, I almost feel sorry for him, but not quite. Has the king forgotten he approved an edict to condemn all Jews to death or did he still not realize it was the Jews he condemned…

Susan: …with one stroke of the quill? Perhaps since he allowed Haman to actually compose and seal that edict, he either truly did not know or it had slipped his mind.

Esther 6:10 "Hurry," said the king to Haman, "and do just as you proposed. Take the robe and the horse to Mordecai the Jew, who is sitting at the king's gate. Do not neglect anything that you have suggested."

Susie: Haman now has the "privilege" of being the one to bestow all these honors on Mordecai.

Susan: I imagine Haman going out of the king's presence stomping his feet up and down and saying under his breath, "Why!? It's so unfair!" just like a spoiled teenager.

Susie: It was really a custom at this time in history to put royal crowns on horses, but to me that sounds like something out of a cartoon. However, this would say to all who saw this one-person parade that he was being treated as if he were the king himself, wearing the king's robe, riding his crowned horse, and being led by one of the king's favorite nobles.

Esther 6:11 So Haman took the robe and the horse, arrayed Mordecai, and paraded him through the city square, crying out before him, "This is what is done for the man whom the king is delighted to honor!"

Susie: The Bible does not tell us anything about Mordecai's reaction to this turn of events, but I am sure he could see the irony of being so honored with his enemy having to lead the horse.

Susan: The Bible does not describe the crowd's reaction either, but I would think they would be absolutely dumbfounded, utterly speechless.

Susie: I agree. The seething enmity between these two men was well known. The people would be gob smacked to see Haman honoring Mordecai.

Susan: The people would be gob smacked to see Haman honoring Mordecai. Therefore, we can be certain there were probably two camps—Haman's Persian friends, and Mordecai's Jewish friends as well as Persians who respected Mordecai.

Esther 6:12-13 Then Mordecai returned to the king's gate. But Haman rushed home, with his head covered in grief. Haman told his wife Zeresh and all his friends everything that had happened. His advisers and his wife Zeresh said to him, "Since Mordecai, before whom your downfall has begun, is Jewish, you will not prevail against him—for surely you will fall before him."

> **6:13** you will not overcome him. Haman's wife and advisers give voice to the belief that the Jewish people were indomitable and, perhaps, even to the view that their God was the living God. See the predictions about the fall of Amalek before Israel (Ex. 17:16; Num. 24:20; Deut. 25:17–19; 1 Sam. 15; 2 Sam. 1:8–16; cf. Dan. 6:26, 27; Josh. 2:11; 9:29; Ezek. 38:23). (58)

Susan: Haman reacts like a wounded dog, hiding his face, with his tail between his legs.

Susie: His mortification now seems complete.

Susan: He told his wife and friends, the same ones who had advised him to have Mordecai executed, what he had been required do for Mordecai on behalf of the king.

Susie: They now offer him advice that is polar opposite to their previous plot. Now they want him to treat Mordecai with kid gloves.

Susan: His advisors now tell him the sad reality of his future. The destruction of the Jews is not eminent, but the destruction of Haman is.

Susie: At this time, Zeresh has no idea how her first advice will backfire on her husband and family.

Esther 6:14 While they were still speaking with Haman, the king's eunuchs arrived and rushed him to the banquet that Esther had prepared.

Susan: All these events have transpired between banquet one and banquet two given by Queen Esther.

Susie: Whereas Haman had been looking forward to the second dinner with the royal couple, there was now a damper on his excitement.

Susan: Haman had no idea how bad this nightmare was going to become.

REVIEW QUESTIONS

1. What did King Xerxes find out when he couldn't sleep and had the royal Chronicles read to him?

   _____
   _____
   _____
   _____
   _____
   _____

2. When the king heard what Mordecai had done for him, he wanted to honor him in some way and asked who was available in the court. Who just "happened" to be there? What had he planned to discuss with the king?

   _____
   _____
   _____
   _____
   _____
   _____

3. What did the king ask Haman? What did Haman wrongly assume?

4. What did Haman propose as a way to honor someone?

5. What did Haman now have the "privilege" of doing for Mordecai?

6. What did Haman's wife and advisors predict after he came home and told them what he had just had to do?

Ponder This...

Haman had a bad habit of thinking himself greater than he really was. His assumption that he was the person the king wished to honor was evidence of his ego. The Apostle Paul cautions believers against this behavior:

> *Romans 12:3 (NLT) Because of the privilege and authority God has given me, I give each of you this warning: Don't think you are better than you really are. Be honest in your evaluation of yourselves, measuring yourselves by the faith God has given us.*
>
> *Philippians 2:3-4 Do nothing out of selfish ambition or empty pride, but in humility consider others more important than yourselves. Each of you should look not only to your own interests, but also to the interests of others.*

We would do well to evaluate our own behavior in light of these admonitions written by Paul under the divine guidance of the Holy Spirit.

Esther

Esther 7 - ESTHER SAVES HER NATION FROM ANNIHILATION

Esther 7:1-2 So the king and Haman went to dine with Esther the queen, and as they drank their wine on that second day, the king asked once more, "Queen Esther, what is your petition? It will be given to you. What is your request? Even up to half the kingdom, it will be fulfilled."

Susie: The king and Haman attended a second banquet hosted by Queen Esther. Once again, she waited until the king made his offer to give her anything "Even up to half of the kingdom" during the after-dinner wine. This was the third time King Xerxes had offered to give Esther up to half the kingdom, but material goods were not her desire.

Esther 7:3-4 Queen Esther replied, "If I have found favor in your sight, O king, and if it pleases the king, grant me my life as my petition, and the lives of my people as my request. For my people and I have been sold out to destruction, death, and annihilation. If we had merely been sold as menservants and maidservants, I would have remained silent, because no such distress would justify burdening the king."

> *Esther 7:4 (VOICE) There are some, my king, who wish to rid your kingdom of us. For my people and I have been sold, marked for destruction and massacre. Now if the plan were simply to sell our men and women into slavery, I would have kept my mouth closed because that would not have been important enough to disturb you, my king.*

Susan: Now that she had the king perfectly primed with two elaborate meals and was assured of his amorous attention, she answered his question with her heart's plea to be spared along with her people. She didn't initially slam the king's favorite official but just said "there are some" who wanted to destroy her people.

Susie: In the original Hebrew, Esther quoted the exact murderous words of the edict that the Jews were to be "destroyed, killed, and annihilated".

Susan: Esther was astute in not naming Haman immediately. She even told King Xerxes that if he were just going to sell or trade them to another owner, she would not have bothered him.

Susie: Her humility probably touched him since he had gone so overboard in showing his favor to the point of offering her up to half of his kingdom.

Susan: Her humble approach disarmed King Xerxes.

Esther 7:5 Then King Xerxes spoke up and asked Queen Esther, "Who is this, and where is the one who would devise such a scheme?"

Susie: The king was a little dense, thick-headed. He either had not put two and two together that his beloved queen was a Jewess, or the edict against the Jews had totally flown out of his brain.

Susan: Since Haman actually composed the edict, the king may not have fully realized what he was approving, or what people the edict targeted.

Esther 7:6 Esther replied, "The adversary and enemy is this wicked man—Haman!"
And Haman stood in terror before the king and queen.

Susan: Esther finally was able to express her true feelings about Haman. Surely after observing the animosity between Haman and her surrogate father, Mordecai, for years, Esther abhorred the king's right-hand man.

Susie: Not only was Haman an enemy to the Jews; but as we have seen, his nation—the Amalekites—and the nation of Israel had always been adversarial. I can almost picture Esther pointing her finger at Haman's face!

Esther 7:7 In his fury, the king arose from drinking his wine and went to the palace garden, while Haman stayed behind to beg Queen Esther for his life, for he realized that the king was planning a terrible fate for him.

Susie: Haman was now shaking in his sandals.

Susan: King Xerxes fumed at the idea that he could be used as a puppet by his most trusted official. Incensed, the king stormed out of the room.

Esther 7:8 Just as the king returned from the palace garden to the banquet hall, Haman was falling on the couch where Esther was reclining. The king exclaimed, "Would he actually assault the queen while I am in the palace?" As soon as the words had left the king's mouth, they covered Haman's face.

Susie: Haman had been reduced to groveling before a Jewish woman.

Susan: One of the very people he viewed as despicable!

Susie: While begging for his life, he threw himself onto the queen's couch. Even daring to touch the queen would be considered as violating her.

Susan: He was seeking mercy in place of justice.

Susie: His timing was horribly unfortunate as the king walked in to see him apparently attacking the queen!

Susan: The king was flabbergasted that Haman would take such outlandish liberties! Cue the dramatic music...

Susie: Haman was now completely sure he was condemned to die.

Esther 7:9 Then Harbonah, one of the eunuchs attending the king, said: "There is a gallows fifty cubits high at Haman's house. He had it built for Mordecai, who gave the report that saved the king." "Hang him on it!" declared the king. So they hanged Haman on the gallows he had prepared for Mordecai. Then the fury of the king subsided.

Susie: The eunuchs must not have appreciated Haman.

Susan: Haman was not a kind overseer which may be the quintessential understatement.

Susie: Harbonah was quick to offer the king a way to dispose of the despised Haman. Harbonah made the king aware of Haman's plot to kill Mordecai and display him on a 75-foot skewer. The king ordered that Haman be shish-kebabbed instead.

Susan: In an ironic twist, Haman became the object of ridicule instead of Mordecai. His wife's prediction came true, and biblical prophecy was fulfilled.

> *Deuteronomy 25:17-19 Remember what the Amalekites did to you along your way from Egypt, how they met you on your journey when you were tired and weary, and they attacked all your stragglers; they had no fear of God. When the LORD your God gives you rest from the enemies around you in the land that He is giving you to possess as an inheritance, you are to* **blot out the memory of Amalek from under heaven.** *Do not forget!*

Susan: Zeresh had not only predicted Haman's demise but had unwittingly proposed the method of his execution.

Susie: The king was no longer hot with anger, but this still had not solved the problem of the upcoming annihilation of the Jews and his queen. Remember, a Persian edict or law cannot be reversed EVEN BY THE KING!

REVIEW QUESTIONS

1. What did King Xerxes offer Esther again after the second banquet?

2. What information did Esther finally divulge to the king?

3. What did the King demand to know?

4. What was Queen Esther's reply?

5. What was the king's initial reaction to the revelation that his trusted right-hand man was the evil mastermind who wrote the edict to annihilate the Jews?

6. What did Haman do? When the king came back into the room, what did he think Haman was doing?

___

7. What did Harbonah suggest to the king? What was the king's response?

___

Ponder This...

Haman had immense power and thought he would destroy his enemies, but God's power was greater. God's providence, His complete sovereignty, is seen throughout the book of Esther. We need to remember that we serve the same sovereign Lord who is able to accomplish all He desires in and through our lives. When things don't seem to be going according to our plan, perhaps we need to wait on the Lord and see that He has a better plan.

Esther

ESTHER CHAPTERS 8-10: GOD ORCHESTRATES THE PRESERVATION OF HIS NATION

Esther 8:1 That same day King Xerxes awarded Queen Esther the estate of Haman, the enemy of the Jews. And Mordecai entered the king's presence because Esther had revealed his relation to her. The king removed the signet ring he had recovered from Haman and presented it to Mordecai. And Esther appointed Mordecai over the estate of Haman.

> **8:1** According to Persian custom, the property of a traitor was confiscated by the crown. (59)

Susie: Haman was a traitor in that he had betrayed the king's confidence by being unjust...

Susan: ...and wickedly advising the king to suit his own purposes rather than for the best for the kingdom. Haman was always looking out for number one, himself. Haman was never thinking in the best interests of the king or the nation of Persia but only for what would elevate Haman.

Susie: King Xerxes made a gift of Haman's confiscated property to Queen Esther. After she explained the relationship between her and Mordecai, the king elevated Mordecai to Haman's former position as second in command to the king.

Susan: Esther gave Mordecai complete charge of his enemy's estate and servants. Just as Joseph had providentially been made second to Pharaoh when he had been captive in Egypt...

Susie: ...and subsequently saved the Jews from drought, Esther and Mordecai are now put in a position to save their people from complete destruction.

Susan: Esther and Mordecai together are now in the same position Joseph was in Egypt. Mordecai has been given the authority to act in the king's name. His wisdom in advising Esther behind the scenes and Esther's respecting his instruction had brought about their ability to redeem Israel. Esther loved and trusted her bonus father, Mordecai.

Esther 8:3 And once again, Esther addressed the king. She fell at his feet weeping and begged him to revoke the evil scheme of Haman the Agagite, which he had devised against the Jews. The king extended the gold scepter toward Esther, and she arose and stood before the king.

Susie: Because the edict written by Haman remained in effect, the Jews still faced annihilation.

So, Esther approached the king again to beg for her people.

Esther 8:5 "If it pleases the king," she said, "and if I have found favor in his sight, and the matter seems proper to the king, and I am pleasing in his sight, may an order be written to revoke the letters that the scheming Haman son of Hammedatha, the Agagite, wrote to destroy the Jews in all the king's provinces. For how could I bear to see the disaster that would befall my people? How could I bear to see the destruction of my kindred?"

Susie: Esther asked the king to please do something to undo the insidious plot put in place by Haman.

Susan: She asked him to break his own laws to lift this unrighteous, catastrophic edict. But if he revoked the edict, he would look weak in the eyes of his own people, the Persians, and his enemies. For this reason, he could not do what his heart longed to do.

Esther 8:7-8 So King Xerxes said to Esther the Queen and Mordecai the Jew, "Behold, I have given Haman's estate to Esther, and he was hanged on the gallows because he attacked the Jews. Now you may write in the king's name as you please regarding the Jews, and seal it with the royal signet ring. For a decree that is written in the name of the king and sealed with the royal signet ring cannot be revoked."

Susie: King Xerxes reminded Esther and Mordecai how he had recompensed them by turning over Haman's property to them. Then the king reminded Esther and Mordecai that once something is sealed with the king's signet ring, it cannot be nullified.

Susan: He gave his blessing for them to write a new order that would rectify the situation and seal ***it*** with his ring. He gave them carte blanche to compose a plan that would save his queen and her people.

Susie: The catch is, they could not revoke the original edict. Therefore, they needed wisdom to find a way to counteract the order to destroy all the Jews.

Esther 8:9 At once the royal scribes were summoned, and on the twenty-third day of the third month (the month of Sivana), they recorded all of Mordecai's orders to the Jews and to the satraps, governors, and princes of the 127 provinces from India to Cush—writing to each province in its own script, to every people in their own language, and to the Jews in their own script and language. Mordecai wrote in the name of King Xerxes and sealed it with the royal signet ring. He sent the documents by mounted couriers riding on swift horses bred from the royal mares.

Susan: Mordecai was the author of these new orders. Surely God instilled wisdom in him to circumvent the previous edict. He had the new orders translated into every dialect spoken in the various provinces, . . .

Susie: . . . including Hebrew so the Jews could read it for themselves.

Susan: Mordecai now had the power Haman once enjoyed—writing an edict in the name of the king and sealing it with the signet ring. This new edict was distributed in much the same way as the edict Haman had written.

Susie: The king dispatched these new orders by the fastest means available, couriers riding the best horses sired by his own stud horse and carried by his own mares.

Susan: He wanted to get the message out quickly for the Jews to have adequate time to prepare.

Esther 8:11-14 By these letters the king permitted the Jews in each and every city the right to assemble and defend themselves, to destroy, kill, and annihilate all the forces of any people or province hostile to them, including women and children, and to plunder their possessions. The single day appointed throughout all the provinces of King Xerxes was the thirteenth day of the twelfth month, the month of Adar. A copy of the text of the edict was to be issued in every province and published to all the people, so that the Jews would be ready on that day to avenge themselves on their enemies. The couriers rode out in haste on their royal horses, pressed on by the command of the king. And the edict was also issued in the citadel of Susa.

Susie: The new edict, worded much the same as the original, gave the Jews the right to fight back and even confiscate the spoils of the battle.

Susan: It would now be a fair fight instead of a virtual slaughter of the Jews.

Susie: The Jews were now given time and the king's permission to arm and defend themselves against Haman's intended slaughter of them.

Susan: Xerxes could not think of a plan himself, so the Lord had him give this task to Esther and Mordecai who definitely rose to the occasion.

Susie: As Mordecai told Esther previously, God had sovereignly and graciously elevated her for the purpose of saving her people. God's redemption of Israel is pictured in the story of their deliverance from Haman's plot.

Susan: Historically, God had protected the nation of Israel many times. This particular time is what makes Esther a "Woman of Christmas" because by God's grace she saved her nation from annihilation.

Esther 8:15 Mordecai went out from the presence of the king in royal garments of blue and white, with a large gold crown and a purple robe of fine linen. And the city of Susa shouted and rejoiced. For the Jews it was a time of light and gladness, of joy and honor. In every prov-

ince and every city, wherever the king's edict and decree reached, there was joy and gladness among the Jews, with feasting and celebrating. And many of the people of the land themselves became Jews, because the fear of the Jews had fallen upon them.

Susie: Mordecai went from sackcloth and ashes to regal robes. Remember that when Haman's edict was heralded, it threw the population of Susa into confusion and chaos. The new edict caused them to burst forth with joy. The Jews could now hold their heads up as the people of the queen!

Susan: The people who had been the Jews' enemies or had even been on the fence suddenly wanted to be their bosom buddies. They wanted to be sure they were on the winning team, the right team, which was God's team.

Susie: They claimed to be Jews out of fear now that the Jews had the upper hand.

Ponder This...

Mordecai demonstrated faith when he prophesied that Esther was promoted to queen for this critical time. Look for how God has used seemingly unrelated circumstances to bring you to your current situation in life. Trust Him to direct your path, and do not take another step without seeking His will and way. Express your gratitude to the Lord for all He has done and is doing in your life.

Esther 9:1 On the thirteenth day of the twelfth month, the month of Adar, the king's command and edict were to be executed. On this day the enemies of the Jews had hoped to overpower them, but their plan was overturned and the Jews overpowered those who hated them. In each of the provinces of King Xerxes, the Jews assembled in their cities to attack those who sought to harm them. No man could withstand them, because the fear of them had fallen upon all peoples.

Susan: Whether they realized it or not, the people were not frightened of the Jews but of the God of the Jews. Just as Rahab had heard of how God empowered His people and feared Him, the people of Persia now had dread of facing the Jews.

Susie: God had shown His sovereign power by orchestrating events to turn the tables on the enemies of the Jews. God gave the Jews victory.

Susan: Instead of the Jews being wiped out as Haman had wanted, the enemies of the Jews were slaughtered by the power the Lord granted His people.

Esther 9:3 And all the officials of the provinces, the satraps, the governors, and the king's administrators helped the Jews, because the fear of Mordecai had fallen upon them. For Mordecai exercised great power in the palace, and his fame spread throughout the provinces as he became more and more powerful.

Susie: Another aspect of this fear of the Jews is that there is now a Jew as second in command and another Jew as queen. Whereas Haman the Agagite (Amalekite) had been in control, now Mordecai has been given that position of authority.

Susan: King Xeres finally figured out who the good guys were.

Susie: God gave not only Esther, but now Mordecai, favor in the eyes of the king.

Esther 9:5-10 The Jews put all their enemies to the sword, killing and destroying them, and they did as they pleased to those who hated them. In the citadel of Susa, the Jews killed and destroyed five hundred men, including Parshandatha, Dalphon, Aspatha, Poratha, Adalia, Aridatha, Parashta, Arisai, Aridai, and Vaizatha. They killed these ten sons of Haman son of Hammedatha, the enemy of the Jews, but they did not lay a hand on the plunder.

Susie: In the capital alone, the Jews killed 500 of their enemies plus all ten of Haman's sons.

Susan: They did not plunder the spoils of their victims because it wasn't about that for them. It was about preserving their nation and saving their very lives.

Susie: The king had given them permission to take what they wanted. However, when God originally told King Saul to demolish the Amalekites, He instructed Saul NOT to take any plunder. Saul disobeyed, which led to his downfall. These Jews may have remembered this story found in 1 Samuel 15 and were careful not to make the same mistake.

Susan: They had learned from Saul's disobedience. Their main goal was preservation of the Jewish nation.

Esther 9:11-12 On that day the number of those killed in the citadel of Susa was reported to the king, who said to Queen Esther, "In the citadel of Susa the Jews have killed and destroyed five hundred men, including Haman's ten sons. What have they done in the rest of the royal provinces? Now what is your petition? It will be given to you. And what further do you request? It will be fulfilled."

Susan: King Xerxes loved Esther so much he was willing to grant her heart's desire as far as is humanly possible.

Susie: The king had probably lost many of his own army as well as many citizens of the capital, yet he gave Esther permission to request something else.

Susan: The king was willing to vindicate Esther perhaps because of the integrity she had always displayed.

Susie: As previously noted, the Lord had given her favor in his eyes. The Lord says, "Vengeance is mine…" Deuteronomy 32:35, but He seems to be using Esther as the instrument of carrying out His wrath on the enemies of the Jews . . .

Susan: . . . and, therefore, God's enemies because the Jews were His chosen people.

Esther 9:13 Esther replied, "If it pleases the king, may the Jews in Susa also have tomorrow to carry out today's edict, and may the bodies of Haman's ten sons be hanged on the gallows." So the king commanded that this be done. An edict was issued in Susa, and they hanged the ten sons of Haman. On the fourteenth day of the month of Adar, the Jews in Susa came together again and put to death three hundred men there, but they did not lay a hand on the plunder.

Susan: The queen always prefaces a request with, "If it pleases the king."

Susie: She makes her request humbly.

Susan: Even when the king is willing to receive her demands, she never uses a demanding tone. She still shows respect for the king's authority.

Susie: Esther asked that Haman's ten sons suffer the ignominious fate of their father, being impaled on a spike, and the king granted her request. All together 810 men were killed by the Jews in Susa, but the Jews still took none of their property.

Susan: They purposefully obeyed the Lord's original command to Saul to not take any spoils from the Amalekites. Even though the words "God" or "Lord" are not used in the book of Esther, we see His sovereign and gracious will carried out by His beloved, chosen people as they obeyed His original orders concerning the Amalekites. It seems that God used Mordecai to clean up the mess that his ancestor Saul had created by not annihilating the Amalekites in the first place!

Esther 9:16 The rest of the Jews in the royal provinces also assembled to defend themselves and rid themselves of their enemies. They killed 75,000 who hated them, but they did not lay a hand on the plunder. This was done on the thirteenth day of the month of Adar, and on the fourteenth day they rested, making it a day of feasting and joy. The Jews in Susa, however, had assembled on the thirteenth and the fourteenth days of the month. So they rested on the fifteenth day, making it a day of feasting and joy. This is why the rural Jews, who live in the villages, observe the fourteenth day of the month of Adar as a day of joy and feasting. It is a holiday for sending gifts to one another.

Susie: After annihilating the enemies who had planned to completely destroy them, the Jews had a big celebration which involved sharing portions of their feasts with their neighbors. Even the rural Jews did not take any of the assets of the conquered.

Susan: The remainder of the book of Esther from chapter 9:20 to the end of chapter 10 reads like the "Cliff Notes" version of the entire story.

Susie: Mordecai kept a journal and wrote letters about the events to Jews in all the provinces. Since Haman had originally cast lots—Purim—to determine the best day to slaughter the Jews, Mordecai and Esther established the annual feast of Purim to commemorate the time when God elevated a Jewess to the position of queen of Persia to save her people from annihilation. According to the notes in the John MacArthur Study Bible, Purim is "the first and last biblically revealed, non-Mosaic festival with perpetual significance." In other words, the other feasts still celebrated by the Jews were established by Moses. The celebration of Purim today still involves giving to others as well as feasting.

REVIEW QUESTIONS

1. What did King Xerxes give Esther after Haman's execution? What did he give to Mordecai?

2. How is Esther's story similar to that of Joseph who was sold by his own brothers?

3. Even with Haman dead, what did Esther still need to beg of the king?

4. What power did the king give Esther and Mordecai in an effort to save the Jews and especially his beloved queen?

5. How did Mordecai send out the new orders?

6. What were the Jews not permitted to do according to what Samuel had told Saul? What happened on the day the Jews were supposed to be annihilated?

7. Whose fame "spread throughout the provinces as he became more and more powerful?"

8. What was the fate Esther requested for Haman's ten sons?

9. What annual Jewish festival commemorates the time when Esther saved her nation from annihilation?

_____
_____
_____
_____

Ponder This...

1. God is always at work protecting His people. Even though he disciplined them through allowing them to be taken captive, He still preserved them. He is also able to preserve you through trials.

2. God is sovereign and cannot be thwarted. He used Esther to save His covenant people thus preserving the nation through whom Jesus, the Messiah, would be born. Therefore, we include Esther as a "Woman of Christmas."

3. O. S. Hawkins in his book *The Bible Code: Finding Jesus in Every Book in the Bible* points out that Jesus can be seen in the character of Mordecai:

   > Through this narrative, time and again, we find Mordecai, behind the scenes, orchestrating deliverance for Esther and, ultimately, all the Jews. With his humble spirit, Mordecai presents to us a beautiful picture of Christ. And, similar to Jesus, it was Mordecai's own initiatives that saved and restored his people in days of darkness and distress. Mordecai's adoption of Esther is a reminder to us of our adoption into the family of God—a gift given to us through no merit or effort of our own. (60)

WORSHIP OPPORTUNITY

Listen to Wayne Watson singing "For Such a Time as This": https://www.youtube.com/watch?v=YmYOQ8h4wsM

SHE SAVED HER NATION FROM ANNIHILATION

- Esther 2:7 And Mordecai had brought up Hadassah (that is, **Esther**), the daughter of his uncle, because she did not have a father or mother. The **young woman** was lovely in form and appearance, and when her father and mother had died, Mordecai had taken her in as his own daughter.

- Esther 2:8-9 When the king's command and edict had been proclaimed, many young women gathered at the citadel of Susa under the care of Hegai. **Esther** was also taken to the palace and placed under the care of Hegai, the custodian of the women. And the **young woman** pleased him and obtained his favor, so he quickly provided her with beauty treatments and the special diet. He assigned to her seven select maidservants from the palace and transferred her with them to the best place in the harem.

- Esther 2:9-11 **Esther** did not reveal her people or her lineage, because Mordecai had instructed her not to do so. And every day Mordecai would walk back and forth in front of the court of the harem to learn about **Esther's** welfare and what was happening to her.

- Esther 2:15 Now **Esther** was the daughter of Abihail, the uncle from whom Mordecai had adopted her as his own daughter. And when it was her turn to go to the king, she did not ask for anything except what Hegai, the king's trusted official in charge of the harem, had advised. And **Esther** found favor in the eyes of everyone who saw her.

- Esther 2:17 And the king loved **Esther** more than all the other women, and she found grace and favor in his sight more than all of the other virgins. So he placed the royal crown upon her head and made her **queen** in place of Vashti.

- Esther 2:18 Then the king held a great banquet, **Esther's** banquet, for all his officials and servants. He proclaimed a tax holiday in the provinces and gave gifts worthy of the king's bounty.

- Esther 2:20 **Esther** still had not revealed her lineage or her people, just as Mordecai had instructed. She obeyed Mordecai's command, as she had done under his care.

- Esther 2:21-22 In those days, while Mordecai was sitting at the king's gate, Bigthane and Teresh, two of the king's eunuchs who guarded the entrance, grew angry and conspired to assassinate King Xerxes. When Mordecai learned of the plot, he reported it to **Queen Esther**, and she informed the king on Mordecai's behalf.

- Esther 4:4 When **Esther's** maidens and eunuchs came and told her about Mordecai, the queen was overcome with distress. She sent clothes for Mordecai to wear instead of his sackcloth, but he would not accept them.

- Esther 4:5 Then **Esther** summoned Hathach, one of the king's eunuchs appointed to her, and she dispatched him to Mordecai to learn what was troubling him and why.

- Esther 4:8-9 Mordecai also gave Hathach a copy of the written decree issued in Susa for the destruction of the Jews, to show and explain to **Esther**, urging her to approach the king, implore his favor, and plead before him for her people. So Hathach went back and relayed Mordecai's response to **Esther**.

- Esther 4:10-11 Then **Esther** spoke to Hathach and instructed him to tell Mordecai, "All the royal officials and the people of the king's provinces know that one law applies to every man or woman who approaches the king in the inner court without being summoned—that he be put to death. Only if the king extends the gold scepter may that person live. But **I** have not been summoned to appear before the king for the past thirty days."

- Esther 4:12-14 When **Esther's** words were relayed to Mordecai, he sent back to her this reply: "Do not imagine that because you are in the king's palace you alone will escape the fate of all the Jews. For if you remain silent at this time, relief and deliverance for the Jews will arise from another place, but you and your father's house will perish. **And who knows if perhaps you have come to the kingdom for such a time as this?"**

- Esther 4:15-16 Then **Esther** sent this reply to Mordecai: "Go and assemble all the Jews who can be found in Susa, and fast for me. Do not eat or drink for three days, night or day, and I and my maidens will fast as you do. After that, I will go to the king, even though it is against the law. **And if I perish, I perish!"**

- Esther 4:17 So Mordecai went and did all that **Esther** had instructed him.

- Esther 5:1 On the third day, **Esther** put on her royal attire and stood in the inner court of the palace across from the king's quarters. The king was sitting on his royal throne in the royal courtroom, facing the entrance.

- Esther 5:2-3 As soon as the king saw **Queen Esther** standing in the court, she found favor in his sight. The king extended the gold scepter in his hand toward Esther, and she approached and touched the tip of the scepter. "What is it, **Queen Esther**?" the king inquired. "What is your request? Even up to half the kingdom, it will be given to you."

- Esther 5:4 "If it pleases the king," **Esther** replied, "may the king and Haman come today to the banquet I have prepared for the king."

- Esther 5:5-6 "Hurry," commanded the king, "and bring Haman, so we can do as **Esther** has requested." So the king and Haman went to the banquet that **Esther** had prepared. And as they drank their wine, the king said to **Esther**, "What is your petition? It will be given to you. What is your request? Even up to half the kingdom, it will be fulfilled."

- Esther 5:7-8 **Esther** replied, "This is my petition and my request: If I have found favor in the sight of the king, and if it pleases the king to grant my petition and fulfill my request, may the king and Haman come tomorrow to the banquet I will prepare for them. Then I will answer the king's question."

- Esther 7:1-2 1So the king and Haman went to dine with **Esther** the queen, and as they drank their wine on that second day, the king asked once more, "Queen **Esther,** what is your petition? It will be given to you. What is your request? Even up to half the kingdom, it will be fulfilled."

- Esther 7:3-4 **Queen Esther** replied, "If I have found favor in your sight, O king, and if it pleases the king, grant me my life as my petition, and the lives of my people as my request. For my people and I have been sold out to destruction, death, and annihilation. If we had merely been sold as menservants and maidservants, I would have remained silent, because no such distress would justify burdening the king."

- Esther 7:5-6 Then King Xerxes spoke up and asked **Queen Esther**, "Who is this, and where is the one who would devise such a scheme?" **Esther** replied, "The adversary and enemy is this wicked man—Haman!" And Haman stood in terror before the king and queen.

- Esther 7:7 In his fury, the king arose from drinking his wine and went to the palace garden, while Haman stayed behind to beg **Queen Esther** for his life, for he realized that the king was planning a terrible fate for him.

- Esther 7:8 Just as the king returned from the palace garden to the banquet hall, Haman was falling on the couch where **Esther** was reclining. The king exclaimed, "Would he actually assault the **queen** while I am in the palace?" As soon as the words had left the king's mouth, they covered Haman's face.

- Esther 8:1-2 That same day King Xerxes awarded **Queen Esther** the estate of Haman, the enemy of the Jews. And Mordecai entered the king's presence because **Esther** had revealed his relation to her. The king removed the signet ring he had recovered from Haman and presented it to Mordecai. And **Esther** appointed Mordecai over the estate of Haman.

- Esther 8:3-4 And once again, **Esther** addressed the king. She fell at his feet weeping and begged him to revoke the evil scheme of Haman the Agagite, which he had devised against the Jews. The king extended the gold scepter toward **Esther**, and she arose and stood before the king.

- Esther 8:4-5 "If it pleases the king," **she** said, "and if I have found favor in his sight, and the matter seems proper to the king, and I am pleasing in his sight, **may an order be written to revoke the letters that the scheming Haman son of Hammedatha, the Agagite, wrote to destroy the Jews in all the king's provinces.** For how could I bear to see the disaster that would befall my people? How could I bear to see the destruction of my kindred?"

- Esther 8:7-8 So King Xerxes said to **Esther the Queen** and Mordecai the Jew, "Behold, I have given Haman's estate to **Esther,** and he was hanged on the gallows because he attacked the Jews. Now you may write in the king's name as you please regarding the Jews, and seal it with the royal signet ring. For a decree that is written in the name of the king and sealed with the royal signet ring cannot be revoked."

- Esther 9:11-13 On that day the number of those killed in the citadel of Susa was reported to the king, who said to **Queen Esther,** "In the citadel of Susa the Jews have killed and destroyed five hundred men, including Haman's ten sons. What have they done in the rest of the royal provinces? Now what is your petition? It will be given to you. And what further do you request? It will be fulfilled." **Esther** replied, "If it pleases the king, may the Jews in Susa also have tomorrow to carry out today's edict, and may the bodies of Haman's ten sons be hanged on the gallows."

- Esther 9:29-32 So **Queen Esther** daughter of Abihail, along with Mordecai the Jew, wrote with full authority to confirm this second letter concerning Purim. And Mordecai sent letters with words of peace and truth to all the Jews in the 127 provinces of the kingdom of Xerxes, in order to confirm these days of Purim at their appointed time, just as Mordecai the Jew and **Queen Esther** had established them and had committed themselves and their descendants to the times of fasting and lamentation. So **Esther's** decree confirmed these regulations about Purim, which were written into the record.

Elizabeth

Luke 1:5-17: AMAZING GRACE ANNOUNCEMENT

Susie: The Lord sent an angel to make three very important announcements concerning two of our Women of Christmas. Zechariah and his barren wife, Elizabeth, would conceive the forerunner of the Messiah, John the Baptist. Gabriel informed first Mary, then Joseph about their roles in the birth of the Messiah. These ordinary people were an essential, integral part of God's extraordinary plan of redemption for a lost and fallen world.

Luke 1:5-6 In the time of Herod king of Judea there was a priest named Zechariah, who belonged to the priestly division of Abijah, and whose wife Elizabeth was a daughter of Aaron. Both of them were righteous in the sight of God, walking blamelessly in all the commandments and decrees of the Lord.

Susan: Zechariah and Elizabeth were both upright people of the utmost integrity. They were both descended from the priestly line of Aaron. Zechariah means "Jehovah has remembered."

Susie: We are about to read exactly how God remembered this couple in their old age.

Susan: Elizabeth means "Consecrated to God" and "My God is Bountiful." Both of these are significant since Elizabeth was barren which was thought in those days to mean a woman was cursed by God.

Susie: But all that was about to be changed.

Luke 1:7 But they had no children, because Elizabeth was barren, and they were both well along in years.

Susan: Not only was Elizabeth barren, but like Sarah, she was way past the age of being able to conceive a child. Her husband, like Abraham, was well up in years.

Susie: However, remember the meaning of Elizabeth's name, "My God is Bountiful."

Luke 1:8-9 One day while Zechariah's division was on duty and he was serving as priest before God, he was chosen by lot, according to the custom of the priesthood, to enter the temple of the Lord and burn incense.

Luke 1:8-9 (VOICE) One day Zechariah was chosen to perform his priestly duties in God's presence, according to the temple's normal schedule and routine. He had been selected from all the priests by the customary procedure of casting lots for a once-in-a-lifetime opportunity to enter the sacred precincts of the temple. There he burned sweet incense . . .

1:8-9 Remember: "The lot is cast into the lap, but its every decision is from the Lord" (Prov 16:33). God is sovereign, working through even seemingly random processes (like the casting of the lot) to accomplish his will. There is no such thing as luck. (61)

1:9 chosen by lot. Because there were so many priests (see note on v. 8), special duties had to be assigned by lot (see note on Ac 1:26). Jewish people believed that God supervised the result of the lot (cf. 1Ch 24:31; 25:8; Ne 10:34). This occasion was likely Zechariah's only opportunity to perform this service during his lifetime. (62)

1:8–17 The priests on duty drew lots to see which ministries they would perform, and Zechariah was chosen to offer incense in the Most Holy Place. This was a high honor that was permitted to a priest but once in a lifetime. The incense was offered daily before the morning sacrifice and after the evening sacrifice, about three o'clock in the afternoon. It was probably the evening offering that was assigned to Zechariah. God often speaks to His people and calls them while they are busy doing their daily tasks. Both Moses and David were caring for sheep, and Gideon was threshing wheat. Peter and his partners were mending nets when Jesus called them. It is difficult to steer a car when the engine is not running. When we get busy, God starts to direct us. (63)

Susie: Zechariah was a priest serving in the temple, taking his turn (the only one in his life) to enter the Holy Place. This is not the "Holy of Holies" where the Ark of the Covenant resided. Only the high priest could enter that area and only once per year.

Susan: His sacred duty was to burn incense to the Lord. Zechariah was not actively seeking anything for himself but was faithfully performing his duty as a priest.

Luke 1:10-12 And at the hour of the incense offering, the whole congregation was praying outside. Just then an angel of the Lord appeared to Zechariah, standing at the right side of the altar of incense. When Zechariah saw him, he was startled and gripped with fear.

Susie: Remember, Zechariah' wife, Elizabeth, was past the age of childbearing; and they had no children. All the people were praying outside while Zechariah prayed inside the Holy Place while burning incense. He was praying for the nation as was his duty, but over the years, we are sure he had prayed for a son.

Susan: Zechariah had the natural reaction to the supernatural appearance of an angel: he was terrified.

Luke 1:13-17 But the angel said to him, "Do not be afraid, Zechariah, because your prayer has been heard. Your wife Elizabeth will bear you a son, and you are to give him the name John. He will be a joy and delight to you, and many will rejoice at his birth, for he will be great in the sight of the Lord. He shall never take wine or strong drink, and he will be filled with the Holy Spirit even from his mother's womb. Many of the sons of Israel he will turn back to the Lord their God. And he will go on before the Lord in the spirit and power of Elijah, to turn the hearts of the fathers to their children and the disobedient to the wisdom of the righteous—to make ready a people prepared for the Lord."

Susan: The angel comforted Zechariah with the words, "Do not be afraid."

Susie: Although the announcement was made to Zechariah, it was God's plan for his wife, Elizabeth, that the angel revealed. God's messenger shocked and surprised him by appearing in the Holy place and speaking to him.

Susan: The angel declared to him that Elizabeth would conceive and have a son who they were to name John which means "God is gracious and merciful." God was giving Elizabeth and Zechariah the gift of a son. Not only a son, but an extremely special son!

Susie: This son came to be known as John the Baptist, who would be the one who announced the beginning of Jesus's ministry. It is significant that Gabriel stated that John would be "filled with the Holy Spirit" even before he was born!

Susan: John was going to prepare the way for the Messiah "in the spirit and power of Elijah, to turn the hearts of the fathers to their children and the disobedient to the wisdom of the righteous—to make ready a people prepared for the Lord." His preaching would soften the hearts of the people and ultimately point them to Jesus as the long-awaited Messiah.

Susie: Later, Jesus would confirm the angel's prophecy had been fulfilled in John the Baptist.

> *Matthew 11:13-14 For all the Prophets and the Law prophesied until John. And if you are willing to accept it, he is the Elijah who was to come.*

LUKE 1:18 "How can I be sure of this?" Zechariah asked the angel. "I am an old man, and my wife is well along in years."

Susan: Zechariah reminds us of what Abraham went through.

Susie: Although he did not laugh as Abraham did, he questioned the validity and certainty of the angel's prophecy. He pointed out the obvious, that he and Elizabeth were way too old to have children.

Luke 1:19 "I am Gabriel," replied the angel. "I stand in the presence of God, and I have been sent to speak to you and to bring you this good news. And now you will be silent and unable to speak until the day this comes to pass, because you did not believe my words, which will be fulfilled at their proper time."

Susan: Gabriel chastised him and basically said, "You can be quiet now," because Zechariah did not believe the word of the Lord that he had been sent to declare to him. Gabriel gave Zechariah a nine-month time out!

Susie: I wonder if this was the root of our southern expression, "Well, shut my mouth!"

Luke 1:21 Meanwhile, the people were waiting for Zechariah and wondering why he took so long in the temple.

Susie: The people were getting a bit concerned since Zechariah was in the temple much longer than the usual time required to offer the sacrifice of incense.

Luke 1:22 When he came out and was unable to speak to them, they realized he had seen a vision in the temple. He kept making signs to them but remained speechless.

Susie: Zechariah, using gestures, was able to get across to the people that he had seen a vision while serving in the temple. It does not appear that he was able to communicate the exact nature of the vision. Or perhaps he felt that he was supposed to keep it a secret since he was unable to speak by the power of the Lord. Perhaps he thought Elizabeth should be the first to know.

Luke 1:23-24 And when the days of his service were complete, he returned home. After these days, his wife Elizabeth became pregnant and for five months remained in seclusion. She declared, "The Lord has done this for me. In these days He has shown me favor and taken away my disgrace among the people."

Susie: After his required time serving as a priest, Zechariah went home to his wife, and it seems she conceived immediately.

Susan: Elizabeth realized that by enabling her to conceive, the Lord was removing her shame of being childless. She remained in seclusion for five months, perhaps in a period of reverent gratitude for how the Lord had smiled upon her.

    1:24 hid herself. Probably an act of devotion out of deep gratitude to the Lord. (64)

    1:24, 25 When Elizabeth became pregnant she went into seclusion in her home for five months, rejoicing within herself that the Lord had seen fit to free her from the reproach of being childless. (65)

REVIEW QUESTIONS

1. What did Elizabeth have in common with Sarah?

2. What are the meanings of the names Zechariah and Elizabeth?

3. Zechariah was chosen by lot for a once-in-a-lifetime duty. What was it?

4. Who or what startled Zechariah?

5. What amazing news did Zechariah receive while serving in the Temple?

6. What would set Zechariah's son apart even before he was born?

7. John would serve the Lord "in the spirit and power of" whom?

8. Why did the angel tell Zechariah he would be unable to talk until the prophecy he gave him came to pass?

9. When Zechariah returned home to Elizabeth, what happened?

Ponder This...

Elizabeth did not yet realize that she would be a significant person in the life of our Lord on earth. Zechariah had been told John would be the forerunner of the Messiah and filled with the Spirit even from conception. How this would manifest itself is yet to be told. Meanwhile Elizabeth worshiped her gracious God. As we have said before, all children are a gift. Imagine the immense gratitude of this mother-to-be who had given up imagining herself as a mom. The idea of giving birth was a forgotten dream. If you have children, praise God, thanking the Lord for entrusting them to you!

Psalm 127:3 Children are indeed a heritage from the LORD, and the fruit of the womb is His reward.

Psalm 113:9 He settles the barren woman in her home as a joyful mother to her children. Hallelujah!

God certainly has the power to answer the prayer of a childless woman. However, His answer may come in unexpected ways. Susie had always wanted children but was divorced, forty years old, and not even dating. The Lord chose to fulfill her desire by having her serve as a nanny to TEENAGERS! Those teenagers eventually thought of her as their mom, and she claims them as her children. God is faithful! Susan found the fulfillment of her mothering nature in being godmother to the children of friends and family. Don't put God in a box!

Mary

LUKE 1:26-38 - BEHOLD THE SERVANT OF THE LORD

Luke 1:26 In the sixth month, God sent the angel Gabriel to a town in Galilee called Nazareth, to a virgin pledged in marriage to a man named Joseph, who was of the house of David. And the virgin's name was Mary.

Susie: Six months after the angel gave Zechariah the news about Elizabeth's pregnancy . . .

Susan: . . . God sent the angel Gabriel on another mission, a second divine assignment.

Susie: Gabriel was dispatched to the small town of Nazareth to make an announcement to a virgin girl named Mary. She was engaged to Joseph who was in the lineage of King David, but they had not yet married.

Susan: They were betrothed, which was legally binding; and any infidelity would be considered adultery against the future spouse.

Luke 1:28 The angel appeared to her and said, "Greetings^{G5463}, you who are highly favored! The Lord is with you."

> G5463 chaírō, khah'-ee-ro; a primary verb; to be "cheer"ful, i.e. calmly happy or well-off; impersonally, especially as salutation (on meeting or parting), be well:— farewell, be glad, God speed, greeting, hail, joy(- fully), rejoice. (66)

Susan: Gabriel greeted Mary with a word that can mean "Rejoice" and told her she was to be unique among all women, specially chosen by God.

Susie: He explained that God was present in her life. Mary was favored in the sense that God extended grace to her for the assignment of bringing forth the Redeemer of the whole world.

Luke 1:29 Mary was greatly troubled at his words and wondered what kind of greeting this might be.

Susie: Mary was a simple peasant girl.

Susan: She was astonished with wonderment at this greeting from the angel.

Luke 1:30-31 So the angel told her, "Do not be afraid, Mary, for you have found favor with God. Behold, you will conceive and give birth to a son, and you are to give Him the name Jesus.

Susie: Gabriel gave Mary the shocking news that she was going to become pregnant and have a son.

Susan: She was to name this son Jesus which means "Jehovah is generous, Jehovah saves."

Susie: Jesus is a derivative of Joshua or Yeshua and was not an uncommon name, but the angel's next statement made clear that this would be no common baby.

Luke 1:32-33 He will be great and will be called the Son of the Most High. The Lord God will give Him the throne of His father David, and He will reign over the house of Jacob forever. His kingdom will never end!"

Susie: Gabriel told Mary that her son would reign on the throne of David FOREVER.

Susan: That throne would continue eternally because Jesus would be the Son of the Most High—the Son of God.

Susie: A descendant of David was not on the throne at this point in history, for Rome had appointed Herod the Great as Israel's king. Herod was not a Jew. His father was from Idumea, and his mother was Arabian. Both Mary and Joseph were in the line of David, but they were poor peasant people. Therefore, this news was shocking.

Luke 1:34 "How can this be," Mary asked the angel, "since I am a virgin?"

Susie: Mary, understandably, was astonished at the news that she would be pregnant since she and Joseph were not married yet, and she was a virgin.

Susan: She must have been terrified and confused. Also, she would have no one to share her troubles with since probably no one would believe her.

Susie: Keep in mind, this was a private conversation between Mary and Gabriel.

Susan: If Mary shared this with anyone else, surely, they would have deemed her crazy.

Susie: Or worse, stoned her as unfaithful to her betrothed.

Luke 1:35-37 The angel replied, "The Holy Spirit will come upon you, and the power of the Most High will overshadow you. So the Holy One to be born will be called the Son of God. Look, even Elizabeth your relative has conceived a son in her old age, and she who was called barren is in her sixth month. For no word from God will ever fail."

Susan: Gabriel answered Mary's question by explaining that this was not going to be the normal exchange between a woman and a man. God was going to personally, miraculously, impregnate her with His Son in the form of an embryo.

Susie: He assured her of God's power to perform this miracle in her by telling her of Elizabeth's pregnancy, miraculous because of her advanced age. I find the statement in verse 37 in the Voice translation particularly comforting: "So the impossible is possible with God." AMEN.

Luke 1:38 "I am the Lord's servant," Mary answered. "May it happen to me according to your word." Then the angel left her.

Susan: Hearing the angel's answer to her question, Mary submitted and committed herself to the process of conception, pregnancy, and birth of the Redeemer Jesus in accordance with the Father's will.

Susie: She must have known she would be subjecting herself to ridicule, gossip, and even the possibility of stoning or banishment, either of which would have been within Joseph's rights to demand.

Susan: At the risk of all these things, she humbly submitted anyway, referring to herself as God's servant. Her God was more important to her than anything, including reputation and even family. Above all else, she wanted to please God.

Susie: Surely, she had an understanding that God was able to do what He was proposing, including protecting her and the child.

REVIEW QUESTIONS

1. How far along in pregnancy was Elizabeth when Gabriel appeared to Mary?
   _____
   _____
   _____
   _____

2. What was Gabriel's greeting to Mary?
   _____
   _____
   _____
   _____

3. When Mary was told she would conceive a son, what was her initial reaction?

   _____
   _____
   _____
   _____
   _____
   _____
   _____

4. What was Gabriel's explanation after Mary voiced her question?

   _____
   _____
   _____
   _____
   _____
   _____
   _____
   _____
   _____
   _____

5. After receiving the news that she was to give birth to the Son of God, what was Mary's humble reply?

   _____
   _____
   _____
   _____
   _____

Ponder This...

Mary's response to God's plan for her was humble. When God uses you in a mighty way, remember to give Him all the glory and credit. You are just the vessel to carry His blessings to others. We are the instrument in God's hand to accomplish the works He has proposed for us to do. The Lord will enable and empower us to fulfill His calling as we humbly surrender to His will.

> *Ephesians 2:10 For we are God's workmanship, created in Christ Jesus to do good works, which God prepared in advance as our way of life.*

> *Philippians 4:13 (AMP) I can do all things [which He has called me to do] through*

Him who strengthens and empowers me [to fulfill His purpose—I am self-sufficient in Christ's sufficiency; I am ready for anything and equal to anything through Him who infuses me with inner strength and confident peace.]

Mary and Elizabeth

LUKE 1:39-56: SPIRIT-FILLED UNBORN BABY JUMPS FOR JOY!

Luke 1:39-40 In those days Mary got ready and hurried to a town in the hill country of Judah, where she entered the home of Zechariah and greeted Elizabeth.

Susan: Mary may have fled Nazareth to avoid prying eyes and whispering lips as her own pregnancy developed.

Susie: But I believe she wanted to see the miracle of Elizabeth's pregnancy in person as well.

Luke 1:41 When Elizabeth heard Mary's greeting, the baby leaped in her womb, and Elizabeth was filled with the Holy Spirit.

Susie: When Mary spoke a greeting to her relative Elizabeth, the unborn baby John jumped for joy!

Susan: Elizabeth was overjoyed as she was overcome by the Spirit of the Lord.

Luke 1:42-45 In a loud voice she exclaimed, "Blessed are you among women, and blessed is the fruit of your womb! And why am I so honored, that the mother of my Lord should come to me? For as soon as the sound of your greeting reached my ears, the baby in my womb leaped for joy. Blessed is she who has believed that the Lord's word to her will be fulfilled."

Susie: John, who Gabriel foretold would be filled with the Spirit in the womb, leapt when Mary greeted His mother.

Susan: An UNBORN baby was the first to recognize the Savior while HE was yet UNBORN. This is a strong argument for the fact that an embryo is already the person God is forming inside their mother.

Susie: Fetus John's reaction caused Elizabeth, who was also filled with the Holy Spirit at the same moment he moved within her, to rejoice as well.

Susan: Elizabeth questioned her worthiness to be visited by the mother of the Son of God, but she boldly prophesied concerning Mary because the Holy Spirit empowered her.

Susie: Elizabeth called Mary "the mother of my Lord," which says that she already believed Jesus would be the Messiah. No human had told her this. Mary had just arrived, so they had not had time to even discuss the fact that Mary was pregnant and all that Gabriel had told Mary. (Remember: Mary could not phone ahead or send Elizabeth a Facebook message or Tweet about her pregnancy).

Susan: The Holy Spirit prompted Elizabeth to honor Mary's faith in entrusting herself to the Lord.

Susie: Somehow, in the moment that baby John moved excitedly in her womb, the Lord caused Elizabeth to know exactly what was going on with her relative, Mary. For this moment in time, the Lord was using Elizabeth as His prophetess. We find it interesting that one of the first people to recognize that Mary's baby was the Son of God was a woman. Jesus continued elevating women throughout His time on earth.

> 1:46–55 Mary's Magnificat (the first word in the Latin translation; see notes on vv. 68–79; 2:29–32) is filled with OT allusions and quotations. It reveals that Mary's heart and mind were saturated with the Word of God. It contains repeated echoes of Hannah's prayers, e.g., 1 Sam. 1:11; 2:1–10. These verses also contain numerous allusions to the law, the psalms, and the prophets. The entire passage is a point-by-point reciting of the covenant promises of God. (67)

Susan: In light of what John MacArthur pointed out about Mary's song, we must remember that girls did not receive formal education at the synagogue which was for boys only. Girls were taught to be good wives and mothers at home with their own mother. Mary had to have been self-motivated to invest time in learning God's word in independent study or with her mother, father, or brother.

> Boys usually began formal schooling at the "house of the book" at age five. He would spend at least a half day, six days a week for about five years, studying at the synagogue. Parents brought their son at daybreak and came for him at midday. While not at school the boy was usually learning a trade, such as farming or carpentry.
> https://www.studylight.org/dictionaries/eng/hbd/e/education-in-bible-times.html

Luke 1:46-47 Then Mary said: "My soul magnifies the Lord, and my spirit rejoices in God my Savior!

Susie: Mary broke out rejoicing in song, humbly praising the Lord for all He was doing through her. This is known as the Magnificat because that is the first word of Mary's praise song in Latin.

Susan: Mary says that her soul magnifies, exalts the Lord. She identifies God as Savior, highlighting the purpose for which Jesus was coming as a man. I think it is significant that the one chosen to bear the Messiah sees her own need for salvation and knows that God is meeting that need. Her own Son would be her Savior!

Luke 1:48-49 For He has looked with favor on the humble state of His servant. From now on all generations will call me blessed. For the Mighty One has done great things for me. Holy is His name.

Susan: Mary viewed herself as God's servant, his "handmaiden" in the King James Version.

Susie: Mary was probably poor, not significant in any way. Therefore, she realized she was extremely blessed to be chosen to conceive and carry her Redeemer in her womb. She acknowledged that this was not her doing but was the choice and work of God in her life.

Susan: God loves to take the insignificant as far as the world's standards and use them in miraculous ways. Mary needed the saving grace of the Seed of God she carried as much as the world He would be born into needed her Baby.

Luke 1:50 His mercy extends to those who fear Him, from generation to generation.

Susie: Mary may have had several passages from the Psalms in mind. We looked up "them that fear him" on www.biblegateway.com and came up with these as well as others: Psalms 25:14, 33:18, 34:7, 34:9, 85:9, 103:11, 13 & 17, 111:5, 145:19, and 147:11. Psalm 103 has been a favorite of mine for a long time:

> *Psalm 103:11 For as high as the heavens are above the earth, so great is His loving devotion for* **those who fear Him**.

> *Psalm 103:13 As a father has compassion on his children, so the LORD has compassion on* **those who fear Him**.

> *Psalm 103:17 But from everlasting to everlasting the loving devotion of the LORD extends to* **those who fear Him**, *and His righteousness to their children's children—*

Luke 1:51-53 He has performed mighty deeds with His arm; He has scattered those who are proud in the thoughts of their hearts. He has brought down rulers from their thrones, but has exalted the humble. He has filled the hungry with good things, but has sent the rich away empty.

> *Psalm 103:5-6 . . . who* **satisfies you with good things**, *so that your youth is renewed like the eagle's. The LORD executes righteousness and justice for all the oppressed.*

Susie: In Jewish thought, riches were a reward from God, which, essentially, they are. However, they believed the opposite was true as well, that poverty was a curse from God. Mary espoused the truth that God would bring down the proud and boastful and elevate the poor and downtrodden.

Susan: In the Magnificat, Mary was announcing prophetic reality that God would bring forth, in the fullness of time, the bringing down of the proud and elevation of the humble. God's salvation would be for ***all*** people who believed.

Luke 1:54-55 He has helped His servant Israel, remembering to be merciful, as He promised to our fathers, to Abraham and his descendants forever."

Susie: God would fulfill His promise to Abraham to redeem His people.

Susan: The time was drawing near for the Messiah to be revealed. The baby Mary was carrying was the long awaited Anointed One promised to Abraham and Sarah, the Savior descended from their son Isaac.

> *Galatians 4:4-5 (NASB) "But when the fullness of the time came, God sent forth His Son, born of a woman, born under the Law, so that He might redeem those who were under the Law, that we might receive the adoption as sons."*

Luke 1:56 Mary stayed with Elizabeth for about three months and then returned home.

Susan: Mary stayed with Elizabeth during her final trimester of pregnancy and probably until John was born.

Susie: Then she went back home to Nazareth.

REVIEW QUESTIONS

1. What happened the moment Mary greeted Elizabeth?

   _____
   _____
   _____
   _____

2. What prophesy given to Zacharias does the baby's reaction fulfill?

   _____
   _____
   _____
   _____

3. Who empowered Elizabeth to prophesy concerning Mary's baby? How did she refer to Mary's unborn child?

   _____
   _____
   _____
   _____
   _____

4. Could reading about the encounter between Mary and Elizabeth change a person's perspective on abortion? Why or why not?

   _____
   _____
   _____
   _____

Ponder This...

Things that assure us that a baby inside the womb is already a human soul even before they take their first gulp of air when born:

1. John was filled with the Spirit even while in his mother's womb.

2. John jumped for joy at the sound of Mary's voice because he recognized by the power of the Spirit that she was carrying the Messiah.

3. Jesus was recognized by John even though Mary was probably not even showing yet, even though by today's modern medical standards Mary's Baby would not be "viable."

Elizabeth

LUKE 1:57-66, 80 - HE SHALL BE CALLED JOHN, NOT ZACH JR.

Luke 1:57 When the time came for Elizabeth to have her child, she gave birth to a son.

Susie: Just as the angel had told Zechariah, Elizabeth gave birth to a boy. Like her ancestor Sarah before her, she had a healthy pregnancy despite being past the age of childbearing.

Susan: This was a miraculous pregnancy by the grace of God, not just the conception at that age, but the health of mother and baby as well.

Luke 1:58 Her neighbors and relatives heard that the Lord had shown her great mercy, and they rejoiced with her.

Susie: As the angel had predicted, this baby brought great joy, not only to Zechariah and Elizabeth, . . .

Susan: ...but also to their extended family and community. Everybody wanted a piece of that baby to love.

Susie: They all recognized God's hand in bring this joy to Zechariah and Elizabeth.

Luke 1:59 On the eighth day, when they came to circumcise the child, they were going to name him after his father Zechariah. But his mother replied, "No! He shall be called John."

Susan: Whoever spoke first wanted to make the baby Zechariah's namesake (Zacharias in some translations)— Zach Jr. if you will, but Elizabeth spoke up and said that he was to be called John instead.

Susie: This must have shocked the midwives because tradition was to name the firstborn after his father.

Susan: However, Elizabeth was obeying what the angel had told Zechariah in the temple.

Susie: Her husband must have communicated this command of the angel to her in writing or by some sort of sign language since he still could not speak.

Luke 1:61–62 They said to her, "There is no one among your relatives who bears this name." So they made signs to his father to find out what he wanted to name the child.

Susie: Not only was John not one of Zechariah's names, but the name was found nowhere in their family tree as far as anyone near them knew. So, in improvised sign language, they asked Zechariah what to name the baby. They did not take Elizabeth's word for it.

Susan: Never make assumptions about someone's limitations. The priests must have assumed that since Zechariah could not speak that he was deaf as well. Wrong.

Luke 1:63–64 Zechariah asked for a tablet and wrote, "His name is John." And they were all amazed. Immediately Zechariah's mouth was opened and his tongue was released, and he began to speak, praising God.

Susie: Zechariah motioned for a writing tablet and let them all know that he wanted to name the baby John just as Elizabeth had said. People were disconcerted at this, but the most astonishing thing happened next. His obedience in naming the child John in accordance with the angel Gabriel's declaration enabled him to speak again!

Susan: This time, instead of doubting, Zechariah affirmed the word of the Lord through his praises.

Luke 1:65–66 All their neighbors were filled with awe, and people throughout the hill country of Judea were talking about these events. And all who heard this wondered in their hearts and asked, "What then will this child become?" For the Lord's hand was with him.

Susan: The neighbors were filled with the fear of the Lord—awe—and spread the news of this miraculous birth everywhere they went.

Susie: They made a point to remember the events of Zechariah being unable to speak and then healed of dumbness as soon as he confirmed the name of baby John. They wondered what John might grow up to be! They probably were *not* envisioning camel hair clothing and locusts and honey for food!

Susan: Those who were discerning, in tune with the Spirit of the Lord, knew that God was with John even throughout his childhood among them.

Susie: In verses 67 through 79, Zechariah praised God and prophesied about his son. We will cover that in some future study since this is about ten **women** of Christmas.

Luke 1:80 And the child grew and became strong in spirit; and he lived in the wilderness until the time of his public appearance to Israel.

Susie: Elizabeth's miracle son grew stronger and stronger in the Lord. As a man, he spent time with God in the desert until it was the appointed time for him to prepare the way of the Messiah.

Susan: John (who became known as the Baptist or the Baptizer) spent much time alone with his God, and God prepared his heart to preach the good news and be the first to point to Jesus as the Perfect Lamb of God. You can read about this in the first few chapters of the Gospel of John (the disciple, not this John).

REVIEW QUESTIONS

1. Compare Luke 1:14 with Luke 1:58. How is verse 58 a fulfillment of the angel's words to Zecharias?

2. What Jewish tradition was carried out on the day the baby John was named?

3. Why were the neighbors surprised when Elizabeth said to name the baby John?

4. What happened when Zacharias confirmed Elizabeth's choice of John for the baby's name?

Ponder This...

Elizabeth and Zechariah were devout Jews. Zechariah may have even been praying about Elizabeth's barrenness when Gabriel spoke to him, yet he was still amazed and unbelieving that the words of the angel could be true. Do we pray expecting an answer and then doubt it when it comes? Not sure where I heard this, but "If you are going to pray for rain, carry your umbrella."

WORSHIP OPPORTUNITY

As we know, Elizabeth and Zechariah's bouncing baby boy grew up to be a prophet "in the spirit of Elijah" who served as the forerunner of the Messiah, encouraging the people to "REPENT, for the Kingdom of God is at hand." May we help to prepare people to understand and accept the Good News that Jesus saves!

Listen to The Ball Brothers singing "John the Baptist":

https://www.youtube.com/watch?v=EYqUTvO1xLk

Elizabeth

Barren Woman Blessed with Bouncing Baby Boy

- Luke 1:5-7 In the time of Herod king of Judea there was a priest named Zechariah, who belonged to the priestly division of Abijah, and whose wife **Elizabeth** was a daughter of Aaron. Both of them were righteous in the sight of God, walking blamelessly in all the commandments and decrees of the Lord. But they had no children, because **Elizabeth** was barren, and they were both well along in years.

- Luke 1:11-13 Just then an angel of the Lord appeared to Zechariah, standing at the right side of the altar of incense. When Zechariah saw him, he was startled and gripped with fear. But the angel said to him, "Do not be afraid, Zechariah, because your prayer has been heard. Your wife **Elizabeth** will bear you a son, and you are to give him the name John."

- Luke 1:18 "How can I be sure of this?" Zechariah asked the angel. "I am an old man, and **my wife** is well along in years."

- Luke 1:24-25 After these days, his wife **Elizabeth** became pregnant and for five months remained in seclusion. She declared, "The Lord has done this for me. In these days He has shown me favor and taken away my disgrace among the people."

- Luke 1:36-37 Look, even **Elizabeth** your relative has conceived a son in her old age, and **she who was called barren** is in her sixth month. For no word from God will ever fail.

- Luke 1:39-40 In those days Mary got ready and hurried to a town in the hill country of Judah, where she entered the home of Zechariah and greeted **Elizabeth**.

- Luke 1:41-45 When **Elizabeth** heard Mary's greeting, the baby leaped in her womb, and **Elizabeth** was filled with the Holy Spirit. In a loud voice she exclaimed, "Blessed are you among women, and blessed is the fruit of your womb! And why am I so honored, that the mother of my Lord should come to me? For as soon as the sound of your greeting reached my ears, the baby in my womb leaped for joy. Blessed is she who has believed that the Lord's word to her will be fulfilled."

- Luke 1:56 Mary stayed with **Elizabeth** for about three months and then returned home.

- Luke 1:57 When the time came for **Elizabeth** to have her child, she gave birth to a son.

- Luke 1:59-60 On the eighth day, when they came to circumcise the child, they were going to name him after his father Zechariah. But **his mother** replied, "No! He shall be called John."

MATTHEW 1:18-25 AND LUKE 2:1-7: MARY'S BABY BORN TO BE SAVIOR

Matthew 1:18–19 This is how the birth of Jesus Christ came about: His mother Mary was pledged in marriage to Joseph, but before they came together, she was found to be with child through the Holy Spirit. Because Joseph her husband was a righteous man and was unwilling to disgrace her publicly, he resolved to divorce her quietly.

Susie: In the Jewish culture of that day, parents chose a mate for their children, sometimes while they were still quite young. From that point, they were considered engaged. When they came of age, a date was set for the wedding and the man began preparing a place for his bride to live. At this point they were considered "betrothed" and if they decided not to marry, the man would need to divorce his wife. With the assumption that Mary had been unfaithful to her betrothed husband, Joseph could have had her publicly humiliated and even STONED TO DEATH as an adulteress! So, Joseph was going to do an extremely kind thing in divorcing her quietly and sending her away from the prying eyes of their hometown.

Susan: Matthew gives us the birth account from Joseph's perspective and shows us the character of the man God chose to raise His only begotten Son. Joseph was merciful even though he did not yet know the true origin of Mary's baby. He knew he was not the father, so the only logical assumption was that she had been unfaithful. Joseph was upright in heart and a man of integrity, but he did not assume a "holier than thou" position. Note that throughout Matthew's narrative, Joseph is seen pondering, thinking things through, rather than behaving rashly with a knee-jerk reaction.

Susie: He was merciful rather than judgmental. Even though this was an arranged marriage, I believe Joseph already loved Mary, his bride to be.

Matthew 1:20–21 But after he had pondered these things, an angel of the Lord appeared to him in a dream and said, "Joseph, son of David, do not be afraid to embrace Mary as your wife, for the One conceived in her is from the Holy Spirit. She will give birth to a Son, and you are to give Him the name Jesus^{G2424}, because He will save His people from their sins."

Susie: God sent an angel to explain the situation to Joseph in a dream. I'm sure Mary had tried to give Joseph an explanation, but he probably found it hard to believe.

Susan: The angel announcer of Heaven was probably Gabriel, sent to let Joseph know not to fear going ahead with marrying Mary because it was part of God's redemptive plan.

Susie: He let Joseph in on a bit of the divine masterplan. He reminded Joseph that he was descended from David as was Mary. Then he pointed out that Mary's pregnancy was orchestrated by the Holy Ghost, making the baby the Son of God, the long-awaited Messiah.

Susan: The angel instructed Joseph to name the baby Jesus meaning "Jehovah is generous, Jehovah saves" because He would save His people from their sins. Jesus would later declare, "I am the way, the truth, and the life: no man cometh unto the Father, but by me." (John 14:6 KJV)

> G2424. Iēsoús; gen. Iēsoú, masc. proper noun transliterated from the Hebr. Yēshūa (3091), Jehovah his help. Jesus, Jehoshua, contracted to Joshua (Neh. 8:17).
> (I) Jesus means Savior (Matt. 1:1, 16, 21). In the gospels, our Savior is designated by the name of Christ alone in nearly 300 passages; by the name of Jesus Christ or Christ Jesus less than 100 times, and by the name of the Lord Jesus Christ less than 50 times. Prior to His resurrection, He was designated as Jesus Christ; after His resurrection, He is often referred to as Christ Jesus (Acts 19:4; Rom. 8:1, 2, 39; 1 Cor. 1:2, 30; Gal. 3:26, 28; Eph. 2:6, 7, 10, 13; Phil. 3:3, 8, 12, 14; Col. 1:4, 28; 1 Tim. 1:12, 14, 15; 2 Tim. 1:1, 2, 13; 1 Pet. 5:10, 14). (68)

Matthew 1:22–23 All this took place to fulfill what the Lord had said through the prophet: "Behold, the virgin will be with child and will give birth to a son, and they will call Him Immanuel"[G1694](which means, "God with us").

Susie: Matthew, who targeted a Jewish audience, makes it clear that this miraculous birth fulfilled one of the many prophecies concerning the Messiah, the Christ, the Anointed One, Jesus.

> *Isaiah 7:14 Therefore the Lord Himself will give you a sign: Behold, the virgin will be with child and will give birth to a son, and will call Him Immanuel[H6005].*

Susan: Immanuel, also spelled Emmanuel, describes who Jesus came to be: God with us! He was born as a human baby, grew as a Jewish boy, and walked with His disciples teaching them about the Kingdom of God.

> H6005 im-maw-noo-ale' – a proper noun designating Immanuel, the name of the child who would serve as a sign to King Ahaz in his day and, in the fuller meaning of the prophecy, as a sign to the Lord's people Israel in the future. The name means "God with us". (69)

> G1694 em-man-oo-ale' – of Hebrew origin (H6005); God with us; Emmanuel, a name of Christ. (70)

Susan: Zechariah and Elizabeth were blessed to be chosen by God to bring forth the forerunner of the Redeemer. Mary and Joseph were given the honor and responsibility of parenting the only begotten Son of God.

Matthew 1:24–25 When Joseph woke up, he did as the angel of the Lord had commanded him, and embraced Mary as his wife. But he had no union with her until she gave birth to a Son. And he gave Him the name Jesus.

Susie: We do not know how much time intervened between the announcement to Mary and Joseph's dream. Joseph may not have been aware of the pregnancy until after Mary returned from a three-month visit with her relative Elizabeth. However, we know that Joseph realized this dream was truly from the Lord God and obeyed what the angel told him.

Susan: Joseph married Mary, but he restrained his natural human desire for intimacy and kept Mary chaste until after Jesus was born. He named the baby Jesus as the angel had instructed him.

Susie: The gospel of Luke gives more details of the birth of Jesus from Mary's perspective.

Luke 2:1–3 Now in those days a decree went out from Caesar Augustus that a census should be taken of the whole empire. This was the first census to take place while Quirinius was governor of Syria. And everyone went to his own town to register.

Susie: Luke sets the birth of the Savior into a timeframe, naming the Caesar of Rome and the governor of Syria for historical accuracy and validation that the birth of Jesus was an actual historical event.

Luke 2:4–5 So Joseph also went up from Nazareth in Galilee to Judea, to the city of David called Bethlehem, since he was from the house and line of David. He went there to register with Mary, who was pledged to him in marriage and was expecting a child.

Susie: The Roman emperor wanted to have an accurate count of every family in order to impose taxes on them. The fact that Joseph had to travel to Bethlehem reiterates that he was descended from King David and fulfills the Old Testament prophecy that the Messiah would be born in Bethlehem.

> *Micah 5:2 (TLB) "O Bethlehem Ephrathah, you are but a small Judean village, yet you will be the birthplace of my King who is alive from everlasting ages past!"*

Susan: Bethlehem in Hebrew means "house of bread". Jesus would later be called the Bread of Life.

Susie: He also compared Himself to manna at one point.

John 6:30-35 So they asked Him, "What sign then will You perform, so that we may see it and believe You? What will You do? Our fathers ate the manna in the wilderness, as it is written: 'He gave them bread from heaven to eat.'" Jesus said to them, "Truly, truly, I tell you, it was not Moses who gave you the bread from heaven, but it is My Father who gives you the true bread from heaven. For the bread of God is He who comes down from heaven and gives life to the world." "Sir," they said, "give us this bread at all times." Jesus answered, "I am the bread of life. Whoever comes to Me will never hunger, and whoever believes in Me will never thirst.

Luke 2:6–7 While they were there, the time came for her Child to be born. And she gave birth to her firstborn, a Son. She wrapped Him in swaddling cloths and laid Him in a manger, because there was no room for them in the inn.

Susie: Mary had traveled with Joseph even in the final month of her pregnancy. By the time they reached Bethlehem, she must have been exhausted, but they had no place to stay except a stable. I am sure the inns were packed because David had many descendants (as the Lord had promised him) that had to travel there.

Susan: Jesus was laid in a feeding trough, which goes back to the Bread of Life again. The Eternal being placed in a feeding trough because He is the food, the life source of man. Sometimes mangers were used to hold water, and Jesus is also the Source of Living Water.

John 4:10 Jesus answered, "If you knew the gift of God and who is asking you for a drink, you would have asked Him, and He would have given you living water."

John 7:38 Whoever believes in Me, as the Scripture has said: 'Streams of living water will flow from within him.'"

REVIEW QUESTIONS

1. What do we learn about Joseph from Matthew's account of the birth of Jesus?

___
___
___
___
___

2. How did God reveal the truth about Mary's pregnancy to Joseph?

3. What is the meaning of the name "Jesus?"

4. What is the meaning of the name Immanuel (Emmanuel)? Tell about a time that Jesus was your Emmanuel.

5. Why did Luke make a point to name the Caesar and the Governor at the time of Christ's birth?

6. Why did Joseph and Mary have to travel to Bethlehem? What prophecy does this fulfill?

7. What does "Bethlehem" mean and why is that significant?

_____
_____
_____
_____
_____

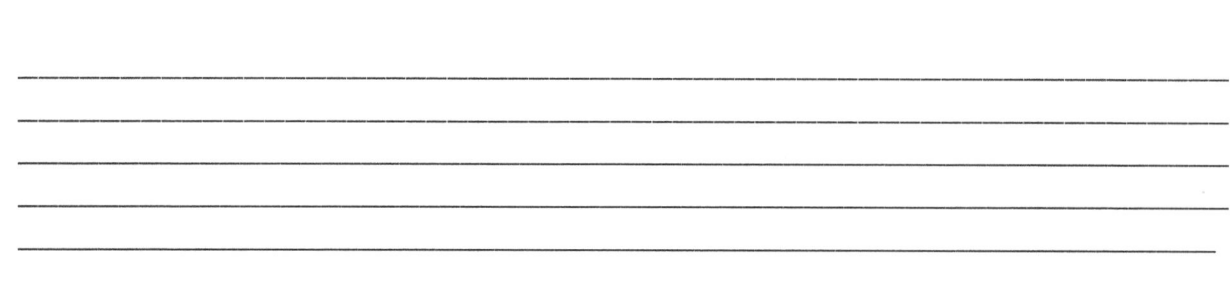

There was no room for the Son of God in the inn, but how often do we have so much "stuff" crammed into the inn of our heart, that Jesus is crowded out of our consciousness? The inn keeper had no idea the mother of the Messiah was seeking shelter, and he turned her away. Do we, who know Jesus as Savior, sometimes turn Him away by replacing intimate time with Him with the modern world's busyness? Do we remember that He is our Emmanuel—God with us?

WORSHIP OPPORTUNITY

Worship along with Michael Card singing "Immanuel".
https://www.youtube.com/watch?v=O7DG3N6rYqk

LUKE 2:8-20: SHEPHERDS HONOR THE GOOD SHEPHERD

Luke 2:8 And there were shepherds residing in the fields nearby, keeping watch over their flocks by night.

Susan: Shepherds were the least esteemed of the working class in that day.

Susie: They were on one of the lowest rungs of society's ladder. These particular shepherds may have been guarding the flocks used for sacrifices in the temple.

Susan: That God chose to announce the birth of His Son first to this group of people shows that He has no favoritism of class. His interest is solely in the hearts of humanity, not where they are on the socio-economic strata.

> *Acts 10:34 Then Peter began to speak: "I now truly understand that God does not show favoritism."*

Susie: He invited the shepherds to be the first to worship the perfect Lamb of God.

Susan: They were allowed VIP access even before the Magi, the wise men, from the east.

> Shepherds were a despised class because their work prevented them from keeping the ceremonial law, and as they moved about the country it was common for them to be regarded as thieves. They were considered unreliable and were not allowed to give evidence in the courts. (71)

Luke 2:9 Just then an angel of the Lord stood before them, and the glory of the Lord shone around them, and they were terrified.

Susan: When angels appear, the first response is to fall on your face afraid.

Susie: Imagine how you would respond if you were out in the middle of nowhere on a pitch-black night, and suddenly the sky lit up like daylight!

Luke 2:10 But the angel said to them, "Do not be afraid! For behold, I bring you good news of great joy that will be for all the people:

Susan: The fact that the good news was for ALL people would be most important to these shepherds who were considered second-class citizens. They were viewed almost as the homeless are today—dirty, unworthy, and possibly criminals.

Luke 2:11–12 Today in the city of David a Savior has been born to you. He is Christ the Lord! And this will be a sign to you: You will find a baby wrapped in swaddling cloths and lying in a manger."

Luke 2:11 (VOICE) Today, in the city of David, a Liberator has been born for you! He is the promised Anointed One, the Supreme Authority!

Susie: Angels almost always begin with "Fear not!" because their appearance can be overwhelming.

Susan: This angel declared he had something good to tell them.

Susie: Joyful news of the Messiah's birth.

Susan: All three names – Liberator (Savior), Anointed One (Christ or Messiah), and Supreme Authority (Lord—used for God in the Old Testament)—were used to describe the baby that had been born in Bethlehem. Jesus was all those things wrapped up in swaddling cloths even though He was not yet demonstrating all the facets of His glorious nature.

Susie: To the shepherds' astonishment, they were told that this Baby King was born in a stable and would actually be lying in a trough where the cattle watered or fed!

Susan: The shepherds themselves had probably been born somewhere better than a stable!

Susie: The God-Man who would identify Himself as the Good Shepherd revealed Himself first to a group of shepherds.

> *John 10:11 I am the good shepherd. The good shepherd lays down His life for the sheep.*

Susan: They, of all people, would eventually understand the words of the prophet Isaiah as they would apply to Jesus before Pilate and on the cross.

> *Isaiah 53:6-7 We all like sheep have gone astray, each one has turned to his own way; and the LORD has laid upon Him the iniquity of us all. He was oppressed and afflicted, yet He did not open His mouth. He was led like a lamb to the slaughter, and as a sheep before her shearers is silent, so He did not open His mouth....*

Luke 2:13–14 And suddenly there appeared with the angel a great multitude of the heavenly host, praising God and saying: "Glory to God in the highest, and on earth peace to men on whom His favor rests!"

> *Luke 2:13-14 (AMPC) Then suddenly there appeared with the angel an army of the troops of heaven (a heavenly knighthood), praising God and saying, Glory to God in the highest [heaven], and on earth peace among men with whom He is well pleased [men of goodwill, of His favor].*

Susie: I imagine the shepherds were now shaking in their sandals. If one angel was terrifying, how much more fearsome would an army of them be?

Susan: But this army was announcing peace, not war. Peace had come for all people who bring pleasure to God. You will have peace when you give God pleasure. When you are not at peace, the question is "are you giving God pleasure or are you breaking His heart because you are not being or becoming what He created you to be?"

Susie: We need to ask ourselves, "What pleases God?"

> *Micah 6:8 (VOICE) "He has shown you, O mortal, what is good. And what does the Lord require of you? To act justly and to love mercy and to walk humbly with your God."*

Susie: Walking humbly with God would involve surrendering to the Lordship of Jesus, in other words receiving the gift of salvation with the full realization that there is no way you could ever earn it. This is how to have peace *with God,* the peace *of God* in your life, and peace *with other people.*

Luke 2:15 When the angels had left them and gone into heaven, the shepherds said to one another, "Let us go to Bethlehem and see this thing that has happened, which the Lord has made known to us."

> *Luke 2:15 (VOICE) As soon as the heavenly messengers disappeared into heaven, the shepherds were buzzing with conversation.* **Shepherds:** *Let's rush down to Bethlehem right now! Let's see what's happening! Let's experience what the Lord has told us about!*

Susan: The shepherds were eager to go and see what the angel had reported to them, this awesome baby King. The shepherds understood the magnitude of what they were allowed to be a part of. They were awestruck!

Susie: They said to each other, "Let's go right now!" They didn't hesitate to head into Bethlehem.

Luke 2:16 So they hurried off and found Mary and Joseph and the Baby, who was lying in the manger.

Susie: The shepherds didn't just talk about going to Bethlehem, they did it right away. They didn't lollygag but traveled quickly. They found everything just as the angel had described it.

Luke 2:17–18 After they had seen the Child, they spread the message they had received about Him. And all who heard it were amazed at what the shepherds said to them.

Susan: Then the shepherds became a holy news crew spreading the Good News to all who would hear them.

Susie: I'm sure the people were wondering, "Could this really be the Messiah?" And, of course, there were probably those who thought, "Can we really believe something *shepherds* are telling us?"

Luke 2:19 But Mary treasured up all these things and pondered them in her heart.

> PON'DER, verb transitive [Latin pondero, from pondo, pondus, a pound; pendeo, pendo, to weigh.] 1. To weigh in the mind; to consider and compare the circumstances or consequences of an event, or the importance of the reasons for or against a decision. (72)

Susan: Mary intentionally filed these memories in her heart, perhaps to be able to recount these wondrous things to Jesus as He grew.

Susie: There were no "baby book albums" in those days, so Mary made a point to commit every occurrence to memory. She considered the weight or importance of everything that was happening. She was probably still amazed at all that had transpired in her life those last few months since Gabriel had appeared to her.

Luke 2:20 The shepherds returned, glorifying and praising God for all they had heard and seen, which was just as the angel had told them.

Susan: The shepherds' response was to glorify God. They did not chalk it all up to some kind of psychological breakdown but realized they had seen something divine and totally real. At some point they may have wondered, "If we tell people this, will anyone believe us, or are we going to be locked away forever?"

Susie: But God revealed Himself to them in such a mighty way that they could not doubt the reality of the encounter, nor could they remain silent about it.

Susan: No matter what happened they were going to faithfully announce this Good News, wherever they went, no matter the consequences.

REVIEW QUESTIONS

1. Why would shepherds seem to be an unlikely choice of audience for the angel's announcement of the Savior's birth?

2. What was the first reaction of the shepherds?

3. What was the good news the angel proclaimed to the shepherds?

4. After the army of angels ascended back to Heaven, what did the shepherds immediately do?

5. After worshiping the Baby Jesus, did the shepherds immediately return to their sheep? Explain.

6. Mary treasured these events and pondered them. Describe what that means in your own words.

Ponder This...

1. Make room amid the busyness of the Christmas season for Jesus to break through into your thoughts and actions. Do not relegate Him to the stable of your life.

2. Do not confine Jesus to two or three holidays in your year or even one day each week. Celebrate and worship every day with your entire being!

3. Remember that Jesus revealed Himself to the lowest of society. We should tell His story with words and actions to **all** people groups.

4. Seek peace with God through a relationship with Jesus and continue to have peace in your life as you obey God.

5. Spread the Gospel even if people discourage you by their responses. As Christians, we are here to please the Audience of One. It is our job to present the way to salvation, but it is the work of the Holy Spirit to draw the person into a relationship with Jesus.

Mary

LUKE 2:21-24: REDEEMING THE LONG-AWAITED REDEEMER

Luke 2:21 When the eight days until His circumcision had passed, He was named Jesus, the name the angel had given Him before He had been conceived.

Susie: Abraham was given instructions concerning circumcision of baby boys who were eight days old as a sign of the covenant between the Lord and His people (Genesis 17:9-14). Therefore, Jesus was circumcised as the Law required on the eighth day.

Susan: In the Bible, numbers have meaning—eight is the number of new beginnings, and Jesus came to bring us the New Covenant. In obedience to what the angel had told both Mary and Joseph, they named Him Jesus which means "Jehovah is generous, Jehovah saves." In the Jewish culture, it was usually the father who named the child. Jesus is the name His heavenly Father had chosen for Him.

Susie: God's free gift of grace was extravagantly purchased by Jesus on the cross to save us from the wrath of God by redeeming us from slavery to sin, a generous gift indeed.

Susan: Before Jesus created the world, before He spoke everything into being, He was "...the Lamb slain from the foundation of the world" Revelation 13:8b. This means that even before Adam and Eve could be deceived and sin, God, in His mercy, had cleaned up the mess of sin, and would reveal this message at the perfect moment in time.

Susie: In God's accounting of time, it was as if Jesus had already gone to the cross.

Luke 1:22–24 And when the time of purification according to the Law of Moses was complete, His parents brought Him to Jerusalem to present Him to the Lord (as it is written in the Law of the Lord: "Every firstborn male shall be consecrated to the Lord"), and to offer the sacrifice specified in the Law of the Lord: "A pair of turtledoves or two young pigeons."

Susie: After Mary waited the required 40 days for purification, Mary and Joseph took the baby to the Temple in Jerusalem.

Susan: As the firstborn male, he was to be dedicated to God as a priest or redeemed by paying two shekels.

Susie: Two turtledoves or two young pigeons was the sacrifice for purification for a mother after birth for poor people who did not own or have the ability to purchase a perfect lamb. However, they were redeeming and dedicating THE PERFECT LAMB!

Susan: Mary did not have the money to purchase a lamb, but her son, the Lamb of God purchased her redemption on the cross!

> *Leviticus 12:1–8 (Complete Jewish Bible) Adonai said to Moses, "Tell the people of Isra'el: 'If a woman conceives and gives birth to a boy, she will be unclean for seven days with the same uncleanness as in niddah, when she is having her menstrual period. On the eighth day, the baby's foreskin is to be circumcised. She is to wait an additional thirty-three days to be purified from her blood; she is not to touch any holy thing or come into the sanctuary until the time of her purification is over. But if she gives birth to a girl, she will be unclean for two weeks, as in her niddah; and she is to wait another sixty-six days to be purified from her blood. "'When the days of her purification are over, whether for a son or for a daughter, she is to bring a lamb in its first year for a burnt offering and a young pigeon or dove for a sin offering to the entrance of the tent of meeting, to the cohen. He will offer it before Adonai and make atonement for her; thus she will be purified from her discharge of blood. Such is the law for a woman who gives birth, whether to a boy or to a girl. If she can't afford a lamb, she is to take two doves or two young pigeons, the one for a burnt offering and the other for a sin offering; the cohen will make atonement for her, and she will be clean.'"*
>
> *Exodus 13:2 (CJB) Set aside for me all the firstborn. Whatever is first from the womb among the people of Israel, both of humans and of animals, belongs to me.*
>
> *Exodus 13:15 (CJB) When Pharaoh was unwilling to let us go, Adonai killed all the firstborn males in the land of Egypt, both the firstborn of humans and the firstborn of animals. This is why I sacrifice to Adonai any male that is first from the womb of an animal, but all the firstborn of my sons I redeem.*
>
> *Numbers 18:16 (CJB) The sum to be paid for redeeming anyone a month old or over is to be five shekels of silver (two ounces), as you value it, using the sanctuary shekel (this is the same as twenty gerahs).*

Susan: Mary and Joseph were devout Jews following all the Law prescribed concerning the Baby Jesus and Mary's purification after childbirth.

Susie: As the following quotation from Galatians points out, Jesus placed Himself under the Law from the moment of His birth. Otherwise, He could not have been the perfect, unblemished, sinless sacrifice for our sin. Therefore, the Redeemer had to be redeemed as a firstborn son.

Galatians 4:4-5 (NIV) But when the set time had fully come, God sent his Son, born of a woman, born under the law, to redeem those under the law, that we might receive adoption to sonship.

REVIEW QUESTIONS

1. Why was Jesus circumcised on the 8th day? (Remember what we learned in our study of Sarah?)

2. What did Joseph and Mary bring as a sacrifice? Why?

3. Why did the Redeemer need to be redeemed?

Ponder This...

Jesus, who was God in the flesh, placed Himself under the law. He was the only man who perfectly obeyed the law, remaining sinless. He who gave the Law to Moses, subjected Himself to it in order to free us from the burden it placed upon humanity. Even as a baby, Jesus had to be redeemed as all firstborn children belonged to God. Mary and Joseph did all the Law required of them concerning Jesus. Imagine—the Redeemer had to be redeemed!

WORSHIP OPPORTUNITY

Jesus was born as a baby "under the Law," lived in perfect obedience to the Law, and even though He was sinless, took our sin upon Himself on the cross and died in our place to free us from slavery to the Law. We now live under grace, and "Therefore, there is now no condemnation for those who are in Christ Jesus" (Romans 8:1). We are, as the Gaither Vocal Band sings "Living in the Rhythm of Grace". Look it up on YouTube™ or follow the link, use closed captioning and worship along with them!

https://www.youtube.com/watch?v=laThTY6fLos

LUKE 2:25-40: INTERCESSOR, PROPHETESS, EVANGELIST

Susie: Simeon and Anna were elderly people who had anticipated the appearance of the Messiah for many years. Here are their stories.

Luke 2:25 Now there was a man in Jerusalem named Simeon, who was righteous and devout. He was waiting for the consolation of Israel, and the Holy Spirit was upon him.

> **Consolation of Israel**. A messianic title, evidently derived from verses like Is. 25:9; 40:1, 2; 66:1–11. (73)
>
> *Isaiah 25:9 And in that day it will be said, "Surely this is our God; we have waited for Him, and He has saved us. This is the LORD for whom we have waited. Let us rejoice and be glad in His salvation.*
>
> *Isaiah 40:1-2 "Comfort, comfort My people," says your God. "Speak tenderly to Jerusalem, and proclaim to her that her forced labor has been completed; her iniquity has been pardoned. For she has received from the hand of the LORD double for all her sins."*

Susan: Simeon means "obedient, listening" in Hebrew.

Susie: Simeon certainly was an obedient listener, hearing the Holy Spirit.

Susan: For us to be enabled to hear the Holy Spirit, we must be obedient listeners. We must listen intently and intentionally and be careful to obey all the Lord instructs us to do.

> *Joshua 1:8 This Book of the Law must not depart from your mouth; meditate on it day and night, so that you may be careful to do everything written in it. For then you will prosper and succeed in all you do.*

Luke 2:26–28 The Holy Spirit had revealed to him that he would not see death before he had seen the Lord's Christ. Led by the Spirit, he went into the temple courts. And when the parents brought in the child Jesus to do for Him what was customary under the Law, Simeon took Him in his arms and blessed God, saying:

Susie: Simeon heard the Spirit in his heart assuring him he would live to see the Messiah. Somehow the Spirit prompted him to go to the temple that very day and hour that Jesus was being dedicated. There he saw baby Jesus in his parents' arms and KNEW by the Spirit's revelation this infant was the Son of God.

Susan: He was filled with hope, peace, and comfort. Joy overwhelmed him as he took the Baby into his arms to bless him.

Luke 2:29–32 "Sovereign Lord, as You have promised, You now dismiss Your servant in peace. For my eyes have seen Your salvation, which You have prepared in the sight of all people, a light for revelation to the Gentiles, and for glory to Your people Israel."

Susan: Simeon now can rest because he not only *believed* that the Lord was in control even before he laid eyes on Jesus, but he had *seen* that the Lord was in control as the Spirit revealed the true identity of the Baby in his arms.

Susie: He had been allowed to see the promised Hope, our freedom.

Susan: The chain breaker, the One who delivers us from the prison of sin.

Susie: He also acknowledged in his speech that Jesus was not for Israel alone. He was to make the message available to other nations, Gentiles included. Simeon referred to the Messiah as a light, and in the gospel of John, we see that Jesus is The Light. Jesus Himself said that He was The Light:

> *John 1:1-5 In the beginning was the Word, and the Word was with God, and the Word was God. He was with God in the beginning. Through Him all things were made, and without Him nothing was made that has been made. In Him was life, and that life was the light of men. The Light shines in the darkness, and the darkness has not overcome it.*
>
> *John 8:12 (ESV) Again Jesus spoke to them, saying, "I am the light of the world. Whoever follows me will not walk in darkness, but will have the light of life."*
>
> *John 9:5 (ESV) As long as I am in the world, I am the light of the world."*

Susie: Simeon was serving the Lord as a prophet while holding the Son of God.

Luke 2:33 The Child's father and mother were amazed at what was spoken about Him.

Susan: Mary and Joseph were receiving confirmation of all the angel had told them. Everything may have begun to make some semblance of sense as Simeon prophesied concerning Jesus's future.

Susie: A total stranger had just come up to them praising God that he had now seen the Messiah, their baby!

Luke 2:34–35 Then Simeon blessed them and said to His mother Mary: "Behold, this Child is appointed to cause the rise and fall of many in Israel, and to be a sign that will be spoken against, so that the thoughts of many hearts will be revealed—and a sword will pierce your soul as well."

Susie: Jesus would have a polarizing effect on people. They would either recognize Him as the Messiah and be raised to walk with God, or they would reject Him and ultimately fall. That He would be a significant person, now seems to be a humongous understatement. Our entire western calendar revolves around Him. Granted, His life was unique, but one ordinary person can have a tremendous impact as well.

Susan: I do not know how many days I have left, but I am determined to use my influence on behalf of God to the fullest extent of God's ability within me. Exposing our secret thoughts is an intimidating and somewhat ominous proposition especially if we have not yet experienced God's saving grace.

Susie: Jesus makes our sin and failure apparent to us in order that we may see our need of Him and the changes He brings about in us when we trust Him.

Susan: And His availability to us when we surrender to Him. Mary's heart would be broken as she saw her innocent Son crucified. As the spear pierced the pericardium, her own heart would feel pierced as well because He was still her beloved Son even though He was the Messiah.

Susie: However, we know the rest of the story, that she would see Him raised from the dead!

Luke 2:36–37 There was also a prophetess named Anna, the daughter of Phanuel, of the tribe of Asher, who was well along in years. She had been married for seven years, and then was a widow to the age of eighty-four. She never left the temple, but worshiped night and day, fasting and praying.

Susan: Anna in Hebrew means "favor or grace, God has favored me".

Susie: God certainly favored Anna in allowing her to see the baby Savior. Anna's husband died when they had been married only a brief time.

Susan: What sustained Anna much of the time was not physical food, but prayer. She made the food for her spirit the priority rather than her physical appetite. She served as an intercessor in the temple and had devoted her life to her Lord.

Luke 2:38 Coming forward at that moment, she gave thanks to God and spoke about the Child to all who were waiting for the redemption of Jerusalem.

Susie: At this point Anna was at least 84 years old. She, like Simeon, immediately knew that Jesus was the Messiah. Therefore, she must have been filled with the Holy Spirit as well. Her service in the temple was not out of duty, but out of love and relationship with the Lord.

Susan: Simeon was now ready to die and be with the Lord, but for Anna, it wasn't time to go and rest even though she, too, was elderly. She now felt compelled to go and share the good news of this Messiah wrapped in the tender skin of a baby. At this point, she is an intercessor, prophetess, and evangelist!

Luke 2:39–40 When Jesus' parents had done everything required by the Law of the Lord, they returned to Galilee, to their own town of Nazareth. And the Child grew and became strong. He was filled with wisdom, and the grace of God was upon Him.

Susie: After a brief sojourn in Egypt after the visit of the Magi (we will read about this in Matthew's gospel), they returned to Nazareth where Joseph worked as a carpenter. Jesus had to grow up and get stronger just like any other child.

Susan: He had to satiate His hunger, hydrate, and eliminate just like the rest of us.

Susie: He had to obey His parents (those He created). He was fully human yet fully divine.

REVIEW QUESTIONS

1. What or whom were both Simeon and Anna awaiting?

2. In what way was Simeon living out the meaning of his name?

3. What could Simeon do now that he had seen the promised Messiah?

4. What prophecy did Simeon give Mary?

5. How did Anna serve the Lord in the Temple?

6. Was Anna ready to die after she beheld Jesus? What did she do?

Ponder This...

1. Remember that Jesus came with the cross already in view. Incarnation is not only about a baby in a manger.

2. Are we expecting Jesus to break through the clouds as if it could be today? And are we excitedly anticipating His moving in our lives right now? Do we have the attitude of expectancy seen in Simeon and Anna?

3. No one knows how many days or years they have left to serve the Lord, but we can choose to live each moment with Jesus' influence flowing through us in this life as Anna did.

4. Anna had lived with an appetite for the Lord. Once she met her Messiah, Jesus, she was

rejuvenated to share about Him with everyone. This reminds us of many of the senior adults at the church we attend. Share the Good News today and every day!

5. Put yourself in the shoes of Simeon or Anna. What do you think your response would be as the Holy Spirit filled you with the knowledge that a little baby being dedicated at the temple was actually God's own Son, the Messiah? What is your emotional response as you try to wrap your mind around the Creator of the universe humbling Himself to be a human baby?

WORSHIP OPPORTUNITY

At over 80 years old, Anna "got all excited" and went out to tell everyone the Messiah had been born! We, who know the rest of the story of His sacrifice on the cross in our place and resurrection from the dead to reign as King of kings, should be enthusiastically spreading the news as well. Worship with the Bill Gaither Trio singing "Get All Excited":
https://www.youtube.com/watch?v=-JVk0gOvBpQ

MATTHEW 2:1-11: TREASURES FOR THE GREATEST TREASURE (REALLY COOL BABY SHOWER!)

Susie: The Magi, the Wise Men, were key visitors and worshipers early in Jesus' life.

Matthew 2:1 After Jesus was born in Bethlehem in Judea, during the time of King Herod, Magi from the east arrived in Jerusalem, . . .

Susan: Herod, whose name means "Son of a hero," was dubbed "The Great" probably due to his planning and financing fantastic building projects including the rebuilding of the Jewish Temple. He was ruthless as proved by his actions later in this passage.

Susie: Herod was identified as being Idumean meaning he descended from the Edomites, the offspring of Esau. The Edomites refused to help Israel against their enemies. Herod was made king over the Israelites by the Roman authorities. According to both the *Reformation Study Bible* and *MacArthur Study Bible* notes the magi were NOT kings but were most likely court advisers who were both astronomers and astrologers. They may have been Zoroastrian wise men. If you want to know more about that religion, there is a brief article here: http://www.religionfacts.com/zoroastrianism/beliefs

Susan: Many scholars believe they may have been from Persia or Babylonia and would have learned of the prophesied Messiah due to Daniel's captivity.

Susie: Another point of view on the Magi insists they were actually Jewish wise men who still lived in Babylon.

> Some have even speculated that these wise men came from a Jewish school that went back to Daniel's day, where the prophets looked to the heavens for the promised arrival of the Messiah. The star in the east was in fact a manifestation of Adonai's Sh'khinah (Divine Presence), marking the arrival of the Son of Man. (74)

Matthew 2:2 . . . asking, "Where is the One who has been born King of the Jews? We saw His star in the east and have come to worship Him."

For ancient people the star confirmed again that Jesus was the Messiah who fulfilled Balaam's star prophecy (Num. 24:17). (75)

Numbers 24:17 I see him, but not now; I behold him, but not near. A star will come forth from Jacob, and a scepter will arise from Israel.

Susie: Scientists have tried to explain the phenomenon of the star by saying it was a conjunction of three planets or a supernova. However, the fact that it moved and rested in one place would negate those theories. Others propose that it may have been some form of the Shekinah glory of God similar to the cloud by day and pillar of light at night which led the Israelites out of Egypt. John MacArthur, Jr., in his book *God With Us, The Miracle of Christmas,* discusses this same theory and states it was the same glory that had shone on the shepherds. (76) At any rate, we believe it was a miraculous, supernatural occurrence.

Susan: I think the star was the Father's personal birthday candle in the sky announcing the birth of His son. The glory of the Father would surely shine at the birth of His only begotten Son!

Susie: The wise men stated that their sole purpose in traveling from the East was to find this Baby and worship Him.

Susan: The wise men may have been only seekers, or they may have been expectant Jewish scholars, anticipating the Messiah's arrival like Simeon and Anna.

Susie: If they were Zoroastrians, they believed in a multiplicity of saviors and may have thought the one born king of the Jews was only one of them. If they were Jewish sages from Babylon as proposed in the *Complete Jewish Study Bible*, then they truly came to worship the Messiah, the Son of God. They did not come desiring gifts *from* Him but bearing gifts *for* Him.

Susan: Their gifts were even of symbolic significance. They did not see this baby King as a cosmic Santa Claus or a supernatural slot machine like many people approach God today. They saw Him as at least an important spiritual figure or more accurately as the promised Messiah, King of the Jews to be worshipped.

Matthew 2:3 When King Herod heard this, he was disturbed, and all Jerusalem with him.

Susie: King Herod was a controlling despot whose reign was one of terror. If King Herod wasn't happy, no one would be happy.

Susan: The Baby was a threat to Herod's dictatorial control over Israel. If this baby were truly to be the king of Israel, it would mean that Herod's sons would not inherit the kingdom. His family dynasty would surely end.

Susie: Instead of being excited about the possibility that the Messiah had arrived, Herod the Great was jealous, green with envy.

Matthew 2:4 And when he had assembled all the chief priests and scribes of the people, he asked them where the Christ was to be born.

Susie: The king of Israel did not have enough interest in the coming Messiah to have studied the scriptures for himself.

Susan: He had to inquire of others who were required by their professions to know these things.

Matthew 2:5–6 "In Bethlehem in Judea," they replied, "for this is what the prophet has written: 'But you, Bethlehem, in the land of Judah, are by no means least among the rulers of Judah, for out of you will come a ruler who will be the shepherd of My people Israel.'"

Susie: This prophecy is found in Micah 5:2. "Ruler" denotes a strong, stern leadership.

> *Micah 5:2 But you, Bethlehem Ephrathah, who are small among the clans of Judah, out of you will come forth for Me One to be ruler over Israel—One whose origins are of old, from the days of eternity.*

Matthew 2:7 Then Herod called the Magi secretly and learned from them the exact time the star had appeared.

Susan: The wise men are not even under Herod the Great's rule, but he privately ordered them to give him information.

Susie: He was trying to ascertain exactly how old the baby Boy was at this time because he had a dastardly deed in mind.

Matthew 2:8 And sending them to Bethlehem, he said: "Go and search carefully for the Child, and when you find Him, report to me, so that I too may go and worship Him."

Susie: Herod had no intention of worshiping the Child. He wanted to eliminate Him as we will see and manipulated the Magi into divulging the Child's possible age.

Susan: He feared Jesus would end his family legacy as well as his own rule.

Susie: We can add blatant, unscrupulous liar to the negative tags associated with the name Herod the Great.

Matthew 2:9–10 After they had heard the king, they went on their way, and the star they had seen in the east went ahead of them until it stood over the place where the Child was. When they saw the star, they rejoiced with great delight.

Susie: The star had disappeared temporarily which is why the Magi had inquired of Herod. Now it re-appeared and led them directly to the house where Jesus was living. I do believe this could have been the glory of God leading them just as He led the Israelites with a pillar of cloud by day and a pillar of fire by night when they fled Egypt. No natural phenomenon would have the ability to disappear, reappear, move, and hover.

Susan: The wise men were not just full of joy when the star came back into view: their joy was exponentially overwhelming. They were ecstatic! It was also a relief that they could now fulfill their mission to worship the baby King.

Susie: Jesus may have been a year to 18 months old by this time (according to the time the wise men told Herod they had first seen the star), and his family had moved to a house in Bethlehem. In other words, the wise men were **not** at the stable as they are so often depicted in artwork and dramatizations.

Matthew 2:11 On coming to the house, they saw the Child with His mother Mary, and they fell down and worshiped Him. Then they opened their treasures and presented Him with gifts of gold and frankincense and myrrh.

Susie: Whenever scripture mentions Jesus and Mary in the same breath, He is always given the position of prominence by being listed first. Joseph must have been at the carpentry workshop since he is not mentioned in these verses.

Susan: The gifts were not just expensive and extravagant. They also had symbolic significance as explained in the notes from *The Voice Bible*.

> These are exceptionally good gifts, for gold is what is given a king, and Jesus is the King of kings; incense is what you expect to be given a priest, and Jesus is the High Priest of all high priests; myrrh ointment is used to heal, and Jesus is a healer. But myrrh is also used to embalm corpses—and Jesus was born to die. (77)

REVIEW QUESTIONS

1. Were the Magi, aka the Wise Men, Kings? Explain.

    _____
    _____
    _____
    _____
    _____
    _____

2. What are the various theoretical explanations of what the Star was? What is your opinion about the Star?

3. What did Herod inquire of the Wise Men?

4. What gifts did the Magi bring to Baby Jesus? What is their symbolic significance?

Ponder This...

1. Are we coming to Jesus to give Him adoration and worship, or are we only interested in what He can give us?

2. Do we understand all Jesus has done for us and can do in and through us, or do we see him (like Herod) as the eternal kill-joy? Jesus came to give us abundant life. His rules are for our protection, peace, and fulfillment; not to limit us.

3. The wise men brought their best gifts to the Savior, not only the physical gifts, but the most important gift—their worship. Are we bringing Him our best? Are we truly engaged in worshiping our Lord as instructed in Scripture, or are we distracted by the world?

MATTHEW 2:12-23: "OUT OF EGYPT I HAVE CALLED MY SON"

Matthew 2:12 And having been warned in a dream not to return to Herod, they withdrew to their country by another route.

Susie: The wise men obeyed the Holy Spirit's message to them in the dream and did not reveal the Baby's location to Herod.

Susan: The Magi were truly wise and were not duped into informing Herod's henchmen where to find the One born to be King of the Jews. They went home by another route in order to avoid passing through Herod's jurisdiction at all.

Matthew 2:13–14 When the Magi had gone, an angel of the Lord appeared to Joseph in a dream. "Get up!" he said. "Take the Child and His mother and flee to Egypt. Stay there until I tell you, for Herod is going to search for the Child to kill Him." So he got up, took the Child and His mother by night, and withdrew to Egypt,

Susan: Angels were protecting the Holy Child and His parents. The Magi obeyed the dream for his protection. Joseph immediately took the family and fled to Egypt in the middle of the night as the angel instructed. Some propose that the expensive gifts from the Magi may have been sold to finance this trip. The way that the Father protected Jesus at every turn should give us great confidence and courage that no matter what we face, if we believe and trust in our God, He will protect us with the same tenacity that He protected His only begotten Son.

Susie: Jesus was here on the mission of the redemption of man. In order to fulfill that, He had to live among us as the perfect God-Man which means He had to grow up!

Susan: God is as eager and intentional for each of us to fulfill our purposes as He was for Jesus to fulfill His.

Susie: When God calls us, it is not for our ease but for us to serve Him and bring others into His kingdom as well.

Matthew 2:15 . . . where he stayed until the death of Herod. This fulfilled what the Lord had spoken through the prophet: "Out of Egypt I called My Son."

Hosea 11:1 (VOICE) Eternal One: When Israel was a child, I loved him; and out of Egypt I called My son.

Susie: Mary, Joseph, and Jesus had to return to the land of Israel's captivity in order to save the Messiah's life. Traveling with a young child is difficult even now. Imagine Mary doing it walking or riding a donkey!

Susan: She's more of a woman than I am, and I'm some kind of woman to be reckoned with!

Susie: Mary and Joseph continued to obey the Lord's leading.

Matthew 2:16 When Herod saw that he had been outwitted by the Magi, he was filled with rage. Sending orders, he put to death all the boys in Bethlehem and its vicinity who were two years old and under, according to the time he had learned from the Magi.

Susie: Herod, seething with anger, commanded that all the boys two and under be slaughtered. He did not care about the innocent lives destroyed. He was intent on killing this One he saw as usurper.

Susan: His plan was thwarted because Joseph, who as we continue to see was listening for the voice of his God, was obedient to the message of the angel in the dream.

Matthew 2:17–18 Then what was spoken through the prophet Jeremiah was fulfilled: "A voice is heard in Ramah, weeping and great mourning, Rachel weeping for her children, and refusing to be comforted, because they are no more."

> *Jeremiah 31:15 This is what the LORD says: "A voice is heard in Ramah, mourning and great weeping, Rachel weeping for her children, and refusing to be comforted, because they are no more."*

Susie: Where is Ramah and why was Rachel weeping since she was not of the tribe of Judah? As with many prophecies, Jeremiah 31:15 was fulfilled when the Israelites were taken into captivity in Babylon. However, it had a further out fulfillment when Herod had the baby boys killed in Bethlehem. This is a bit of a rabbit trail, so we will give you the link to an excellent article in case you are curious as I was.
https://www.biblestudy.org/prophecy/rachel-ramah-birth-of-jesus.html

Susan: Imagine the anguish of all those mothers who lost their sons to a murderous annihilator!

Matthew 2:19–20 After Herod died, an angel of the Lord appeared in a dream to Joseph in Egypt. "Get up!" he said. "Take the Child and His mother and go to the land of Israel, for those seeking the Child's life are now dead."

Susie: Just as an angel had warned Joseph to flee to Egypt, one now informs him that it is safe to return to Israel with Mary and Jesus.

Matthew 2:21–23 So Joseph got up, took the Child and His mother, and went to the land of Israel. But when he learned that Archelaus was reigning in Judea in place of his father Herod, he was afraid to go there. And having been warned in a dream, he withdrew to the district of Galilee, and he went and lived in a town called Nazareth. So was fulfilled what was spoken through the prophets: "He will be called a Nazarene."

Susie: Joseph and Mary returned to Israel, but not to Bethlehem since Herod's son was now on the throne. Instead, they took Jesus back to their hometown of Nazareth.

Susan: Joseph, being a devout man, needed no further explanation than the angel telling him to get up and go. He did not need to set out a fleece or wait for some type of confirmation. He recognized God's instructions when he heard them. Then he followed the instructions immediately.

REVIEW QUESTIONS

1. Why did the Magi return home by a different route rather than going back to Herod?

2. Where did the angel tell Joseph to take Jesus and Mary for their safety?

3. What prophecy did their time in that country fulfill?

4. What age range of children did Herod order to be executed in Bethlehem?

5. What prophecy did this "slaughter of the innocents" fulfill?

   _____
   _____
   _____
   _____
   _____
   _____

6. When Joseph, Mary, and Jesus returned from Egypt, in what city did they make their home? What prophecy was fulfilled by this location?

   _____
   _____
   _____
   _____
   _____

Ponder This...

1. Do we seek the Lord's wisdom as we travel this earth, trusting Him to guide our steps?

2. We need to fully rely on the Lord to fulfill His purposes in and through us as He did through the "Ten Women of Christmas" we have studied. Could you be an ordinary person that God wishes to use in an extraordinary way?

Humble but Courageous Servant of the Lord

- Matthew 1:16 . . . and Jacob the father of Joseph, the husband of **Mary**, of whom was born Jesus, who is called Christ.

- Matthew 1:18-19 This is how the birth of Jesus Christ came about: His mother **Mary** was pledged in marriage to Joseph, but before they came together, she was found to be with child through the Holy Spirit. Because Joseph her husband was a righteous man and was unwilling to disgrace her publicly, he resolved to **divorce her** quietly.

- Matthew 1:20-21 But after he had pondered these things, an angel of the Lord appeared to him in a dream and said, "Joseph, son of David, do not be afraid to embrace **Mary** as your wife, for the One conceived in her is from the Holy Spirit. **She** will give birth to a Son, and you are to give Him the name Jesus, because He will save His people from their sins."

- Matthew 1:24-25 When Joseph woke up, he did as the angel of the Lord had commanded him, and embraced **Mary** as his wife. But he had no union with her until **she** gave birth to a Son. And he gave Him the name Jesus.

- Matthew 2:11 On coming to the house, they saw the Child with His mother **Mary**, and they fell down and worshiped Him. Then they opened their treasures and presented Him with gifts of gold and frankincense and myrrh.

- Matthew 2:13-15 When the Magi had gone, an angel of the Lord appeared to Joseph in a dream. "Get up!" he said. "Take the Child and **His mother** and flee to Egypt. Stay there until I tell you, for Herod is going to search for the Child to kill Him." So he got up, took the Child and **His mother** by night, and withdrew to Egypt, where he stayed until the death of Herod. This fulfilled what the Lord had spoken through the prophet: "Out of Egypt I called My Son."

- Matthew 2:19 After Herod died, an angel of the Lord appeared in a dream to Joseph in Egypt. "Get up!" he said. "Take the Child and **His mother** and go to the land of Israel, for those seeking the Child's life are now dead."

- Matthew 2:21 So Joseph got up, took the Child and **His mother**, and went to the land of Israel.

- Luke 1:26 In the sixth month, God sent the angel Gabriel to a town in Galilee called Nazareth, to a **virgin** pledged in marriage to a man named Joseph, who was of the house of David. And the virgin's name was **Mary**.

- Luke 1:29-33 **Mary** was greatly troubled at his words and wondered what kind of greeting this might be. So the angel told her, "Do not be afraid, **Mary,** for you have found favor with God. Behold, you will conceive and give birth to a son, and you are to give Him the name Jesus. He will be great and will be called the Son of the Most High. The Lord God will give Him the throne of His father David, and He will reign over the house of Jacob forever. His kingdom will never end!"

- Luke 1:34-35 "How can this be," **Mary** asked the angel, "since I am a virgin?" The angel replied, "The Holy Spirit will come upon you, and the power of the Most High will overshadow you. So the Holy One to be born will be called the Son of God.

- Luke 1:38 "I am the Lord's servant," **Mary** answered. "May it happen to me according to your word." Then the angel left her.

- Luke 1:39 In those days **Mary** got ready and hurried to a town in the hill country of Judah, where she entered the home of Zechariah and greeted Elizabeth.

- Luke 1:41 When Elizabeth heard **Mary's** greeting, the baby leaped in her womb, and Elizabeth was filled with the Holy Spirit.

- Luke 1:46-47 Then **Mary** said: "My soul magnifies the Lord, and my spirit rejoices in God my Savior! . . .

- Luke 1:56 **Mary** stayed with Elizabeth for about three months and then returned home.

- Luke 2:4-5 So Joseph also went up from Nazareth in Galilee to Judea, to the city of David called Bethlehem, since he was from the house and line of David. He went there to register with **Mary**, who was pledged to him in marriage and was expecting a child.

- Luke 2:6-7 While they were there, the time came for **her** Child to be born. And **she** gave birth to her firstborn, a Son. **She** wrapped Him in swaddling cloths and laid Him in a manger, because there was no room for them in the inn.

- Luke 2:16-19 So they hurried off and found **Mary** and Joseph and the Baby, who was lying in the manger. After they had seen the Child, they spread the message they had received about Him. And all who heard it were amazed at what the shepherds said to them. But **Mary** treasured up all these things and pondered them in her heart.

- Luke 2:22-24 And when the time of purification according to the Law of Moses was complete, **His parents** brought Him to Jerusalem to present Him to the Lord (as it is written in the

Law of the Lord: "Every firstborn male shall be consecrated to the Lord"), and to offer the sacrifice specified in the Law of the Lord: "A pair of turtledoves or two young pigeons."

- Luke 2:33-35 The Child's father and **mother** were amazed at what was spoken about Him. Then Simeon blessed them and said to His **mother Mary**: "Behold, this Child is appointed to cause the rise and fall of many in Israel, and to be a sign that will be spoken against, so that the thoughts of many hearts will be revealed—and a sword will pierce your soul as well."

- Luke 2:39 When **Jesus' parents** had done everything required by the Law of the Lord, they returned to Galilee, to their own town of Nazareth.

God's Sovereignty, Grace, and Redemption
REVEALED IN TEN WOMEN OF CHRISTMAS
SUMMARY

In the pages of this book, we have studied Ten Women of Christmas. Some may think we were "stretching" to include a few of them, and others may be wondering why we left someone out. However, we believe we studied exactly what we should have for this point in time.

We have examined Eve, Sarah, Tamar, Rahab, Ruth, Bathsheba, Esther, Elizabeth, Mary, and Anna. Let's recap what makes each of these an integral part of the Christmas story.

EVE – GENESIS CHAPTERS 1-3

1. As mother of all living, the entire human race— including Mary, the mother of Jesus— sprang from Eve.
2. Eve was the first to receive the hope and the promise of redemption when the Lord told her that the serpent's seed would bruise the heel, but her Seed (Messiah) would crush His head.

SARAH – GENESIS 17-18, 21-22

1. Sarah was the mother of God's chosen people, the nation of Israel, because the Lord insisted that Abraham had to father the child Isaac specifically through Sarah. She is specified as the matriarch of the Jewish people twelve times in Scripture.
2. Her son, Isaac, was also a "type" of Christ when Abraham was willing to sacrifice him as a burnt offering but God provided a ram for Himself instead. The ram was a foreshadowing of the Perfect Lamb provided by God to cover our sins.
3. Sarah is the most mentioned woman in the Bible, referred to fifty-six times.

TAMAR – GENESIS 38

1. Tamar made sure that the family line of Judah did not end with the death of his two older sons and his unwillingness to give the younger in marriage as he had promised.
2. The baby she had after posing as a prostitute to deceive her father-in-law Judah would be in the direct line of the Messiah, the Lion of the tribe of Judah.
3. We also saw God's grace demonstrated in that she was not killed as an adulteress and/or for committing incest.

RAHAB – JOSHUA CHAPTERS 2 & 6

1. Rahab was identified as a harlot, but when she hid the two spies sent by Joshua, by God's grace, her family was saved from destruction.
2. After she converted to Judaism, she married a Jewish man named Salmon and gave birth to Boaz who became Ruth's kinsman-redeemer.
3. Rahab was a great-great-grandmother of David.

RUTH – BOOK OF RUTH

1. Ruth was the Moabite widow of a Jewish man who was the son of Naomi. The characteristics listed in Proverbs 31 could have been based on Ruth.
2. Since she loved her Mother-in-law, Naomi, so deeply, she traveled back to Bethlehem with her, converted to Judaism, and led the life of a poor widow, gleaning in someone else's field.
3. In God's providence, the field belonged to Boaz who, as the kinsman-redeemer, married Ruth and cared for both her and Naomi.
4. Ruth's son Obed was the father of Jesse who was the father of King David; and the Messiah was to be his descendant.

BATHSHEBA – 2 SAMUEL 11 & 12
1 KINGS CHAPTER 1

1. Bathsheba committed adultery with King David who subsequently made sure her husband Uriah was killed in battle. The child of that adulterous union died as the cost of their sin.
2. However, David repented, and God in His grace, allowed Bathsheba and David to have Solomon through whom the kingship continued.
3. The Messiah is the final and eternal king to sit on the throne of His ancestors David and Solomon.

ESTHER – EXCERPTS FROM THE BOOK OF ESTHER

1. Esther was a young Jewish girl who God sovereignly elevated to the position of Queen of Persia in order to redeem the Jewish nation by His grace.
2. She was willing to risk her life to approach the king, and thus, saved her nation from annihilation. Without Esther and her wise cousin, Mordecai, the forefathers of Mary and Joseph would surely have been killed.

ELIZABETH – LUKE 1:1-25, 39-80

1. Elizabeth, like Sarah, gave birth to a very special baby boy in her old age even though she had been barren.
2. Her baby, John, jumped for joy in her womb when Mary, pregnant with Jesus, visited her. A fetus was one of the first to recognize the Messiah when He, too, was still and

embryo.
3. Elizabeth's son became known as John the Baptist and was the forerunner of the Messiah that had been prophesied.

MARY – LUKE 1:39-56, MATTHEW 1:18-25, LUKE 2:8-40, and MATTHEW 2:1-23

1. Mary was God the Father's chosen vessel to bring God the Son into the world.
2. Her heart was pure, and she was consecrated and devoted to the Lord as evidenced by all the scriptural references in her song of praise known as the Magnificat.
3. Mary and her husband Joseph were given the tremendous responsibility of parenting Jesus, the Son of the Most-High, until He became an adult and began to fulfill His purpose on earth.

ANNA – LUKE 2:25-40

1. Anna was widowed at a young age, but she decided rather than go man-hunting, she would serve the Lord wholeheartedly in the temple, living passionately for God and waiting expectantly for the Messiah.
2. When she recognized the Baby Jesus as the Messiah, she was so bursting with joy that she could no longer remain inside the temple but had to take her devotion to God out into the streets and share that the Messiah had finally come.
3. Anna was a prophetess, intercessor, and evangelist who spread the word that the Messiah was born to all who had been awaiting His appearance.

WORSHIP OPPORTUNITY

These ten women experienced the Sovereignty, Grace, and Redemption of God. Throughout their stories, we see God working for their good as well as His glory. We serve a GOOD GOD! Join CeCe Winans in singing "Goodness of God":

https://www.youtube.com/watch?v=y81yIo1_3o8

IN THE STUDY OF

God's Sovereignty, Grace, and Redemption REVEALED IN TEN WOMEN OF CHRISTMAS,

WE FIND:

- 1 first woman created and mother of all living – **Eve**
- 2 prostitutes - **Tamar** and **Rahab**
- 4 widows – **Naomi**, **Ruth**, **Bathsheba**, and **Anna**
- 2 Levirate marriages – **Tamar** with Judah and **Ruth** with Boaz
- 2 barren women who conceived – **Sarah** and **Elizabeth**
- 2 adulteresses – **Tamar** and **Bathsheba**
- 1 incident of incest – **Tamar** and her father-in-law Judah
- 2 murders – Cain killed his brother Abel and King David had **Bathsheba's** husband Uriah the Hittite killed
- 2 unwed mothers – Judah married **Tamar** *after* her pregnancy became known and she identified him as the father. **Mary** was pregnant with the Messiah before she and Joseph were married.
- 5 virtuous women – **Sarah**, **Ruth**, **Esther**, **Elizabeth**, **Mary**, and **Anna**

They were women from varied walks of life, varying degrees of respectability, and varied amounts of faith; but all of them were shown God's sovereign grace as He included them in His redemptive purpose. Five of them were listed in Matthew's genealogy of Jesus – Tamar, Rahab, Ruth, Bathsheba, and Mary. However, we believe we have demonstrated that the other five belong in the Christmas story as well.

JEWELS OF SALVATION

- *Romans 3:22-24 And this righteousness from God comes through faith in Jesus Christ to all who believe. There is no distinction, **for all have sinned and fall short of the glory of God** and are justified freely by His grace through the redemption that is in Christ Jesus.*

Everyone on earth has sinned. Sin is both doing things that go against what God tells us to do in the Bible and failing to do the good things He instructs us to do. This failure brings the wrath of God on us, and Jesus is the **only way** to make peace with God. John 14:6 "Jesus answered, 'I am the way and the truth and the life. No one comes to the Father except through Me.'"

- *Romans 6:20-23 For when you were slaves to sin, you were free of obligation to righteousness. What fruit did you reap at that time from the things of which you are now ashamed? The outcome of those things is death. But now that you have been set free from sin and have become slaves to God, the fruit you reap leads to holiness, and the outcome is eternal life. **For the wages of sin is death, but the gift of God is eternal life in Christ Jesus our Lord.***

The punishment for sin is death. The official term is "substitutionary atonement" which simply means you were sentenced to the death penalty, but Jesus volunteered to die on the cross in your place in order for you to be set free. Jesus died a painful death to redeem you from slavery to sin and spare you from the wrath of the righteous, Holy God.

- *Romans 5:6-8 For at just the right time, while we were still powerless, Christ died for the ungodly. Very rarely will anyone die for a righteous man, though for a good man someone might possibly dare to die. **But God proves His love for us in this: While we were still sinners, Christ died for us.***

Jesus died while we were still sinners. "For God so loved the world that **He gave His one and only Son**, that everyone who believes in Him shall not perish but have eternal life." John 3:16.

- *Romans 10:8-10 But what does it say? "The word is near you; it is in your mouth and in your heart," that is, the word of faith we are proclaiming: that **if you confess with your mouth, "Jesus is Lord," and believe in your heart that God raised Him from the dead, you will be saved.** For with your heart you believe and are justified, and with your mouth you confess and are saved.*

1 Corinthians 15:3-4 "For what I received I passed on to you as of first importance: that Christ died for our sins according to the Scriptures, that He was buried, that He was raised on the third day according to the Scriptures . . ." If you believe that Jesus is the Son of God who died for you and was raised to life, then trust in—rely on—Him to save you from the wrath of God, you can belong to Jesus.

- ❖ *Romans 10:11-13 It is just as the Scripture says: "Anyone who believes in Him will never be put to shame." For there is no difference between Jew and Greek: The same Lord is Lord of all, and gives richly to all who call on Him, for,* **"Everyone who calls on the name of the Lord will be saved."**

How do you become a member of the family of God? Pray—talk to God admitting that you cannot be good enough because you could *never* perfectly obey all His commands. Tell Him you trust that Jesus died on the cross to save you from slavery to sin and the wrath of God. Ask God to place His Holy Spirit in you and change you from the inside out. Thank Him for giving you life in His presence forever.

BELIEVERS' BENEFITS

The obvious benefit of trusting in Jesus, the Son of God who died for you and was raised from the grave to return to the right hand of His Father, and surrendering your life to him, is that instead of spending eternity separated from God and all that is good you will live in His presence in complete peace and joy. However, those who become the Lord's children by relying on Jesus gain many other things in this current life on earth. Here are a few:

- **Lord, we thank you for freeing us from slavery to sin and providing a way to flee temptation!** *Romans 6:6 "We know that our old self was crucified with Him so that the body of sin might be rendered powerless, that **we should no longer be slaves to sin."*** This does *not* mean that a believer will never sin again. It means he/she now has a choice to tap into the Holy Spirit's power to resist the urge to give in to temptation. *"No temptation has seized you except what is common to man. And God is faithful; He will not let you be tempted beyond what you can bear. But **when you are tempted, He will also provide an escape,** so that you can stand up under it" (1 Corinthians 10:13).*

- **Lord, thank You that nothing can separate us from Your love!** *"For I am convinced that neither death nor life, neither angels nor principalities, neither the present nor the future, nor any powers, neither height nor depth, nor anything else in all creation, will be able to separate us from the love of God that is in Christ Jesus our Lord" (Romans 8:38-39).*

- **Lord, thank You that our salvation is secure and cannot be lost!** *John 10:27-29 "My sheep listen to My voice; I know them, and they follow Me. I give them eternal life, and they will never perish. **No one can snatch them out of My hand.** My Father who has given them to Me is ^{great}er than all. No one can snatch them out of My Father's hand."*

- **Lord thank you for empowering us to do whatever You call us to do!** *Philippians 4:13 (AMP) "I can do all things [which He has called me to do] through Him who strengthens and empowers me [to fulfill His purpose—I am self-sufficient in Christ's sufficiency; I am ready for anything and equal to anything **through Him who infuses me with inner strength and confident peace.**]*

- **Lord, thank You for giving us brothers and sisters all over the world!** *"Respect everyone, and love the **family of believers."** 1 Peter 2:17a (NLT).*

Notes

1. Easton, M. G., M.A., D.D., *Illustrated Bible Dictionary,* Third Edition, published by Thomas Nelson, 1897.

2. Swindoll, Charles R., *Galatians, Ephesians: Swindoll's Living Insights Commentary,* Tyndale House, 2015.

3. Silver, Moises and Tenney Merrill C., *The Zondervan Encyclopedia of the Bible, 5 Volume Set,* Zondervan, 2010.

4. MacArthur, John, Twelve Extraordinary Women: How God Shaped Women of the Bible and What He Wants to Do with You, (Thomas Nelson, 2005) p. xi.

5. Green, Steve and High, Bill, *This Beautiful Book: An Exploration of the Bible's Incredible Story Line and Why It Matters Today,* (Zondervan, 2019).

6. Baker, Warren and Eugene E. Carpenter, *The Complete Word Study Dictionary: Old Testament* (Chattanooga, TN: AMG Publishers, 2003), 952.

7. Baker, Warren and Eugene E. Carpenter, *The Complete Word Study Dictionary: Old Testament* (Chattanooga, TN: AMG Publishers, 2003). H1823.

8. Swindoll, Charles R., *The Swindoll Study Bible NLT,* (Tyndale House, 2017, EPUB).

9. Warren Baker and Eugene E. Carpenter, *The Complete Word Study Dictionary: Old Testament* (Chattanooga, TN: AMG Publishers, 2003), 822.

10. Warren Baker and Eugene E. Carpenter, *The Complete Word Study Dictionary: Old Testament* (Chattanooga, TN: AMG Publishers, 2003), 704.

11. Webster, Noah, *The American Dictionary of the English Language, 1828.* as found at https://webstersdictionary1828.com/.

12. Warren Baker and Eugene E. Carpenter, *The Complete Word Study Dictionary: Old Testament* (Chattanooga, TN: AMG Publishers, 2003), 104–318.

13. Warren Baker and Eugene E. Carpenter, *The Complete Word Study Dictionary: Old Testament* (Chattanooga, TN: AMG Publishers, 2003), 104–318.

14. Warren Baker and Eugene E. Carpenter, *The Complete Word Study Dictionary: Old Testament* (Chattanooga, TN: AMG Publishers, 2003), 1009.

15. Wiersbe, Warren W., *NKJV Wiersbe Study Bible,* (Thomas Nelson, 2021). As found at www.biblegateway.com

16. McGee, J. Vernon, *Thru the Bible: Genesis through Revelation,* (Thomas Nelson, 1984, EPUB) as found at www.biblegateway.com

17. Hawkins, O.S., *The Bible Code: Finding Jesus in Every Book in the Bible,* (Thomas Nelson, 2020).

18. Patterson, Dorothy Kelly and Kelly, Rhonda Harrington, Eds., *NIV Women's Study Bible,* (Thomas Nelson, 2017) as found on www.biblegateway.com

19. MacArthur, John, *NKJV MacArthur Study Bible, 2nd Edition,* (Thomas Nelson, 1997, 2006, 2019), as quoted on www.biblegateway.com

20. Lockyear, Herbert, *All the Women of the Bible,* (Zondervan, 2016, EPUB).

21. Barker, Kenneth L. and John R. Kohlenberger III, *Expositor's Bible Commentary,* (Zondervan, 2004) as found as www.biblegateway.com

22. Garrett, Duane A.; Kaiser, Walter C., Jr., eds. *Archaeological Study Bible-NIV: An Illustrated Walk Through Biblical History and Culture,* (Zondervan, 2006).

23. MacArthur, John, *NKJV MacArthur Study Bible, 2nd Edition,* (Thomas Nelson, 1997, 2006, 2019), as quoted on www.biblegateway.com

24. MacArthur, John, *NKJV MacArthur Study Bible, 2nd Edition,* (Thomas Nelson, 1997, 2006, 2019), as quoted on www.biblegateway.com

25. MacArthur, John, *NKJV MacArthur Study Bible, 2nd Edition,* (Thomas Nelson, 1997, 2006, 2019), as quoted on www.biblegateway.com

26. Strong, James, *The New Strong's Exhaustive Concordance of the Bible,* (Thomas Nelson, 2009).

27. *Berean Standard Bible* (BSB) © 2016, 2020 by Bible Hub and Berean.Bible. Note on Joshua 6:17.

28. MacDonald, William, *Believer's Bible Commentary,* (Thomas Nelson, 2016).

29. MacDonald, William, *Believer's Bible Commentary,* (Thomas Nelson, 2016).

30. Barker, Kenneth L. and John R. Kohlenberger III, *Expositor's Bible Commentary*, (Zondervan, 2004) as found as www.biblegateway.com

31. MacArthur, John, *The MacArthur Bible Commentary,* (Thomas Nelson, 2005).

32. MacArthur, John, *The MacArthur Bible Commentary,* (Thomas Nelson, 2005).

33. MacArthur, John, *NKJV MacArthur Study Bible, 2nd Edition,* (Thomas Nelson, 1997, 2006, 2019), as quoted on www.biblegateway.com

34. MacArthur, John, *NKJV MacArthur Study Bible, 2nd Edition,* (Thomas Nelson, 1997, 2006, 2019), as quoted on www.biblegateway.com

35. Strong, James, *The New Strong's Exhaustive Concordance of the Bible,* (Thomas Nelson, 2009).

36. MacArthur, John, *NKJV MacArthur Study Bible, 2nd Edition,* (Thomas Nelson, 1997, 2006, 2019), as quoted on www.biblegateway.com

37. Henry, Matthew, *Matthew Henry's Commentary on the Whole Bible,* (Hendrickson Publishers, 2014) as found at www.biblegateway.com

38. *Berean Standard Bible* (BSB) © 2016, 2020 by Bible Hub and Berean.Bible.

39. MacArthur, John, NKJV MacArthur Study Bible, 2nd Edition, (Thomas Nelson, 1997, 2006, 2019), as quoted on www.biblegateway.com

40. Smith, William, *Smith's Bible Dictionary,* (Hendrickson Publishers, 1993).

41. MacArthur, John, *NKJV MacArthur Study Bible*, 2nd Edition, (Thomas Nelson, 1997, 2006, 2019), as quoted on www.biblegateway.com

42. MacArthur, John, *NKJV MacArthur Study Bible*, 2nd Edition, (Thomas Nelson, 1997, 2006, 2019), as quoted on www.biblegateway.com

43. MacArthur, John, *NKJV MacArthur Study Bible*, 2nd Edition, (Thomas Nelson, 1997, 2006, 2019), as quoted on www.biblegateway.com

44. MacArthur, John, *NKJV MacArthur Study Bible*, 2nd Edition, (Thomas Nelson, 1997, 2006, 2019), as quoted on www.biblegateway.com

45. Sproul, R. C. *ESV Reformation Study Bible*, (Reformation Trust Publishing of Ligonier

46. Henry, Matthew, *Matthew Henry's Commentary on the Whole Bible,* (Hendrickson Publishers, 2014) as found at www.biblegateway.com

47. Lucado, Max, *You Were Made for this Moment: Courage for Today and Hope for Tomorrow,* (Thomas Nelson, 2021), p. 8.

48. *The Voice*™. (Ecclesia Bible Society, 2008) note on Esther 1:1-4.

49. Lockyear, Herbert, *All the Women of the Bible,* (Zondervan, 2016, EPUB).

50. Patterson, Dorothy Kelly and Kelly, Rhonda Harrington, Eds., *NIV Women's Study Bible,* (Thomas Nelson, 2017) as found on www.biblegateway.com

51. Lockyear, Herbert, *All the Women of the Bible,* (Zondervan, 2016, EPUB).

52. Lucado, Max, *You Were Made for this Moment: Courage for Today and Hope for Tomorrow,* (Thomas Nelson, 2021), p. 53.

53. Sproul, R. C. *ESV Reformation Study Bible,* (Reformation Trust Publishing of Ligonier Ministries, 2021).

54. Sproul, R. C. *ESV Reformation Study Bible,* (Reformation Trust Publishing of Ligonier Ministries, 2021).

55. *The Voice*™. (Ecclesia Bible Society, 2008) note on Esther 4:12-14.

56. *Berean Standard Bible* (BSB) © 2016, 2020 by Bible Hub and Berean.Bible, note on Esther 5:14.

57. Keener, Craig and Walton, John, *NIV Cultural Backgrounds Study Bible,* (Zondervan, 2016), note on Esther 5:14.

58. Sproul, R. C. *ESV Reformation Study Bible,* (Reformation Trust Publishing of Ligonier Ministries, 2021).

59. Sproul, R. C. *ESV Reformation Study Bible,* (Reformation Trust Publishing of Ligonier Ministries, 2021).

60. Hawkins, O.S., *The Bible Code: Finding Jesus in Every Book in the Bible,* (Thomas Nelson, 2020).

61. Evans, Tony, *The Tony Evans Study Bible: Advancing God's Kingdom Agenda,* (Holman Bible Publishers, 2019).

62. Keener, Craig and Walton, John, *NIV Cultural Backgrounds Study Bible,* (Zondervan, 2016), note on Esther 5:14.

63. Wiersbe, Warren W., *NKJV Wiersbe Study Bible,* (Thomas Nelson, 2021). As found at www.biblegateway.com

64. MacArthur, John, *NKJV MacArthur Study Bible,* 2nd Edition, (Thomas Nelson, 1997, 2006, 2019), as quoted on www.biblegateway.com

65. MacDonald, William, *Believer's Bible Commentary,* (Thomas Nelson, 2016).

66. Strong, James, *The New Strong's Exhaustive Concordance of the Bible,* (Thomas Nelson, 2009). G5463

67. MacArthur, John, *NKJV MacArthur Study Bible,* 2nd Edition, (Thomas Nelson, 1997, 2006, 2019), as quoted on www.biblegateway.com

68. Zodhiates, Spiros, ed., *The Complete Word Study Dictionary: New Testament* (Chattanooga, TN: AMG Publishers, 2000).

69. Warren Baker and Eugene E. Carpenter, *The Complete Word Study Dictionary: Old Testament* (Chattanooga, TN: AMG Publishers, 2003),

70. Strong, James, *The New Strong's Exhaustive Concordance of the Bible,* (Thomas Nelson, 2009), G1694.

71. Sproul, R. C. *ESV Reformation Study Bible,* (Reformation Trust Publishing of Ligonier Ministries, 2021).

72. Webster, Noah, *The American Dictionary of the English Language, 1828.* as found at https://webstersdictionary1828.com/.

73. MacArthur, John, *NKJV MacArthur Study Bible,* 2nd Edition, (Thomas Nelson, 1997, 2006, 2019), as quoted on www.biblegateway.com

74. Rubin, Rabbi Barry, *The Complete Jewish Study Bible,* (Hendrickson Publishers, 2016).

75. *The NKJV Chronological Study Bible,* (Thomas Nelson, 2008).

76. MacArthur, John, *God With Us: The Miracle of Christmas,* (Zondervan, 1989).

77. *The Voice*™. (Ecclesia Bible Society, 2008), note on Matthew 2:11.

BIBLIOGRAPHY

Baker, Warren and Carpenter, Eugene, eds., *The Complete Word Study Dictionary: Old Testament,* (Chattanooga, TN: AMG Publishers, 2003).

Barker, Kenneth L. and John R. Kohlenberger III, *Expositor's Bible Commentary,* (Zondervan, 2004) as found as www.biblegateway.com

Easton, M. G., M.A., D.D., *Illustrated Bible Dictionary,* Third Edition, published by Thomas Nelson, 1897. At www.biblegateway.com

Evans, Tony, *The Tony Evans Study Bible: Advancing God's Kingdom Agenda,* (Holman Bible Publishers, 2019).

Garrett, Duane A.; Kaiser, Walter C., Jr., eds. *Archaeological Study Bible-NIV: An Illustrated Walk Through Biblical History and Culture,* (Zondervan, 2006).

Green, Steve and High, Bill, *This Beautiful Book: An Exploration of the Bible's Incredible Story Line and Why It Matters Today,* (Zondervan, 2019).

Hawkins, O.S., *The Bible Code: Finding Jesus in Every Book in the Bible,* (Thomas Nelson, 2020)

Henry, Matthew, *Matthew Henry's Commentary on the Whole Bible,* (Hendrickson Publishers, 2014) as found at www.biblegateway.com

Keener, Craig and Walton, John, *NIV Cultural Backgrounds Study Bible,* (Zondervan, 2016).

Lockyear, Herbert, *All the Women of the Bible,* (Zondervan, 2016, EPUB).

Lucado, Max, *You Were Made for this Moment: Courage for Today and Hope for Tomorrow,* (Thomas Nelson, 2021).

MacDonald, William, *Believer's Bible Commentary,* (Thomas Nelson, 2016).

MacArthur, John, *God With Us: The Miracle of Christmas,* (Zondervan, 1989).

MacArthur, John, *NKJV MacArthur Study Bible, 2nd Edition,* (Thomas Nelson, 1997, 2006, 2019), as quoted on www.biblegateway.com

MacArthur, John, *The MacArthur Bible Commentary,* (Thomas Nelson, 2005).

MacArthur, John, *Twelve Extraordinary Women: How God Shaped Women of the Bible and What He Wants to Do with You,* (Thomas Nelson, 2005)

McGee, J. Vernon, *Thru the Bible: Genesis through Revelation,* (Thomas Nelson, 1984, EPUB) as found at www.biblegateway.com

The NKJV Chronological Study Bible, (Thomas Nelson, 2008).

Patterson, Dorothy Kelly and Kelly, Rhonda Harrington, Eds., *NIV Women's Study Bible,* (Thomas Nelson, 2017) as found on www.biblegateway.com

Rubin, Rabbi Barry, *The Complete Jewish Study Bible,* (Hendrickson Publishers, 2016).

Silver, Moises and Tenney Merrill C., *The Zondervan Encyclopedia of the Bible, 5 Volume Set,* Zondervan, 2010.

Smith, William, *Smith's Bible Dictionary,* (Hendrickson Publishers, 1993).

Sproul, R. C. *ESV Reformation Study Bible,* (Reformation Trust Publishing of Ligonier Ministries, 2021).

Strong, James, *The New Strong's Exhaustive Concordance of the Bible,* (Thomas Nelson, 2009).

Swindoll, Charles R., *The Swindoll Study Bible NLT,* (Tyndale House, 2017, EPUB).

Webster, Noah, *The American Dictionary of the English Language, 1828.* as found at https://webstersdictionary1828.com/

Wiersbe, Warren W., *NKJV Wiersbe Study Bible,* (Thomas Nelson, 2021).

Zodhiates, Spiros, ed., *The Complete Word Study Dictionary: New Testament* (Chattanooga, TN: AMG Publishers, 2000).

You have a story.
We want to publish it.

Everyone has as a story to tell. It might be about something you know how to do, or what has happened in your life, or it may be a thrilling, or romantic, or intriguing, or heartwarming, or suspenseful story, starring a cast of characters that have been swimming around in your imagination.

And at Wyatt & Sons Publishers, we can get your story onto the pages of a book just like the one you are holding in your hand. With professional interior design and a custom, professionally designed cover built just for you from the start, you can finally see your dream of being an author become reality. Then, you will see your book listed with retailers all over the world as people are able to buy your book from wherever they are and have it delivered to their home or their e-reader.

So what are you waiting for? This is your time.

visit us at

www.wyattpublishing.com

for details on how to get started becoming a
published author right away.

www.ingramcontent.com/pod-product-compliance
Lightning Source LLC
Chambersburg PA
CBHW061118170426
43199CB00027B/2960